Applying Business Capabilities in a Corporate Buyer M&A Process

Andreas Freitag

Applying Business Capabilities in a Corporate Buyer M&A Process

Springer Gabler

Andreas Freitag
Garching, Germany

Dissertation, Technische Universität München, Germany, 2014

ISBN 978-3-658-07281-0 ISBN 978-3-658-07282-7 (eBook)
DOI 10.1007/978-3-658-07282-7

The Deutsche Nationalbibliothek lists this publication in the Deutsche Nationalbibliografie; detailed bibliographic data are available in the Internet at http://dnb.d-nb.de.

Library of Congress Control Number: 2014949922

Springer Gabler

Printed on acid-free paper

Springer Gabler is a brand of Springer DE.
Springer DE is part of Springer Science+Business Media.
www.springer-gabler.de

Acknowledgements

This thesis is the result of my activities as an external PhD student at the Chair for Informatics 19 (sebis) at the Department of Informatics of the Technische Universität München. There have been many ways of assistance during the journey of a doctoral thesis like discussing, proofreading, or just being there. Here, I would like to express my gratitude to all of you, who supported me in my research in the one way or another.

First and foremost, I would like to thank my supervisor, Prof. Dr. Florian Matthes, for providing the opportunity to work on this interesting and challenging research topic. His constant support, insightful suggestions, guidance, and advice greatly contributed to the success of this work. I would also like to thank Prof. Dr. Helmut Krcmar for our conversations about the subject and for being the second reviewer of my thesis.

This work is part of a research project on Mergers & Acquisitions and Enterprise Architecture Management, which has provided an excellent environment for my research. Thus, I would like to thank my colleagues at the "chair for software engineering for business information systems" (sebis) for their passion in discussing ideas, their patience in developing a suitable research approach, and joint writing of publications. My thanks especially go to Dr. Sabine Buckl, Sascha Roth, and Christopher Schulz.

I would also like to thank Dr. Verena Schmidtmann and Uwe Weber. They supported my research with valuable ideas and suggestions. Equally important, they helped to adapt my working environment at Detecon International GmbH to my research activities.

Discussing the developed ideas, as well as preliminary and final results with practitioners greatly contributed to my research. Thus, my thanks also goes to all interviewees and workshop participants who gave me the opportunity to discuss my work with them.

And lastly, but most of all, I thank my family, my partner Anna, and my friends for their support and encouragement during this journey.

Garching b. München Andreas Freitag

Acknowledgements

Contents

List of Figures

List of Tables

1 Motivation, Introduction and Overview

1.1 Motivation

Mergers and Acquisitions (M&A) are a common event in today's business environment. Along the past merger waves, they became established as a strategic management instrument to generate value through external growth. Despite this development, enterprises still struggle to manage M&A efficiently and a significant number of merger projects do not reach the expected goals or fail completely [GS09]. The high amount of unsuccessful M&A in the past shows that there are difficulties in the management of M&A. The success of an M&A initiative is strongly depending on the outcome of the integration and the realization of expected synergies [Ja08]. In addition, inaccurate planning can lead to wrong expectations, for example due to an overestimation of synergies or an underestimation of integration costs. Even if expected business benefits and the purchase price look promising, a poor integration procedure will diminish overall transaction performance [BC08, GS09]. Jansen [JB08] especially emphasizes the need to integrate pre-merger planning and post-merger integration. At the same time, he reveals that there are no reliable contributions from academia for this challenge.

Many enterprises recognized that a professional M&A practice can be a competitive advantage if an enterprise's corporate strategy includes external growth [MS00, Pi08c]. Nevertheless, many enterprises struggle to provide consistent information for decision making throughout the M&A process in an efficient manner. From the buyer perspective, the setup of a professional M&A practice is key to improve the success of M&A [GS09, JB08, WS06]. Already some time ago, it has been shown that a comprehensive preparation of M&A increases the success rate and it provides an essential basis for the subsequent integration [HJ92, Hu99]. Therefore, large enterprises follow the idea of achieving "merger readiness" and they build up an M&A practice by establishing the skills, organization, processes and methods to support their M&A activities. The M&A process is a central element of any M&A management approach [JS86, KHG06].

Enterprise Architecture Management (EA Management) is a business and IT planning discipline [Th09]. It is an approach for analyzing, planning, and controlling as-is and target states of the enterprise in terms of business, information systems, and technology architecture [Au11]. Consequently, EA Management should provide a *"holistic and integrated view of the strategic direction, business practices, information flows, and technology resources"* [Be05]. While early EA approaches like Zachman [Za87] had their roots in business planning, many practitioners applied EA Management with a limited scope for IT architecture management and alignment of business and IT (e.g. [ARW08, Ke06, Ni08]). Over the last decade, the majority of large enterprises has adopted EA methods and models to analyze and plan their IT landscape.

Currently, experienced enterprises and thought leaders recollect the roots of EA Management and place special emphasis on the value of EA Management to manage business transformation activities. Ross et al. [RWR06] explicitly propose EA Management as a holistic approach for business transformation. M&A are one type of complex business transformation projects, which affects a large part of the enterprise and include massive re-engineering and integration efforts [Ja08, GS09, PP00]. Furthermore, some of the success factors for M&A activities are also referred to as benefits of an EA Management approach, e.g. a clear business vision, coordinated and holistic planning of business and IT, consistent decisions, and stakeholder management.

Business capabilities describe the functional building blocks of an enterprise's business model as part of the business architecture. Today, business capability models are an essential element of a state of the art EA Management approach and frequently used to work collaboratively with business and IT stakeholders [Au11, SCA10]. Furthermore, there is an enormous interest among academics and practitioners, reflected in a growing number of publications dealing with the concept and application of business capabilities. Additionally, they have been addressed in many presentations, workshops, and discussions during EA practitioner conferences (e.g. [Ne10, Th11]). However, due to the innovative character of business capability approaches, many issues have not been subject to structured research yet. Hence, several authors (e.g. [BBH07, Ke09a]) demand for a consistent theoretical foundation.

Some large international enterprises identified the potential of an EA Management approach in the context of M&A (e.g. [Ne10, Th11]) and a few pioneers start to gain first experiences in applying EA models or methods during post merger integration projects (e.g. [De07]). But so far, the application of EA Management methods and models in the context of M&A has not been subject to explicit research.

Business capabilities are the most business-oriented element in today's EA Management approaches [Au11]. Additionally, they are a central reference structure for stakeholders from different disciplines, providing a common language to exchange information. Therefore, they promise to provide a good starting point for the support of M&A with EA Management. One important element of a comprehensive M&A practice is a professional M&A process comprising the overall scope from early pre-merger planning to full completion of integration. As an additional challenge, this process has to integrate the perspective of multidisciplinary experts and stakeholders to establish a common approach to M&A [PP00]. Bringing together both disciplines, this thesis investigates the end-to-end applicability of business capability models in the M&A process of a corporate buyer organization as a starting point for the support of M&A with EA Management methods and models.

1.2 Goal of Thesis and Research Questions

The goal of this thesis is to evaluate the applicability of EA Management methods and models in the context of M&A. Thus, we analyze if EA Management methods and models help to improve the M&A practice of a corporate buyer organization. As this thesis constitutes a first attempt to interlink both disciplines, we focus on an architecture element promising to connect both research domains. We investigate if business capabilities can be used as a boundary object between the EA practice and other management disciplines during the M&A process of a corporate buyer organization.

The central question of this thesis is:

Can business capabilities be used as a boundary object between EA practice and other management disciplines during the M&A process?

The formulated goal is addressed by investigating the application of business capability models in the M&A process of a corporate buyer organization. The conducted research aims on identification and evaluation of potential benefits of applying business capabilities to close the gap between strategic merger planning and post merger integration (PMI) and to improve communication between experts and stakeholders from different management disciplines. Figure 1.1 charts this idea of interlinking the domains of EA Management and M&A with a business capability approach.

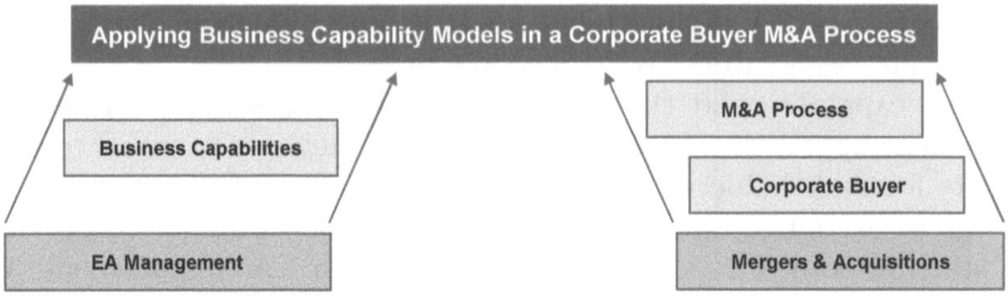

Figure 1.1: EA Management and M&A

The following six research questions are addressed in the course of this work.

Research Question 1:

What are the characteristics of a typical corporate buyer scenario?

This research question aims to formalize the context and characteristics of a typical M&A scenario in a buyer organization. Given the broad scope of the M&A research domain, it aims at defining a homogeneous group of enterprises with similar boundary conditions and resulting transformation challenges. The corporate buyer scenario needs to describe this scenario in terms of motivation, acquisition object, and integration goals driving the design of the M&A process and the application of business capability models. It determines the overall scope of the process, as well as the activities constituting each phase. Additionally, it defines the criteria to identify relevant participants for the evaluation of the developed artifacts.

Research Question 2:

What are transformation challenges of a corporate buyer organization during M&A?

This research question aims to substantiate the corporate buyer's challenges that may be addressed by establishing business capabilities as a central reference structure for stakeholders from different disciplines. We aim at identifying transformation challenges from literature and practitioner feedback, including business and IT aspects. These transformation challenges can be relevant for one or more process phases of the M&A process or for the communication between experts and stakeholders from different management disciplines. They are taken into account during the design of the M&A process. Transformation challenges that can be addressed with a capability approach have to be considered during the evaluation of research results.

Research Question 3:

What are the elements of an M&A process for a typical corporate buyer organization?

This research question aims to identify the elements of an M&A process which is suitable for the corporate buyer scenario. From a horizontal perspective on the process, the research question addresses the scope according to formulated goals in a corporate buyer scenario and the selection of the right structure for activities and deliverables. From a vertical perspective, it aims to identify matching management dimensions representing participating experts and stakeholders. Additionally, an adequate documentation structure has to be selected. A reasonable degree of detail has to ensure balance between providing a guiding structure for the overall progress and offering adequate degrees of freedom for efficient transformation work. A documented M&A process is a prerequisite to identify anchor points for the application of business capability models.

Research Question 4:

How does a definition of a business capability concept and its management context look like?

This research question focuses on the need to provide a theoretical foundation for the business capability concept. Due to the innovative character of business capability concepts in EA Management, many issues have not been subject to structured research yet. Therefore, a structured overview on the different understandings, as well as available definitions and graphical representations is needed. The research question aims at providing a solid foundation for the business capability concept, which can be used for the remainder of this thesis, but also for future research in this domain. Besides a definition for business capabilities, relationships to the business side and IT side have to be clarified.

Research Question 5:

Can business capability models be beneficially applied in single steps of the M&A process?

This research question focuses on single activities and methods that are part of the M&A process. We assume that business capabilities are relevant for several parts of the M&A process. However this does not apply to all activities and deliverables of the process. Therefore, this research question aims at identification of potential anchor points for the application of business capability models by following the sequence of the developed M&A process. As a prerequisite, a basic business capability map has to be described and adequate visualization methods have to be selected. Furthermore, this research question aims at demonstrating the applicability with example business capability maps.

Research Question 6:

Can business capability models help to close the gap between strategic planning of M&A and post merger integration (PMI)?

With a horizontal view on the M&A process of a corporate buyer, this research question focuses on the end-to-end availability of information across the single phases. We assume that business capability models can be applied as a common reference structure for the end-to-end process, supporting strategy development, transaction, and implementation of the integration plan. It has to be proven that business capabilities can be applied for a series of activities along the process. A complete support of all activities is not reasonable. Consequently, the focus lies on investigating applicability across the different process phases, which today are partially performed independently from each other, leading to knowledge loss.

Research Question 7:

Can business capability models improve the information exchange between experts and stakeholders from different disciplines?

This research question focuses on the availability of information across multiple disciplines and from an overarching perspective. It focuses on the vertical view on the M&A process of a corporate buyer and how business capability models can be applied as a common reference structure and common language for experts and stakeholders from different management disciplines. It aims at investigating the comprehensiveness and the acceptance of the capability concept for participants of the M&A process that are not familiar to the concept so far.

1.3 Research Approach

The research documented in this thesis follows a design science approach. The goal of design science research is to contribute to the identified area of research through the building and evaluation of innovative artifacts designed to meet identified business needs [He04]. Several authors (e.g. [He04, MS95, Of09, Pe07]) provide single elements of design science research methodologies or attempt to create design science research frameworks. In all, rigor and relevance are generally accepted as requirements in design science.

According to March and Smith [MS95] and Hevner et al. [He04], an artifact refers to all innovations attempting to create utility for an organization, which can be constructs, models, methods, and instantiations. Constructs form the vocabulary and symbols applied to describe problems and to specify respective solutions for a domain. Models are the abstractions and representations describing the problem domain and relationships between constructs. They can represent problems or solutions. Methods are algorithms and guidelines mainly used to perform problem-solving activities. Instantiations are the realization of an artifact in its environment. These artifacts may be represented by formal logic, software, or mathematic formulas, but also in informal language descriptions [He04].

A research process is the application of scientific methods to the complex task of discovering solutions (answers) to identified problems (questions) [NMP91]. Offermann et al. [Of09] have developed a research process for design science, based on existing processes and findings from a multitude of resources on design research. It provides a recommendation for research steps and their sequence, as well as hints regarding the accomplishment of the single steps. The goal of following the research process shown in figure 1.2 is to produce viable results by combining qualitative and quantitative research and to apply well-known research methods for problem identification, artifact design, and evaluation. The process ensures relevance and scientific rigor by the interaction of practitioners and researchers, in order to foster the quality of created artifacts.

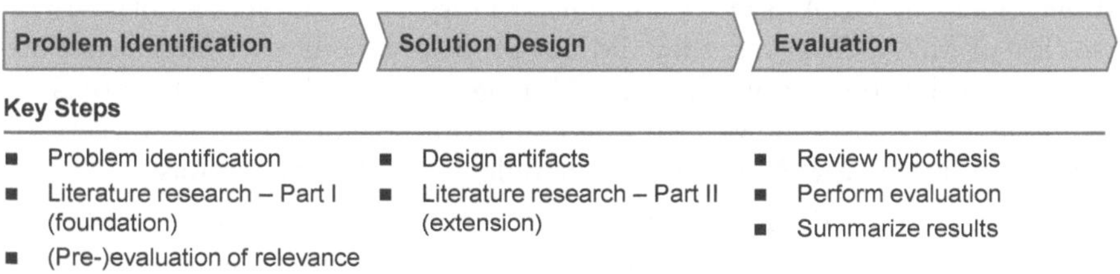

Figure 1.2: Research Process, following [Of09]

In all, the research activities conducted to develop the contributions presented in this thesis follow Hevner et al.'s [He04] guidelines for understanding, executing and evaluating research. These guidelines provide practice rules for conducting design science research by describing the key characteristics of research conducted in a well-ordered manner. Therefore, they have been taken into consideration as follows.

Design as an Artifact: The research presented in this thesis is structured along a set of artifacts that are developed to interlink the domains of EA Management and M&A with a business capability approach. We present a theoretical foundation for business capabilities, a description of the corporate buyer scenario, an integrated end-to-end M&A process for the corporate buyer scenario (CBMA Process), a set of 13 business capability models to support the CMBA process, as well as three business capability based methods for the initial development of a business capability model and the application of the model during dependency analysis and PMI planning.

Problem Relevance: The problem relevance arises from findings from a literature study, from practitioner's feedback collected during expert interviews, workshops and from a survey. The presented research is part of a research project on "EA Management in the context of M&A" at our chair[1]. Our research team performed a comprehensive literature study to get a insight into the M&A domain [FMS11]. As already stated in the motivation (see section 1.1), the relevance of the research arises from the fact that M&A are a common event in today's business environment but enterprises struggle to realize the aspired benefits. Based on the findings of our initial literature studies, we performed two empirical studies to complement the picture from an IT and an EA Management perspective. First, we performed a series of expert interviews on the role of IT in the context of M&A [FMS10b, FMS11]. The study revealed a list of transformation challenges which underpin the problem relevance. Second, we conducted a survey on the role of EA Management in M&A (see section 3.4). Enterprise architects identified the use case of M&A. However, they did not propose concrete artifacts or report about experiences in applying EA Management methods and models so far. The study also shows that the aspiration of enterprise architects to participate in the M&A process is not reflected in practice today.

Design Evaluation: The artifacts have been evaluated with a multiperspective approach. Based on a fictional case study, open discussions and a questionnaire, we performed three workshops with 14 representatives from different management disciplines. We discussed the developed approach with enterprise architects working in the EA practice or ongoing M&A projects of large international companies. They are familiar with the concept of business capabilities and they are willing to apply EA Management methods and models during M&A. In addition, we discussed the approach with representatives from other management disciplines like process management, compliance,

[1] Software Engineering for Business Information Systems (sebis) (`http://wwwmatthes.in.tum.de`)

and security who are experienced in M&A, but had no experiences with the capability concept or EA Management so far.

Research Contributions: With this thesis, we contribute to the domains of EA Management and M&A. As a first contribution, a theoretical foundation for business capabilities is presented. Even though there is an enormous interest in business capabilities among academics and practitioners, many issues have not been subject to structured research yet. Accounting for the innovative character of this approach, the theoretical foundation is based on a structured analysis of business capability literature and related work from strategic management. The second contribution is the Corporate Buyer M&A Process (CBMA Process), an integrated end-to-end M&A process for a corporate buyer scenario. Building on the goals of efficient integration and holistic optimization, the CBMA Process comprises the three phases, Pre-Merger Phase, Transaction Phase, and Post-Merger Phase, as well as eight management dimensions. Each phase is described including its steps, the methods applied and resulting deliverables. As a third contribution of this thesis, the applicability of business capability models is evaluated along the developed CBMA Process. Based on the theoretical foundation for business capabilities, a set of 13 business capability models is presented and their application in the process is shown. Furthermore, three business capability based methods are included. They support the initial development of a business capability model and illustrate the application of the model during dependency analysis and PMI planning.

Research Rigor: The research was conducted according to the research process as proposed by Offermann et al. [Of09] shown in figure 1.2. During literature research we followed the guidelines of Webster and Watson [WW02]. Expert interviews have been prepared and results have been analyzed according to the manual proposed by Kanwischer [Ka05]. For the survey setup we followed the questionnaire design process suggested by Frazer and Lawley [FL00]. Evaluation work widely followed the textbook of Bortz and Döring [BD09], providing methods and suggestions for evaluation setup, conduction, and documentation. The findings from interviews and evaluation workshops have been systematically transcribed, consolidated, and analyzed. To ensure consistency of terminology while working with German and international documents, translations are taken from technical dictionaries (e.g. [KK01]).

Design as a Search Process: Our research aimed at combining EA Management and M&A perspectives, incorporating knowledge from different management disciplines with inputs from academia and from practitioners.

The artifacts have been designed iteratively, incorporating feedback collected from practitioners working in the real-world business environment. This applies equally to the development of artifacts (see section 6.1) and the evaluation of the approach (see sections 5.2 and 8.3). Due to confidentiality reasons, we refrain from any references to interview and workshop partners and their organizations.

Communication of Research: The artifacts are published in this thesis to make them available to both management and technology audiences. Results of this thesis have been published and discussed at various academic and practitioner conferences, e.g. [FMS10a, FMS10b, FMS11, Fr11, Fr12, FS12, Ne10, Th11].

1.4 Document Structure

The structure of this thesis is depicted in figure 1.3.

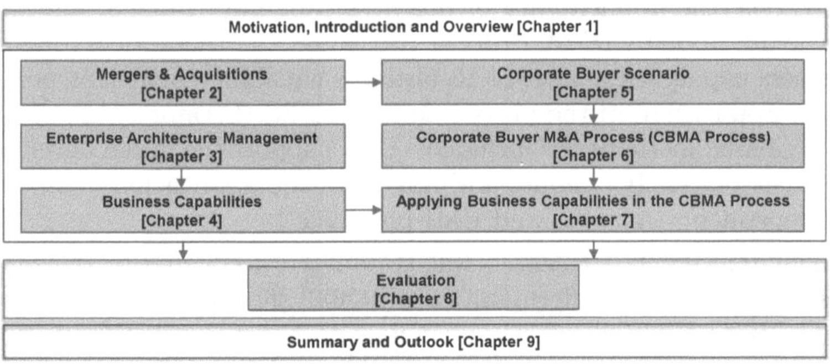

Figure 1.3: Structure of Thesis

With chapter 2, we ensure the linkage of our research into the M&A domain. It presents a summary of rationales for M&A and key challenges to proof relevance of the conducted research and to position our work. We describe different forms of M&A and typical participants in an M&A transaction. We identify merger readiness as motivation and the M&A process as one key concept to improve the M&A practice. The foundation is completed with IT transformation challenges and IT integration strategies during M&A.

In chapter 3, we analyze the state-of-the-art of EA Management in the context of M&A. We provide an overview on related work and a short clarification of our understanding of the discipline. Then, we examine the current progress of application of EA Management in M&A from an academic and a practitioner's perspective. We present the findings of an analysis of the topic M&A in EA Management literature and the results of an expert survey on the role of EA Management in M&A. Additionally, we included a short description of the architecture viewpoint concept, which is the underlying theory for capability maps.

In chapter 4, we present a theoretical foundation for business capabilities. Accounting for the innovative character of this approach, we present the findings of a structured analysis of the existing body of knowledge. We describe the relationship between the business model, the capability map, and a single capability. Additionally, it comprises a definition for business capabilities, its characteristics, attributes for description, and the dimensions that together provide the capability. Furthermore, we present the status-quo of business capabilities in EA Management and present three architecture viewpoints related to business capabilities: the capability map, the business entity map, and the information ownership map.

In chapter 5, we describe the corporate buyer scenario according to the target group of enterprises for the capability-based approach developed in this thesis. We present the resulting M&A classification scheme for the corporate buyer scenario and a list of nine transformation challenges. To substantiate the corporate buyer scenario, we include findings from a series of expert interviews and a practitioner workshop.

In chapter 6, we present the Corporate Buyer M&A Process (CBMA Process), a structured representation of work in the M&A discipline for the corporate buyer scenario. To identify anchor points for the application of EA Management and especially for business capabilities, we need a complete M&A process with a balanced level of detail for activities and deliverables along the phases, which is not available today.

In chapter 7, we connect the domain of M&A with EA Management and the concept of business capabilities. We present the Company Business Capability Map (C-BCM), four visualization concepts, and a set of 13 business capability maps to support the CBMA Process. Following the sequence of the developed CBMA Process, a structured analysis indicates which methods and deliverables are anchor points for the application of business capability maps. Furthermore, we present three business capability based methods. They support the initial development of a business capability model and illustrate the application of the model during dependency analysis and PMI planning.

Chapter 8 documents the evaluation of the developed artifacts with a multi-perspective approach. We describe the research environment and the setup of the evaluation approach, which is based on a fictional case study, open discussions and a questionnaire. Then we present the findings from three workshops with 14 representatives from different management disciplines and discuss limitations and prerequisites for introducing the approach in practice. Finally, we review our findings with regards to the identified transformation challenges.

Finally, Chapter 9 gives a summary of our key findings, a critical reflection of our work, and suggestions for further research.

2 Introduction to Mergers & Acquisitions

2.1 The Rationale behind M&A

2.1.1 Economic Drivers for M&A

The recurrent appearance of Mergers and Acquisitions (M&A) over the last decade has lead to increasing attention for this phenomenon in today's corporate world [Ja08]. Numerous publications around this topic are contributed by academia. M&A became a standard instrument for strategic management [TB08]. This applies equally to large international corporations and to small and medium sized enterprises. At the same time, the perception of M&A in our society is mostly negative as it is related to cost cutting and loss of workplaces [TB08].

Reflecting the importance of the topic and the demand for consolidated knowledge, a group of comprehensive M&A management handbooks have been published, e.g. by Jansen [Ja08], Picot [Pi08b], or Wirtz [Wi06b]. These books give a comprehensive and broad overview on the topic of M&A. While differentiating between a strategic planning, an execution, and an integration phase, the single contributions thoroughly investigate on the different forms, activities, organizational impacts, constraints, and artifacts of M&A.

It is important to understand the external drivers coming from the economic environment and the individual business goals that can lead to a decision for a merger or an acquisition. Therefore, in the following a short overview of the external economic conditions and company business goals that may lead to M&A are given. Even though it is useful to elaborate on the external drivers and internal motivation separately, it has to be noticed that the external drivers strongly influence the strategic direction and thus internal management decisions of an enterprise.

Changing market conditions constantly lead to new opportunities and challenges in today's highly dynamic business environment. Examples are technological, economical, cultural, and political changes [Ja08, WS06]. Increasingly, modern enterprises leverage the strategic instrument of M&A

to take advantage of opportunities and adapt to the altering enterprise environment [GS09, WS06]. The general expectation is that M&A allow for faster adaption than an evolutionary approach with internal resources. According to established M&A literature resources [Ja08, LM02, Pi08b, Wi06b], in addition to the general change of the environment, the following three economic effects are commonly agreed as drivers to M&A transaction.

Internationalization and Globalization Effects: An increase in internationalization or globalization in a market is a driver for M&A [Ja08]. Despite the phenomenon of globalization in many industries, single countries show strong differences regarding economic, legal, and regulatory regulations. Thus, the acquisition of a locally operating company is one option to establish an adequate market presence in a new country [LM02].

Competitive Markets: A high level of competition in a market does also foster M&A [TB08, WS06]. The increasing convergence of available technologies, customer need structures, consumer proclivities for all market players leads to highly standardized products in mass production and small profit margins [LM02]. At the same time, companies require flexible corporate structures in order to realize first mover benefits when market conditions change. In this case, M&A are again one option to adapt.

Industry Consolidation: The level of M&A activity in a certain industry follows patterns as a consequence of market consolidation [TB08]. Based on a comprehensive empirical study, Deans et al. developed the "merger endgames" graph describing the consolidation of an industry along four phases over a total time frame of 25 years [DKZ02]. Phase 1, the "opening phase" is the starting point, where companies enter the industry, trying to expand their market share and to establish market entry barriers. It closes with first consolidation tendencies. During phase 2, the "scale phase", companies try to realize economies of scale through growth, leading to major consolidations. In phase 3, the "focus phase", the main consolidation activities are completed. The resulting group of enterprises begins to expand their core business. The number of M&A transaction decreases while their volume increases leading to potential "mega deals". In phase 4, the "balance phase", only a small number of key players dominates an industry. In this phase, strategic alliances are more likely than M&A transactions. In their 2002 book, they allocated utilities, textile, recreation, construction, real estate, railways, telecommunication, and insurance industry in the first phase (opening), indicating a high relevance of M&A for the future.

2.1.2 Company Business Goals

An enterprise has the general goal of continually increasing its long-term value in a sustainable manner. In order to reach this goal, an enterprise has to create and capitalize competitive advantages. M&A can be one alternative to achieve this goal [Li06]. It is important to understand the business theory and economic concepts leading to M&A from an enterprise perspective. Summarizing [BU05, Ja08, Li06, LM02, Wi06b], the business goals of an individual company that can lead to M&A may be grouped into:

- Strategic matters:
  A strategic motivation may be market-oriented (e.g. growth in market share, increased market power, reduction of competitors, or access to new markets), access to resources or knowledge (e.g. new technologies or special competencies), economies of scale and adaption of the internal structure, as well as changes in the value chain setup (e.g. vertical or horizontal integration).
- Financial matters:
  Financial transactions are beneficial if the estimated value of a target company (represented in its net present value or future cash flow[2]) is higher than the acquisition price to be paid. Additional financial motivations may arise from stock market effects or tax benefits.
- Management reasons:
  An enterprise's management team may have personal motivation to enter into an M&A deal. These may be the prevention of a hostile takeover or investment of free cash flows, but also very egoistic goals like their status, power, self-fulfillment, or remuneration effects.
- Others:
  Other motivations include succession (follow-up) planning, regulatory enforcements, or capitalization of asynchronous information.

Within one enterprise, there may be different and sometimes contradictory motivations. This also applies for M&A, as individual stakeholders may have different motivations to enter into a merger or an acquisition [Li06]. Shareholders, for example may have more finance driven and short term oriented motivation than employees that yield for job stability in the long term. However, this aspect is not in scope of this work. A detailed discussion of different motivations and explanatory models can be found in [Ja08, LM02]. In the following, the focus is laid on strategic motivations which are relevant

[2] For details on financial valuation methods see [DS09, EST10, Wi10].

to this work. Certainly, a concrete decision for M&A will always be driven by a set of motivations [FM06].

The production of products and services is conducted along a chain of value creating activities. Each enterprise decides on the scope of the section it occupies in the value chain, trying to maximize profits [FM06]. Today, enterprises operate within complex and dynamic value chains in order to address consumer requirements [Ja08]. In the long run, enterprises do not only change their internal structures such as business units, branch networks, or organizational structures, but also manage their external relationships or completely redefine their external boundaries [Ja08].

According to Porter [Po04a], the value chain of an enterprise is the central element to gain competitive advantage. He defines two types of competitive advantage, either low cost or differentiation. The resulting level of competitive advantage is strongly driven by the relative position of the enterprise compared to its competitors within the industry. To achieve an above-average performance in the long run, an enterprise has to build up and protect its sustainable competitive advantage.

Based on the two types of competitive advantage, Porter defines three generic competitive strategies to achieve above-average performance: cost leadership, differentiation, and focus [Po04a]. The generic strategies can be characterized according to their type of competitive advantage (cost vs. differentiation) and their competitive scope (broad target market vs. narrow target market). While cost leadership and differentiation strategies cover a broad range of industry segments, focus strategies (cost focus or differentiation focus) address a narrow segment[3].

The following set of theory models are regularly applied to support enterprises in pursuing a certain strategy. The realization of each strategic positioning can be supported by M&A [FM06, Ja08]. In each case, external growth can have significant advantages compared to organic (internal) growth, for example in terms of time-to-market [TB08].

Cost Leadership Strategy: In a cost leadership strategy, an enterprise tries to position itself as the low-cost producer in a certain industry. The broad competitive scope covers many industry segments or may also be cross-industry. Cost leaders often rely strongly on economies of scale, achieved by high volume business and large company size. Therefore, growth is a central element of their business strategies. Cost leadership may also

[3] Some economists argue that growth is the only strategy for long time success (survival) of a company, in opposite to Porter, who does also see a benefit in a differentiating niche strategy.

arise from proprietary technologies or special access to raw material. M&A can foster the realization of increased market power through inorganic growth, leading to economies of scale and relative cost reductions or revenue enhancements [Li06]. An M&A strategy with direct competitors leads to instant growth in market share, increased market power, and obviously to a reduction of competitors in the market. Moreover, new markets may be accessed through the enlargement of the product and service portfolio targeting at economies of scope [PP00]. M&A can also be a means to get access to technologies, production resources, knowledge as well as consumer or supplier channels.

Differentiation Strategy: In a differentiation strategy, an enterprise tries to establish a unique position, addressing special consumer needs. In opposite to the cost leader, this company may realize higher prices and margins for its unique products or services. Other differentiating factors can be a special marketing approach, an excellent delivery system, or the brand image. M&A can be a means to establish new internal business capabilities that lead to a competitive advantage through differentiation [Li06]. An external acquisition can complement existing capabilities to use them more efficiently, or even comprise completely new capabilities.

Focus Strategy: When choosing a focus strategy, an enterprise approaches a selected rather small industry segment with a focused cost or differentiation strategy in order to achieve a competitive advantage in this part of the market. Consequently, the company does not try to achieve an overall competitive advantage. A cost focus may help to exploit a segment with a special cost behavior, whereas a differentiation focus is a strategy to exploit a niche with special consumer needs. Therefore, M&A can help to achieve a focus strategy as described for the two strategies above.

2.1.3 History and Current Relevance

Before looking at the current state of M&A, a short retrospective view provides informative insights as a foundation for the subsequent work. In the past, the global M&A activity was characterized by cyclical ups and downs. The initial appearance of intensive M&A activities began in the end of the 19th century in the USA. Müller-Stewens and Jansen [JB08, LM02, MS00] identified six so called "merger waves" during the last century. Each wave was driven by different strategic goals, which have been influenced by those theories for competitive advantage which were accepted at this time.

Table 2.1 gives an overview on the merger waves, the leading strategy, the resulting integration requirements and an indication about the required level of post merger competence. It shows, that the two most recent waves demand an especially high level of integration competence.

Table 2.1: Historical M&A Waves, following [JB08]

Wave (Timeframe)	Strategic Direction	Post Merger Competence
Wave 1 (1897 – 1904)		
Strategy	Monopoly formation through horizontal integration	low
Integration Requirement	Pool market power	
Wave 2 (1916 – 1929)		
Strategy	Control value chain through vertical integration	medium
Integration Requirement	Optimize interfaces	
Wave 3 (1965 – 1969)		
Strategy	Anti-cyclic portfolio to absorb weak economy	low
Integration Requirement	None (unrelated conglomerates)	
Wave 4 (1984 – 1989)		
Strategy I	Focus on core business disinvestments and financial transactions	low
Integration Requirement	Limited horizontal acquisitions	
Strategy II	Financial transactions	low
Integration Requirement	Only financial motivation	
Wave 5 (1993 – 2000)		
Strategy I	Global shareholder value	high
Integration Requirement	Horizontal integration of core competencies and regional integration	
Strategy II	Talents and technology, new economy	high
Integration Requirement	Entrepreneurial spirit, innovation and people driven	
Wave 6 (2002 – 20??)		
Strategy I	Industry consolidation	high
Integration Requirement	horizontal integration of core competencies and global integration	
Strategy II	Financial investors, growth and efficiency focus	low-high
Integration Requirement	Buy-and-build strategies	

Additionally to these five historic waves that can be clearly defined as completed, several authors report on a sixth merger wave starting in 2002. There was a deterioration of M&A activities during the financial crisis around 2008. In the following years, enterprises that performed well during the crisis will have good opportunities to strengthen their position in the market through acquisition of organizations which have been seriously harmed by the crisis. As there is no consensus about the end of this sixth wave and current market reports still indicate a high level of activity on the M&A market, it can be assumed that it is still ongoing.

Complementing the view on the past, Jansen [JB08] formulated six trends which characterize today's M&A transactions. They also help to understand the resulting integration requirements:

- Size of target enterprise:
  The size of a target enterprise can be measured in turnover or stock market value. Medium sized transactions are more likely for the near future than so-called mega deals as they appeared in the past.
- Type of integration:
  The dominant type is horizontal integration without a product portfolio extension, leading to market consolidation in certain industries. Vertical integration and conglomerates are less relevant.
- Cross-border deals:
  Cross-border deals are mainly conducted by small and medium enterprises.
- Financing of transaction:
  "Cash offers" became more relevant than "share swaps". The purchasing power of one of the two currencies is strongly depending on the share prices (underpriced/overpriced) and the availability of free cash flows.
- Development of (price) premium:
  Todays price premium in M&A transactions are much lower than they have been during the fifth merger wave (new economy). After a peak during 2006, the premium stabilized on the level observed at the beginning of the sixth wave.
- New actors on acquisition side:
  The participation of private equity companies has increased during the last years as they are equipped with strong liquidity from their fonds.

The M&A report regularly published by Bloomberg [Bl11] comprises key M&A activity statistics from various perspectives. Besides in-depth data on deal-making activity for different deal types, regions, and industry sectors, it contains results from an extensive survey among M&A professionals. According to the data presented, global M&A activity has strongly recovered with aggregated deal count and deal volume figures higher than the 2009 levels. Complementing this trend, more than 80% of survey respondents expect an increase of M&A activity for the next years. The study also revealed a trend towards M&A transactions beyond domestic borders. In 2010 the authors identified more than 8100 cross border deals, worth about 945 billion USD, which is a 41% increase in volume compared to the year before. In line with these figures, 75% of survey respondents favor these deals over domestic transactions. In 2010, 49% of global M&A volume is generated by cross-border transactions (compared to 39% in 2009 and 30% in

2004). Regarding the relevance of certain industries, the report reveals that in 2010, the financial sector had the highest level of M&A activity, followed by energy. For the next year, survey participants expect the highest level of M&A activity for energy, industrials, and the financial sector. Bloomberg's study also shows the actual trend for M&A activities in Europe in relation to other regions. Europe follows the global trend of increased M&A activity. For the near future, survey participants expect the most active buyers in Asia Pacific and North America, followed by Central Asia. Noteworthy, the most attractive acquisition targets are expected in North America, Asia Pacific, and Western Europe.

In summary, it has been shown that the relevance of M&A is high and that the volume of M&A follows a series of merger waves. Each of these waves is driven by a particular strategy leading to different types of transactions and to different integration requirements. The more recent waves lead to transactions which require an integration of business on regional or global level. Therefore, a buyer's ability to perform this integration gets more important.

2.2 Key Challenges in M&A

2.2.1 M&A Success and Failure

Despite the increasing relevance, M&A still have low success rates [GS09]. Enterprises struggle to manage M&A and consequently fail to achieve the planned benefits [Ja08, Wi06b]. The expected benefits of an M&A transaction are estimated before the deal is performed and are reflected in the purchase price, but the overall success of an M&A transaction is strongly depending on the outcome of the integration and the realization of expected synergies [BC08].

In the course of this work, success is understood as achievement of formulated goals and realization of the aspired value contribution of an M&A transaction. According to Hommel and Grass [HG08], the value contribution of the M&A transaction is the value of the target candidate, plus synergies, minus the purchase price to be paid and transaction costs as depicted in figure 2.1. Consequently, the subjective value for the acquiring enterprise can be increased in two dimensions. Either a better estimation of the expected value of an acquisition, or by decreasing integration costs. As this thesis aims to improve an enterprise's M&A capability, it does primarily focus on the second dimension.

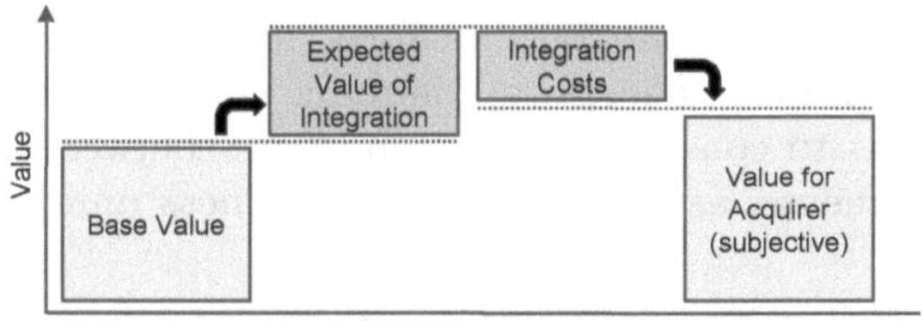

Figure 2.1: Value of an Acquisition (Buyer Perspective), following [BU05]

Several empirical studies evaluate success and failure rates of M&A transactions. The authors base their respective work on highly diverse definitions of success. According to Lucks and Meckl [LM02], the success criteria can be grouped into effects on turnover, the achievement of communicated goals, effects on the capital market returns, and impacts on the annual financial statements. The applicability of single success criteria depends on the individual position of a participant in an M&A transaction. A strategic corporate buyer will be interested in long-term effects on the overall enterprise performance, while a financial investor judges the value of a deal according to its short-term financial outcome. Nevertheless, the following example results of M&A success and failure rates indicate a rather low performance overall:

- A Deutsche Bundesbank report states that approximately every second merger is a success from an efficiency point of view, comparing efficiency levels and changes of merging versus non-merging banks [Ko05a].
- ComputerWeekly reports that 70% of mergers and acquisitions fail to achieve anticipated results, mainly because of IT problems [Br01].
- McKinsey reports a 50% failure rate (from the buyer's perspective) for 507 international mergers or acquisitions between 1996 and 1998 [LM02].

2.2.2 M&A Boundary Conditions & Constraints

A merger project is performed under a set of special boundary conditions and constraints that influence the working environment. We need to understand these boundary conditions to develop artifacts that are useful for enterprises working in the special setting of these challenging business transformation projects. In the following, we present a summary of key characteristics of M&A projects.

Enterprise Scope: A merger is a complex business transformation project, affecting large parts of the enterprise [Lu02]. It includes massive changes through restructuring and integration efforts, leading to an unstable working environment [LM02]. Therefore, planning and implementation of the transformation has to consider interdependencies between business units, functional departments, as well as between business units and IT departments.

High Complexity of Transformation Tasks: As the M&A transaction affects almost every element of an enterprise, such as strategy, products, organization, business processes, IT, and infrastructure, the transformation represents a highly complex effort and dependencies between the single elements have to be incorporated. Therefore, the integration of an acquired enterprise with the buyer organization is a challenging process [AF01].

Strong External Influences (Law & Regulations): In addition, a merger is typically performed under a multifaceted set of boundary conditions given by legal regulations (e.g. company law, labor legislation, fiscal law, and competition law) and the regulatory environment (e.g. market regulations or corporate governance guidelines) [Pi08b]. As a result, the scope for decision making is often limited.

Project Character and Time Constraints: Like every other project, a merger is performed and completed within the interdependent constraints of given scope, time, and costs, the dimensions of the so called project management triangle [Ke09b, Le06]. Thereby, integration steps with outside visibility are often seen as more time critical than internal restructuring work. For example, the establishment of a common presence in the market in terms of brand, products, and customer services.

Multidisciplinary Stakeholders and Information Demands: Additionally, a merger project has to incorporate a large number of stakeholders from multiple disciplines [LM02, Me06]. Each of these disciplines has individual concerns and goals during the planning and implementation of the merger. Furthermore, they may have a different background, for example mismatching company or national cultures, or languages [SH09].

Changing Priorities in Merger Phases: The long duration of M&A projects leads to additional challenges, as the enterprise's business strategy may change during this time or other initiatives are started which may have interdependencies with the ongoing integration work (e.g. another acquisition). Furthermore, the people initially planning the integration may not be available during the integration phase anymore. This especially applies to external advisers and consultants [LM02].

2.2.3 M&A Success Factors

Several studies evaluate risks and common pitfalls in order to identify key success factors for M&A planning and PMI projects. Gerds and Schewe, for example, performed a profound study on 45 factors for success of Post Merger Integration [GS09]. Other examples can be found in the M&A handbooks (e.g. Jansen [Ja08], Picot [Pi08b], or Wirtz [Wi06b]).

The literature study on success factors for M&A of our research team resulted in the subsequent list. The single items can be found in the majority of publications (e.g [Ep04, Gö06, HKT02, LM02, Pi08b, PP00]), even though their work is sometimes based on different languages and slightly differing terminology:

- Clear business vision - committed, explicitly described, and measurable
- High aspiration level, definite directions, and common performance indicators
- Stakeholder management, effective communication, and corporate cultures
- Project organization (structures and processes)
- Coordinated and holistic planning of business and IT
- Consistent decisions for business and IT
- Continuous knowledge management
- Adequate risk management
- Realize growth and demonstrate early wins

Instead of elaborating on single success factors in detail, we use this condensed list as an input to substantiate the scenario of a corporate buyer in chapter 5. As stated above, detailed descriptions and empirical studies can be found in [Ep04, Gö06, HKT02, LM02, Pi08b, PP00].

2.3 Different Forms of M&A

2.3.1 M&A Classification Scheme

Each of the comprehensive M&A books offers some kind of classification to document and analyze different appearances of M&A and their characteristics, e.g. [Ja08, LM02, Pi08b, Wi06b]. In summary, the different forms of M&A can be structured according to five main attributes which are transaction type (merger or acquisition), direction of integration (horizontal, vertical, or conglomerate), distribution of power (merger of equals vs. leader role), deal setting (hostile vs. friendly), and deal motivation (strategic vs. financial).

Additional differences characterizing a certain form of M&A may be the selected payment method (share deal vs. asset deal), the channel of offer submission (e.g. auction, bidding procedure, direct offer to target, or indirect offer via a broker), internationality of the transaction (national or cross-border transaction), as well as the exit of investor (e.g. no exit, trade sale, public offering (IPO), or trade sale to a third party) [Ja08, LM02].

Figure 2.2 shows the condensed M&A classification scheme that is applied in this work. It consists in the five main characteristics mentioned above, while additional differences are summarized into a free text attribute "other".

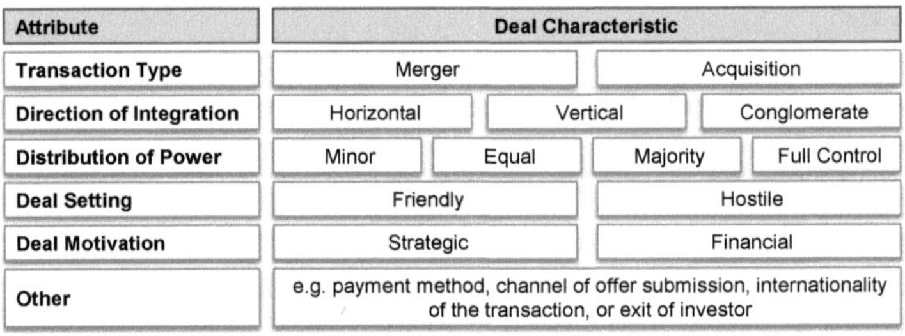

Figure 2.2: M&A Classification Scheme

The concrete characteristics of a company's regular M&A transactions have implications on the set-up of an M&A practice and an the M&A process in an organization. For example, as a financial investor's core business is acquiring and selling companies, the company will focus on different activities than a strategic buyer that is trying to optimally integrate an acquired company into its enterprise structure. The elements of the M&A classification scheme are described in section 2.3.2. Our work focuses on the buyer perspective. In chapter 5, we describe the corporate buyer scenario and its characteristics in more detail using the M&A classification scheme.

2.3.2 M&A Characteristics

Transaction Type: Although the two words "merger" and "acquisition" in M&A are often used synonymously, both terms have different meanings [De09, LM02, Ja08]. Actually, the differentiation of both terms has not reached complete consensus in literature. Jansen [Ja08], for example, elaborates on the different terminology in US/Anglo-Saxon and German language areas. While the terms are sufficiently defined and consistently applied in the Anglo-

Saxon publications (especially in the United States), German literature still lacks a commonly accepted distinction between both concepts. From a commercial law perspective, Picot [Pi98] states that this problem arises from the missing definition of an enterprise in German law. Becker [Be94] refers to the payment method in order to differentiate both transactions. Thereby, a cash payment is an acquisition, whereas a merger is typically a share transaction.

In summary, both terms can be defined as follows. A *"merger"* refers to a transaction, where two separate enterprises agree to form a common corporate entity. Thereby, one enterprise may be merged into a second or the fusion may result in a new enterprise. An *"acquisition"* refers to a takeover of a target enterprise by a buyer enterprise by purchasing the complete target enterprise. Acquiring a company can be carried out either by purchase of capital shares, asset shares, or a different type of agreement. A detailed discussion on both terms and definitions can be found in general M&A literature, e.g. [GS09, Ja08, LM02, Wi06b]. M&A can be seen as a generic term for transactions that include the transfer of management and supervisory authority [LM02]. Therefore, it may be applied for mergers and acquisitions as long as the differences between both do not impede research results. Being aware of M&A being a very broad topic and that there are considerable differences between mergers and acquisitions, this work does not elaborate on these aspects in detail. As the scope of this work is the applicability of business capability models in a concrete corporate buyer scenario, the focus is laid on providing the foundation to define this scenario. For the ease of reading, the terms "M&A", "merger", and "acquisition" are applied interchangeably in this document.

Direction of Integration: An M&A transaction results in either a horizontal integration, a vertical integration, or in conglomerates [FM06, LM02]. Horizontal integration refers to a situation where both enterprises offer products or services in the same market. Often they are closely related companies, e.g. regional competitors [LM02]. A vertical integration refers to an M&A involving enterprises from different stages in the value chain. In this case, it results in an adaption of a company's vertical range of manufacture. Vertical M&A can be forward, towards the final purchaser facing the customer (e.g. a manufacturer acquiring a distribution network), or backwards in direction of the raw material suppliers (e.g. a manufacturer acquiring a supplier) [LM02]. Conglomerate integration refers to M&A across industries where the companies involved do not share a value chain or market [Ja08].

Distribution of Power: The decision power can be differently distributed among the companies that enter into an M&A. A special case is the so-called merger of equals, in which both enterprises have a similar size and decision power [GH10]. In practice, the internal decision power will be defined with the assignment of management positions in the new structure [LM02]. However, from an external point of view, the involved parties try to prevent an image of a victim, taken over by a superior organization. Even though this situation is called a merger of equals, the concrete transaction in the background may also be an acquisition. A prominent example for a merger of equals with the typical challenges is the DaimlerCrysler case. The level of decision power for the buyer enterprise, can be categorized as minor (smaller than 50%), equal (50%), majority (more than 50%, less than 100%), and full control (100%) [Sc00]. The rights arising from an investment differ from country to country. There are different stages (in percentage) that imply certain rights, even in a minor role [LM02].

Deal Setting: The basic setting for an M&A deal can be a friendly or hostile takeover [Ja08]. Hostile takeovers usually involve a big enterprise that acquires a smaller one. Jansen [Ja08] discusses the effects of a hostile mode on various aspects of the M&A process such as negotiations and communication. Additionally he provides an overview on defense strategies on the side of the target enterprise. A hostile takeover brings along additional challenges for performing the transaction. In the past, they where relatively rare, especially in Germany [HJ06]. The deal setting can also change during the transaction. Some prominent examples that started in a hostile manner turned out as friendly acquisitions, e.g. the Vodafone/Mannesmann case.

Deal Motivation: The motivation for an M&A can be basically differentiated into strategic and financial transactions [Ja08, LM02]. In the first case, so called strategic investors seek to support their strategic business goals by choosing the instrument of M&A as described in section 2.1.2. In the second case, financial investors or private equity firms acquire companies partly or completely in order to realize financial returns through resale.

2.4 Participants in an M&A Transaction

The planning and execution of an M&A project involves a high quantity and heterogeneity of tasks [LM02, Me06]. These tasks are performed by a multitude of different groups and individuals with multifaceted, sometimes competing goals and concerns [LM02]. Consequently, each of these stakeholder groups has its own perspective on the M&A transaction. M&A

literature (e.g. [Ja08, LM02, Pi08b, Wi06b]) structures the participants of an M&A into three groups: the buyer organization, the target enterprise, and external participants. To make the M&A process successful, it is essential to balance the diverging or conflicting goals and concerns among the participants between both enterprises and within the groups in each enterprise [LM02, Me06]. An appropriate organization and well-organized communication are key to successful M&A (see section 2.2) [GSV06, Lu02]. Therefore, appropriate governance is critical to success since it defines decision rights, accountability, communication lines, and escalation paths to direct participants during the integration.

Buyer Organization: The buyer organization is the company acquiring the target enterprise. The roles and individuals relevant to a M&A and thus influencing the success of a transaction are not limited to the owners (shareholder) of the enterprise and top management (executive board). Operational management (e.g. business unit management, executive staff, department heads) as well as the company's employees are also important. They may be not participating in the deal directly, but are affected by the results. Thus, they care about their personal role in future (e.g. staffing of key positions in the target organization), security of their jobs, salary, location changes, and social benefits [LM02]. Moreover they will be responsible for business operations after completion of the merger. Uncertainty or dissatisfaction can lead to fluctuation, especially among high-potentials [LM02].

Target Enterprise: Comparable with the buyer organization, the target enterprise does also include the roles mentioned above. Especially relevant are those roles and individuals that can negatively influence the progress or outcome of the integration. These can be identified from top level to the level of a single employee. Executives and top management, as one example, can defend the company against hostile takeover and strongly influence the successful implementation of the integration plan and willingness of employees [LM02]. A second important group is the target enterprise's key staff and carriers of special knowledge, a high level of uncertainty can lead to a substantial loss of knowledge, if key staff can not be convinced to contribute to success of the target organization [GS09].

Externals: External participants comprise competitors, suppliers, clients, regulatory authorities, M&A advisers, and investors. Competitors will try to take advantage of a moment of uncertainty, for example by alienating customers [Ho00b] or recruiting high-potential employees and their expert knowledge [GS09, LM02]. Suppliers will try to at least secure price structure and delivery conditions. Depending on the relationship between the enterprises involved in the M&A and its suppliers, several effect may occur [LM02]. If a supplier serves both enterprises, the increased market power of the merged enterprise can result in lower prices and worse conditions for the supplier. If the supplier is only serving the buyer organization, he also fears increased market power, but expects a higher volume. A supplier for the target enterprise has to fear loosing a client through procurement synergies of the merged enterprise. Although sometimes underestimated, clients are not indifferent about the supplier company for their preferred products and services [Ho00b]. From a consumer's perspective, increased market power of merged enterprise may result in higher prices. Especially for clients of the target enterprise, there is an uncertainty about the continuation of production and sales of certain products or services and the availability of personal contacts [LM02].

Another group of external participants are the relevant national and international authorities and bodies, as well as economic and social partners [GS09]. These include public institutions like government, administration, courts, and antitrust agency, but also employee representations (e.g. labor union, employee's association) that bundle individual interests to give them more power and influence. External M&A advisers can be distinguished between consultants that cover the whole M&A process (like investment banks and large management consultancies) and M&A consultants who specialize on certain process phases (e.g. auditors, tax advisers, and lawyers) [GS09, LM02]. Investors provide debt capital and will be requesting a high attractiveness of the deal. Other external participants may be commercial traders, commercial brokers, institutional investors (e.g. private equity firm, hedge fond), or M&A boutiques.

2.5 Merger Readiness

From a buyer point of view there is an apparent need to improve the outcome of M&A activities [GH08, GS09, LM02]. This challenge is addressed with the concept of "merger readiness", originating from the idea of an improved ability to successfully manage M&A. According to Meier and Spang, "merger readiness" can be defined as *"a systematic preparation of the entire company for the execution of a merger or acquisition"* [MS00].

In line with the idea of achieving merger readiness, enterprises establish and evolve an M&A practice supporting corporate management in successful integration of an acquired entity [LM02]. Jansen [JB08] also identified the need for a comprehensive M&A management capability to improve success of M&A and especially emphasizes the need to professionalize this capability regarding pre-merger planning and post-merger integration. In the same breath, he reveals that there are no reliable contributions from academia for this challenge. In other words, merger readiness demands for a certain maturity of an enterprise's M&A capability. And the goal of establishing a profound M&A capability is to improve planning of the merger and implementation of the integration. Thus, it contributes to M&A success regarding both dimensions, the better estimation of the value of an acquisition and to decreasing integration costs (see figure 2.1). One important element of the M&A capability is a professional M&A process comprising the overall scope from early pre-merger planning to full completion of integration [Ja08, LM02].

2.6 Basic M&A Process Structure

Even back in in 1986, Jemison and Sitkin [JS86] positioned the M&A process as a critical determinant for M&A success. In line with this statement, several authors showed that a professional M&A process can be a competitive advantage if an enterprise's corporate strategy includes external growth [MS00, Pi08b]. There is consensus, that a professional M&A process comprises the overall scope from early pre-merger planning to full completion of integration [Ja08, LM02]. Along this way, it includes activities relating to different interdependent management disciplines including a variety of special experts as well as internal and external stakeholders [LM02, Me06]. As M&A comprises multiple process dimensions, views and terminologies which have to be differentiated and integrated for a professional proceeding, the process has to be part of an actively managed M&A capability to ensure efficient operation.

The planning and execution of an M&A project along this process involves a high quantity and heterogeneity of tasks [LM02]. These tasks are performed by a multitude of different groups and individuals with multifaceted, sometimes competing goals and concerns [LM02]. Additionally, a merger project has to incorporate a large number of stakeholders from multiple disciplines [PP00]. In order to make the M&A process successful, it is essential to balance the diverging or conflicting goals and concerns among the participants between both enterprises and within the groups in each enterprise [LM02]. With the division of the M&A process into sub-areas, and the definition of individual tasks that have to be performed in these areas, a conceptual framework is created which allows a simplification of the often very complex M&A projects [LM02]. Figure 2.3 depicts a typical M&A process with three phases and multiple management dimensions.

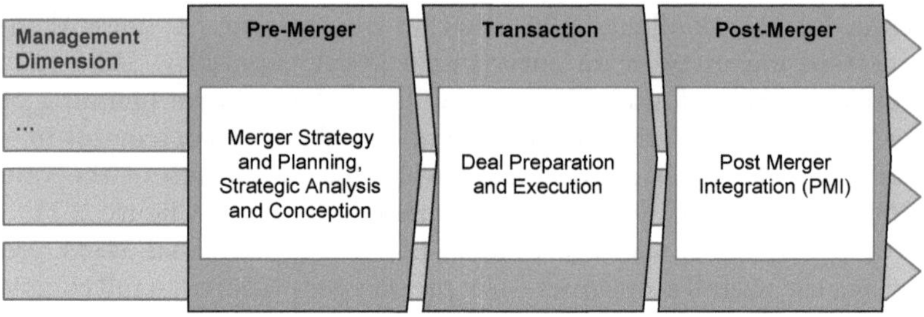

Figure 2.3: M&A Process

On the top level, an M&A process is divided into three distinct phases: merger planning, transaction, and post merger integration (PMI) [BU05, Ja08, KHG06, Lu03, Me06, Pi08b, Wi06b]. More process models can be found in publications from practitioners and academics, for example in [Br90, Ho96, Ju99, LM02, St93b]. They represent additional perspectives on the process or elaborate on different steps, activities, or methods in more detail. Some authors (e.g. [Gi97]) reduce the transaction phase to the concrete deal execution, thus they allocate deal preparation activities like the due diligence to the pre-merger phase. However, none of them provides a complete reference model with the same level of detail for activities and deliverables along the phases. In this thesis, we adhere to the broadly accepted structure of three phases and use the terms "Pre-Merger Phase", "Transaction Phase", and "Post-Merger Phase".

Complementing the process phases, an M&A process comprises a number of different interdependent management dimensions [LM02, Me06]. Different authors define different boundaries for the single management dimensions, thus the single definitions are not always selective. Additionally, different terminology is applied to describe different groups of stakeholders or activities, e.g. "(sub-)process" [LM02], "management issues" [Me06], or "key tasks" [GS09]. Typical management dimensions are "strategy", "finance", "legal", "human resources", or "processes". Furthermore, some authors (e.g. [LM02]) differentiate between core activities and supporting activities.

In order to start to identify anchor points for the application of EA Management and especially for the application of business capabilities, we need a complete M&A process reference model with a balanced level of detail for activities and deliverables along the phases. As this kind of M&A

process reference model is not available today, we consolidate available approaches into the "Corporate Buyer M&A Process" (CBMA Process), which is presented in chapter 6.

2.7 IT Transformation during M&A

The impact of IT on a company's performance is an enduring research question in the information systems (IS) literature [Ca03]. Regarding the role and importance of IT during M&A, an analysis of literature reveals differing, but nonetheless well-founded statements. The different opinions originate from different perspectives on the enterprise and on IT. On top level management, IT is not a high priority during planning and transaction of M&A [PP00]. Primary activities are implementation of the new organizational structures, realization of quick wins, and implementation the strategy of the new enterprise [LM02, GS09]. Therefore, a well-structured approach to IT integration is not always part of top priority activities. But, from the perspective of an IT manager, it is the personal area of responsibility and thus receives primary attention [KS02, PP00].

Several studies on past mergers have shown that success of M&A can be strongly influences by IT and IT integration work. They reveal high M&A failure rates resulting from IT-related problems. On the basis of several empirical studies in the banking industry, Gartner [Mo09] summarizes that at least 50% of PMI fail due to the large scope and high IT complexity as well as a lack of IT due diligence and planning prior to acquisitions. Brown [Br01] states that even 70% of M&A fail to achieve the anticipated results, mainly due to IT problems.

Today, IT is a key enabler for most business processes and therefore an integral part of business operations. Hence, in merger situations IT has to be considered carefully [Br01, Pe99]. During an M&A, poor IT integration can significantly disrupt business operations with potential negative implications for customer retention and regulatory compliance [An09]. During a merger, IT has to fulfill three important roles. IT has to provide the backbone of daily business operations, it is the basis for business process target design, and at the same time IT is subject for integration and rationalization [SB09]. During the whole M&A process, appropriate IT support is essential for business operations [Gi97, MM95]. However, the importance of IT during M&A is also depending on the industry, the involved companies operate in. If IT is getting more and more important in an industry, it also influences integration processes - positively or negatively. Consequently, the successful integration of IT during M&A is vital for the overall success.

When trying to identify resources addressing the challenge of IT integration during M&A, valuable contributions may come from the business and the IT domain. Business literature tends to put more emphasis on the overall M&A process from a management point of view, while IT-related contributions tend to address IT challenges considering M&A as context.

Approaching the topic of IT integration during M&A from a business perspective, the comprehensive M&A management handbooks of Jansen [Ja08], Picot [Pi08b], and Wirtz [Wi06b] can provide a starting point. But, due to their business focus, these publications set the overall context of the merger but do not provide specific artifacts for the consolidation of IT. Mostly, IT is not in the focus of these publications. In Picot's book [Pi08b] for example, the role and importance of IT is only addressed by a high level IT due diligence checklist.

Approaching the topic of IT integration during M&A from an IT perspective, more contributions are available. However, little literature exists, both in academia as well as in practice, providing specific artifacts facilitating the integration of IT in the course of M&A projects [MB07, WL04, JY96]. Furthermore, most resources focus on the challenges of and solutions for PMI of IT [AH08]. The need for improved planning of IT integration has been identified, but is rarely addressed explicitly so far [An09]. Alaranta and Henningsson [AH08] state, that IT integration is one of the most challenging tasks during M&A. The authors propose an approach to analyze and plan PMI of IT that extends general theory for IT planning with specific characteristics of the M&A context. It comprises a process for IT PMI planning and decisions that have to be considered for designing an IT integration plan. Furthermore, they emphasize the need to embed IT PMI in overall PMI. Anello [An09] states, that knowledge of the strategic rationale, knowledge of decisions for the M&A activity, and an understanding of the effects on the enterprise IT are key for successful M&A. This should be promoted by early involvement of IT within the M&A process and alignment of planning and activities between business areas and IT. Depending on the form of a merger, IT should be viewed as an enabling mechanism for achieving the aspired merger goals. This can imply the reduction of costs or the goal of increasing revenues while minimizing risks. According to Anello, it is important to recognize that IT itself does not make a significant contribution to cost reduction during mergers and that revenue enhancement through IT is a longer-term objective. Buck-Lew et al. [BLWP92] propose, that the so-called "IT fit" should be explicitly considered during the analysis of corporate acquisitions. They argue that data and information technology can be considered as a management resource equally important as financial and human resources. According to the authors, an assessment of IT fit should cover the IT environments of the two joining companies, the IT contribution each of them can bring to the combined enterprise, and the role of IT in negotiations of the acquisition price and during PMI. Cypra, Fletcher and Piché [CFP07] especially stress the importance of an early involvement of IT representatives in the M&A process. They state that today the CIO is often not involved prior to due diligence and PMI planning and thus missing to contribute information to more accurate IT integration planning in terms of synergies and costs. Larsen [La05b] conducted a review of literature from academics and practitioners and performed a case exemplification at a company from the financial service industry. The author concludes that planning of information and communication technologies in early stages of the integration process is vital to the realization of benefits of an M&A. McKiernan and Merali [MM95] state that IT integration is one of the main challenges during PMI leading to poor overall M&A performance. The authors differentiate between a reactive and a pro-active role of IT during M&A. While IT is adapted to changed operational considerations in a reactive role, it facilitates other organizational changes in a pro-active role. If a company's IT is the primary motivation for an acquisition, the authors also speak of a pro-active role. Miklitz and Buxmann [MB07] point out four different integration strategies for application landscapes. The authors present a decision model for selecting target applications aiming at the standardization of the landscape. Penzel and Pietig [PP00] published a book labeled the "Merger Guide" containing experiences from bank mergers. The authors explicitly take IT into account as one dimension in the overall M&A process. They spend a dedicated chapter dealing with IT during M&A. Besides pointing out relevant system integration strategies, system transition plans, and a layer model of a bank's system architecture, the work also considers data migration and the shutdown of obsolete systems.

2.8 IT Integration Strategies

A transaction may not succeed if IT planning is inappropriate or not aligned with the overall integration strategy, since appropriate IT support is essential for business operation [RS99, SJR96]. Therefore, the selection of an IT integration strategy is strongly dependent on the chosen overall integration strategy [Wi06a].

The overall integration strategy is predominantly driven by the type, direction of integration, and individual goals of the transaction [MS06] (see also section 2.3). Haspelagh and Jemison [HJ92] describe three integration types depending on the required degree of organizational autonomy and demand for strategic interdependencies. In their so-called "contingency matrix", the authors suggest four distinct strategies. A holding implies low autonomy and low strategic interdependence, a symbiotic strategy is characterized by high autonomy and high strategic interdependence, preservation entails high autonomy and low strategic interdependence, and an absorption strategy results in low autonomy and high strategic interdependence. These general strategies are generally agreed in literature and provide a foundation for several contributions, for example the approaches to PMI [Kr06] or the intensity of organizational change [MM10]. Regarding the different depth of integration in certain functional areas, Jansen [JB08] proposes three integration types on enterprise level. According to the author, a back-end merger is characterized by low integration depth, concentrating on supporting activities like administration, human resources, or finance. An operational merger requires middle to high integration depth for example in the areas of operations, procurement, or manufacturing. A front-end merger involves middle to high integration depth for consumer-facing activities like marketing, sales, and distribution.

During M&A, the enterprise is confronted with at least two IT landscapes that have to be integrated [OWB09]. Literature documents four commonly agreed strategies for IT integration: co-existence, absorption, best-of-breed, and greenfield [Ke06, MB07], illustrated in figure 2.4.

Compared to one another, each strategy has certain characteristics regarding the overall effort, time and budget needed, and risk involved during the execution of the implementation. Noteworthy, the single strategies may also be combined [Gu10], for example an absorption strategy can be complemented with selective best-of breed or selective greenfield.

Co-existence refers to a strategy where both IT landscapes are left independent and are operated in parallel. Where necessary, interfaces between are implemented primarily for information exchange. According to literature, with a co-existence strategy effort is rather low [MB07] and implementation of the changes requires a shorter time [CL09, Gu10, MB07, Wi06a]. Therefore, required budgets are smaller [CL09, Gu10, HC06] and risk are rather low [JY96].

Absorption implies that business applications of one merging partner are chosen as target application landscape for the merged company. Alternatively, the name "steam-roller" [Ke06] or "complete integration" [Wi06a] is used.

According to literature, with an absorption strategy involved effort is rather limited [JY96, MB07] and implementation of the changes requires a shorter time [BS08, Gu10, JY96, Ke04, MB07, Po01, Wi06a]. Hence, required budgets are smaller [JY96, Gu10, Ke04, MB07, Wi06a] and risk are rather low [Br06, Gu10, JY96, Ke04, MB07].

In a best-of-breed strategy, the best solutions are selected from both existing IT landscapes. Occasionally, this approach is also called "cherry-picking" [Ke06] or "partial integration" [Wi06a]. According to literature, involved effort is rather high [DT07, Gu10, WL04] and implementation of the changes requires longer [BS08, Gu10, JY96, Ke04, MB07, Wi06a] when selecting a best-of-breed strategy. Hence, required budgets are rather high [Gu10, JY96, Ke04, MB07] and risk can be high [Br06, MB07].

Greenfield describes a strategy where the target IT landscape is developed from scratch, while decommissioning the existing solutions [MB07]. Some authors refer to this strategy as "new-build". According to literature, involved effort is rather high [Gu10] and implementation of the changes requires longer [BS08, Gu10, Ke04, MB07, Wi06a, WL04]. Consequently, required budgets are rather high [Br06, BS08, FMS11, Gu10, Ke04, MB07]. Regarding involved risks, literature statements range from limited [MB07] to rather high [Gu10, Ke04] risks.

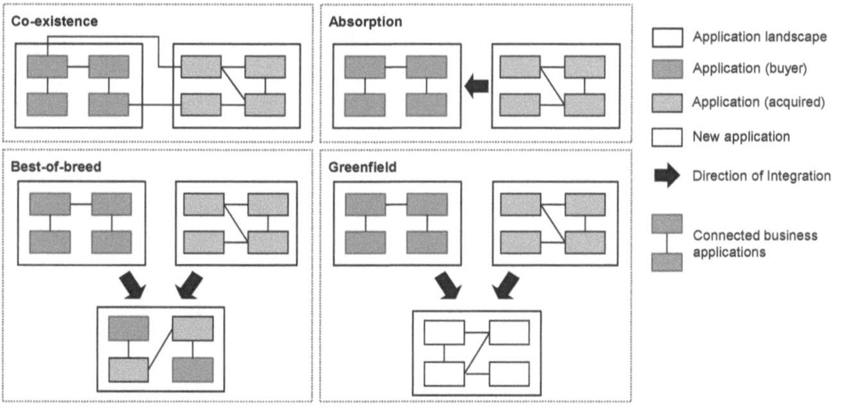

Figure 2.4: IT Integration Strategies [Ec12]

3 State-of-the-Art of EA Management in the Context of M&A

3.1 EA Management Resources and Related Work

In recent years, the topic Enterprise Architecture (EA) and Enterprise Architecture Management (EA Management) has gained considerable importance as well as acceptance in practice and academia [Bu11]. At the same time, EA Management became an established management discipline with formal organization units in many international enterprises. Even small and medium sized companies adopt EA Management.

A multitude of EA Management publications have been issued by various research groups and practitioners over the last decade. Unlike to other traditional management disciplines, the core literature for the area of EA Management is not known and the fundamental sources on the subject of EA Management, which provide an introduction are not clearly identified [My11]. Zachman [Za87] published one of the first major publications on EA Management in 1987, which is still seen as relevant by many research groups and practitioners. Since then, a plurality of approaches to EA Management have been proposed by different groups of researchers, practitioners, and standardization bodies, which vary widely in respect to their methods, models, and languages [Ka08, My11]. However, recent research is moving towards a mutual understanding of EA [SW09].

Recently, several literature reviews have been released, helping to structure existing resources and to make contributions comparable. Mykhashchuk et al. [My11] performed an extensive literature study, structuring and documenting the state-of-the-art in EA Management. The authors analyzed the distribution of papers over time, their geographical origin, the type of publication, the number of references of an article, and the author groups involved. Three years before, in 2008, Aier et al. published their work on

EA Management literature which included a survey on the common EA practice [ARW08]. In the same year, Schönherr et al. [Sc08b] published their work, analyzing 126 references regarding their definitions for EA or EA Management. Kappelman et al. [Ka08] provide an overview of existing research and practice regarding EA Management and present key functions and benefits of EA as seen by IT professionals based on the results of a survey. Schelp and Winter [SW09] focus on EA research, especially the research methodologies applied by the respective academic groups forming so-called language communities. Both, Schönherr et al. as well as Schelp and Winter identified the need to establish a common terminology in the discipline of EA Management.

The amount of EA-related literature is even larger, when including literature from related disciplines, such as business/IT alignment or IT architecture management, which is not explicitly labeled as EA related literature [Ka08]. In general, available literature can be grouped into different classes, for example their geographical origin, maturity level, language (terminology) group, theory-oriented vs. practice-oriented character, intended target group of readers, as well as the continuity of contributions from a certain group. However, boundaries between single categories are not always selective.

Single research results on EA Management have been published in workshop and conference proceedings, journal articles (mainly IS journals), reports, and academic theses [My11]. Summarized findings of continuous research work and practical experiences have been published in dedicated EA Management books and EA Management frameworks [Ma11]. Since 2004, dedicated EA Management books have been published by academics, e.g. Bernard [Be05], Berg and Steenbergen [BS10], Johnson and Ekstedt [JE07], Land et al. [La08], Lankhorst [La05a], Ross et al. [RWR06], Schekkerman [Sc08a], and Wagter et al. [Wa05], as well as by practitioners, e.g. Engels et al. [En08], Hanschke [Ha09c], Keller [Ke06], Niemann [Ni08], and Schwarzer [Sc09]. Related work analysis for the majority of EA Management books mentioned above can be found in [Bu11], [Er09], and [My11].

The most relevant EA Management frameworks in the corporate environment are "The Open Group Architecture Framework (TOGAF)" [Th09] and the "Zachman Framework" [Za87, SZ92, Za01]. Administration, government, and military also apply the "Federal Enterprise Architecture Framework (FEAF)" [US99], the "Department of Defense Architecture Framework (DoDAF)" [US10], and the "NATO Architecture Framework (NAF)" [No07]. "Building Blocks of Enterprise Architecture Management (BEAMS)" is a relatively new academic approach, which aims at complementing TOGAF with more detailed artifacts [BMS11].

In the following, the focus is laid on related work addressing the application of EA Management in M&A. Before we can start with this analysis, the basic definitions and terminology are introduced in the subsequent section.

3.2 Key Definitions and Terminology

As mentioned above, various definitions are available for the concepts of Enterprise Architecture (EA) and Enterprise Architecture Management (EA Management). These definitions vary regarding the general scope and the level of detail, reflecting different understandings of EA Management that can also be found among practitioners. The scope ranges from a technology-oriented view, over alignment of information technology (IT) with business requirements, to a holistic planning discipline comprising business and IT architectures. While some definitions have a strong focus on strategy, others have a very operational character. Some definitions are model-oriented, emphasizing the EA model and its construction, while others are process-driven, thus focusing on the EA Management function to enable planning & controlling of the EA. As a result, the different definitions lead to the absence of a generally accepted definition [Er09, Sc08b, SW09].

Therefore, definitions in this work are selected from industry standards which are widely accepted in academia and practice. Furthermore, these standards are referenced in the majority of publications that build the foundation for the research conducted in this thesis. In general, EA Management is seen as a holistic management discipline, covering both business and IT. The remainder of this section introduces the basic definitions relevant to the EA Management discipline as considered in this thesis.

The International Organization for Standardization (ISO) published the "Standard for Systems and Software Engineering - Architectural Description" (ISO/IEC 42010) [In07]. This document serves as a general foundation. The standard is complemented with additional definitions where needed. TOGAF, for example embraces but does not strictly adhere to the terminology of ISO/IEC 42010 [Th09]. However, the following definitions are commonly agreed among the member companies of The Open Group's Architecture Forum and widely applied in practice.

ISO/IEC 42010 defines *"architecture"* as *"the fundamental organization of a system, embodied in its components, their relationships to each other and the environment, and the principles governing its design and evolution"* [In07]. In a system-oriented approach, an enterprise can also be seen as a system that consists in other systems [Ha05], e.g. its organizational units or a group of enterprises. Therefore, the definition in ISO/IEC 42010 can also be used for enterprises.

TOGAF expands the architecture definitions of ISO/IEC 42010 standards into an enterprise architecture view. TOGAF defines *"enterprise"* as *"any collection of organizations that has a common set of goals"* and further specifies it as *"the highest level (typically) of description of an organization and typically covers all missions and functions. An enterprise will often span multiple organizations"* [Th09][4]. According to these definitions, an enterprise could be a government agency, a whole corporation, a division of a corporation, a single department, or a chain of geographically distant organizations which are linked together by common ownership. Consequently, it may also represent the extended enterprise, including partners, suppliers, customers, and internal business units [Th09].

Building on ISO/IEC 42010, TOGAF distinguishes between two definitions for *"architecture"* depending on the context. The first definition focuses on implementation issues and defines an architecture as *"a formal description of a system, or a detailed plan of the system at component level to guide its implementation"* [Th09]. The second definition in TOGAF focuses on structural issues and guidelines. In this case, an architecture is *"the structure of components, their inter-relationships, and the principles and guidelines governing their design and evolution over time"* [Th09].

Consequently, the *"Enterprise Architecture (EA)"* can be defined as *"the fundamental conception of the enterprise in its environment embodied in its elements, their relationships to each other and to its environment, and the principles guiding its design and evolution"* [Bu11, Er09].

While the structure of an enterprise is represented in the EA, EA Management considers the management activity of "architecting" on the basis of this representation [Er09]. Correspondingly, Buckl defines *"EA Management"* as *"a continuous and self maintaining management function seeking to improve the alignment of business and IT and to guide the managed evolution of an (virtual) enterprise. Based on a holistic perspective on the enterprise furnished with information from other enterprise-level management functions it provides input to, exerts control over, and defines guidelines for these enterprise-level management functions"* [Bu11]. In other words, EA Management is an approach for analyzing, planning, and controlling as-is and target states of the enterprise in terms of business, information systems, and technology architecture, based on an overarching EA model. Often, the

[4] This definition shares commonalities with ISO/EC 15704, defining an enterprise as *"one or more organizations sharing a definite mission, goals and objectives to offer an output such as a product or a service"* [CDV08].

definitions for EA and EA Management are not selective[5]. Being aware of the overlaps, both concepts are separated in a way they can be used jointly.

In order to perform architectural activity effectively within an enterprise, TOGAF also defines the *"EA capability"* as *"an appropriate business capability for architecture, through organization structures, roles, responsibilities, skills, and processes"* [Th09]. The *"EA capability"* is supported by the establishment of a corresponding functional unit, the so-called *"EA Management function"*.

3.3 M&A in EA Management Literature

As mentioned above, the body of knowledge of EA Management matured steadily. However, the application of this knowledge in M&A just starts to be subject of research. To get an overview on available related work, we conducted a literature study focusing on the contribution of EA Management literature towards M&A (see 3.3.1). Due to the limited availability of dedicated contributions, we also analyzed thirteen recent English and German EA Management books published between 2005 and 2011 (see section 3.3.2) and three EA Management frameworks (see section 3.3.3). These resources are consulted frequently by EA practitioners willing to apply EA methods and models in real-world situations, which is also the case for M&A.

3.3.1 Literature Study

We performed an online search to identify relevant conference proceedings, journal articles, reports, and academic theses. The search was performed in 2011. It was focused on online databases, e.g. ACM digital library, CiteSeerX, Google scholar, as well as the electronic libraries of our university. We applied the key words "M&A", "merger", and "acquisition", in different combinations with "EA", "EA Management", and "enterprise architecture". The search was performed with the English terms and their respective German translations.

In each publication, we examined the relationship between EA Management and M&A from general to specific. First, we checked if there is a general reference to M&A in EA Management literature. In a next step,

[5] As one example, Lankhorst proposes a definition with explicit reference to a strategic dimension of EA: *"Enterprise Architecture (EA)"* is *"a coherent set of principles, methods, and models that are used in the design and realization of an enterprise's organizational structure, business processes, information systems, and technology infrastructure with respect to corporate strategy"* [La05a].

we analyzed which phases of an M&A process are referenced and if there are typical EA Management tasks mentioned that are carried out during M&A. If this is the case, we tried to identify EA Management artifacts that are used to perform these tasks and investigated if these artifacts have been designed and/or evaluated by empirical means. Whenever a publications did not discuss the topic in enough detail, only the first aspect is documented.

Table 3.1 structures the identified publications according to author, citation key, year, and type of work. Additionally, it indicates on which pages the topic of M&A is addressed and, if applicable, the specific M&A process phase the author refers to.

Table 3.1: M&A in EA Management - Online Search Results

Publication			Basic Info		M&A	M&A Phases		
Author	Title	Cit.	Type	Year	mentioned	Pl.	Tr.	PMI
Aier, S.; Fischer, C.; Winter, R.	Construction and Evaluation of a Meta-Model for Enterprise Architecture Design Principles	AFW11	Academic	2011	p. 643			
Assmann, M.	Model-Based Evaluation of Service-Oriented Enterprise Architectures	As09	Academic	2009	p. 5, 46			
Bucher, T.; Fischer, R.; Kurpjuweit, S.; Winter, R.	Analysis and Application Scenarios of Enterprise Architecture: An Exploratory Study	Bu06	Academic	2006	p. 4, 7			X
Buckl et al.	EA Management Patterns for Consolidations after Mergers	Bu09	Academic	2009	p. 1-12 (all)			X
Braun, C.; Winter, R.	Integration of IT Service Management into Enterprise Architecture	BW07	Academic	2007	p. 1			X
Dudas, M.; Tobisson, P.	Information Systems Integration in Mergers and Acquisitions	DT07	Academic	2007	throughout			X
van Houwelingen, J. W.	Relevance and Usability of Enterprise Architectures during Post Merger IT Integrations	Ho08	Academic	2008	throughout			X
Kamogawa, T.; Okada, H.	Enterprise Architecture Create Business Value	KO09	Academic	2009	p 205, 207			
Larsen, M.	ICT Integration in an M&A Process	La05b	Academic	2005	throughout		X	X
Mo, J.; Nemes, L.	Issues in using Enterprise Architecture for Mergers and Acquisitions	MN09	Academic	2009	p. 239-266 (all)	X	X	X
Namba, Y.	City Planning Approach for Rebuilding Enterprise Information Systems	Na05	Academic	2005	p. 6, 77			
Vaniya, N.	Building Preparedness for Mergers and Acquisitions - The role of Enterprise Architecture Practice	Va11	Academic	2011	throughout	X		X
de Vries, M.; van Rensburg, A. C.	Enterprise Architecture - New Business Value Perspectives	VV08	Academic	2008	p. 1			

The online search resulted in two groups of publications. The first group establishes a linkage between EA Management and M&A (section 3.3.1). These publications mention M&A as a driver for EA Management or state that support of M&A is a task of the EA Management discipline. Often, M&A is an example business driver for change that leads to challenges for the management of IT. However, these publications do not address the application of EA Management during M&A in detail. The second group of publications address the application of EA Management in the case of M&A (section 3.3.1).

According to the scope of this work (see section 2.3.1), we did not include publications that focus on carve-outs in our analysis (e.g. [Fä10a, Fä10b]). Furthermore, our online search identified some commercial publications describing consultancy service offerings (e.g. [Ga01, GB09, Gu09a]), consultant's case studies (e.g. [Gu09b]), or EA Management tool capabilities (e.g. [Al11a, Tr11]). These publications are not evaluated in detail.

Linkage between EA Management and M&A

The publication of Aier et al. [AFW11] is focused on principles in EA Management. The authors analyze existing definitions for EA principles and propose a meta-model defining EA design principles. The developed model is evaluated in two case studies. One of the case studies is a company resulting form a series of mergers of regional IT service providers. Noteworthy, the authors mention that this company follows a very strict top-down EA Management approach and state that this is a result from the history of several post merger integration scenarios.

Assmann [As09] approaches EA Management from an Service-Oriented Architecture (SOA) perspective. He addresses technical challenges (e.g. manage technologies, develop services) of SOA and governance challenges (e.g. stakeholder management, financial management, and change management for processes). The author proposes a model-based approach to EA, based on the eclipse modeling framework (EMF). This approach allows to evaluate the service orientation of an enterprise with the help of service orientation quality criteria. M&A is only mentioned as an example scenario for merging two divisions in which SOA is beneficial.

The work of Bucher et al. [Bu06] aims at a systematization of analysis techniques in EA Management. The authors identify these techniques (e.g. dependency analysis, compliance analysis, cost analysis) and describe application scenarios (e.g. business continuity planning, sourcing decisions, project initialization). According to the authors, EA Management techniques can be applied during post merger integration to unify or consolidate processes, organizational structures, applications, and IT systems. They also mention that a comparison of two EA models helps to compare enterprises in terms of similarities, differences, overlaps, and gaps. The identified techniques and application scenarios are then evaluated in an exploratory study with 51 responses. For the application scenarios, the authors applied a five-tiered Likert scale to the statement "EA is a critical success factor for realizing the scenario" (minimum value (1) means "scenario not supported by EA at all", maximum value (5) means "EA is a critical success factor for realizing the scenario"). The scenario "Post Merger Integration" is rated in a range between 1.5 and 3.5, depending on industry (manufacturing 3.5, telecommunications and software/IT 2.0, and finance/insurance 1.5). The authors do not elaborate on this finding in detail. However, the scenario is one of the lowest ratings. Therefore, it can be assumed that it is not a well established application scenario in practice, today.

Braun and Winter [BW07] focus on the integration of IT service management into EA Management. When describing the activities and value of EA Management as an introduction, the authors reference to [Bu06] and state that EA Management supports PMI. They do not elaborate on the application of EA Management during M&A.

In his master thesis, van Houwelingen [Ho08] analyzes the relevance and usability of EA Management for IT integration during PMI. The author develops a conceptual model and evaluates results from three case studies in the banking and insurance industry. He focuses on the topics communication, decision making and project management, and describes information requirements of selected stakeholder groups regarding the different architecture layers. The case study analysis reveals, that not all required information is provided by EA Management. Sometimes information is missing, in other cases it is not presented in the suitable level of detail for the respective stakeholder. Van Houwelingen concludes, that EA frameworks provide a set of methods to facilitate the IT integration process. Additionally, he states that communication profits most from EA Management, followed by project management. Decision making shows a diversified picture, depending on the stakeholder. Finally, the author motivates the advancement of EA frameworks to better support IT integration during M&A. Again, the work supports the idea of applying EA Management in M&A, but does not describe how to do it.

Kamogawa and Okada [KO09] discuss EA Management as an approach to increase the ability of organizations to adapt to changes in the business environment. The focus of the paper lies on a discussion of its influence on the creation of business value for Japanese enterprises. They present a conceptual model which links EA Management to financial measures (e.g. return on assets, return on sales) and the results of an online questionnaire. From these figures, the authors conclude that an implemented EA can improve business performance. The work does not really address M&A. During the motivation, they mention acquisitions as one type of change that can be supported by EA Management. Additionally, "pliability for acquisition" and "facilitating system mergers" are two of more than 40 observation variables in their work.

Larsen [La05b] (already been mentioned previously, see section 2.7) investigates the representation of ICT integration in an M&A process ("what", "why" and "how"). In his paper, he presents a review of literature and results of one interview on a case study from the finance industry. The author elaborates on the role of ICT during the M&A process and presents a collection of best practice approaches of leading consultancies. During the presentation of the case study, Larsen refers to EA Management as one management process for ICT which is a lever for standardization. The author states that the realization of benefits of an M&A process requires planning of ICT in early stages of the integration process. He does not describe a concrete linkage between EA Management and M&A.

Namba [Na05] focuses on the analogy between EA Management and city planning. The author mentions M&A as one type of business change and as a reason for a complex IT architecture in the background information of a case study. The presented research does not address the application of EA Management during M&A at all.

De Vries and van Rensburg [VV08] propose EA Management as a new management approach to create synergies in conglomerate organization structures resulting from M&A. According to the authors, EA Management helps to align the diverse businesses, processes and system landscapes of the single units. In their work, they combine the EA objectives per operating model defined by Ross et al. [RWR06] with Norton's Balanced Scorecard (BSC) approach [KN96]. With this approach, they provide a structure to assess the value of EA Management in an organization. The authors conclude, that the short-term return is overemphasized today. Instead, an EA initiative should be regarded as a bundle of activities addressing multiple strategic goals.

Application of EA Management in M&A

Buckl et al. [Bu09] document EA Management patterns for consolidations after mergers. The authors present a best practice approach for IT consolidation during post merger integration, describing a methodology together with a supporting viewpoint on the EA (V-pattern). Additionally they describe an information model, outlining the information demands for execution of the method. The business domain-driven approach to architecture planning during post-merger integration of two enterprises is documented on a very high-level. However, it could be used as a starting point to develop more concrete artifacts.

Dudas and Tobinson [DT07] address the topic of information systems integration in M&A from an EA perspective. The authors state that existing EA Management approaches do not provide a sufficient link between the business and technology level to facilitate IT integration during M&A. As a contribution to fill this gap, they propose a framework that addresses the relationship between integration on business activity level and information systems integration. The result is a relational model in form of a matrix that helps to visualize integration approaches for information systems according to business integration needs. The authors conclude that both, the analysis level of business activities and the EA perspective, are well suited to analyze and describe information systems integration in specific M&A situations.

Mo and Nemes [MN09] explore, how EA Management can support analysis before and after the purchase in M&A. As one chapter in a book on coherency management, M&A is seen as one type of change in an organization for this discipline. The contribution is primarily research based. The authors state, that an EA model should be used as a tool for coherency management during the merger, especially to ensure a coherent integration process, but also on a regular basis in the new enterprise. They reference to Bernus et al. [BNW96], who state that the volatility during an M&A process violates many fundamental principles that EA theories are based on. The authors identify the inflexibility of strict top-down approaches of current EA implementations as a major drawback to support the M&A process. As a solution, they propose a DNA-based[6] approach to modeling the enterprise. The authors illustrate their argumentation with the example that EA assumes a consistent mission which is, in their option, not the case with a new enterprise resulting from two merging entities. Obviously, the authors understand EA as a tool to manage the integration more than as a tool to plan a merger or an acquisition. In this case, the mission would be consistent and it would include the goal of external growth. However, the authors state that architecture design and early modeling should be started during feasibility studies in early phases of the M&A process.

In his master thesis, Vania [Va11] addresses the role of EA Management in achieving merger readiness. The author argues that enterprises need to achieve "preparedness", used as a synonym for readiness, for M&A before deciding on a transaction. He proposes EA Management as an approach to support management in achieving the required level of preparedness, for

[6] DNA: Deoxyribonucleic acid (Biology)

example for the major issue of long-term integration planning. M&A are seen as one type of organizational change in his work. In the course of the thesis, the author discusses how an EA framework can be used to manage this change and to build the M&A preparedness. Therefore, he develops a meta-methodology and discusses the researcher and a practitioner perspective on the topic. Vania selected the GERAM (Generalised Enterprise Reference Architecture) [IF99] framework as a basis for his work. According to the author, the TOGAF framework [Th09] and the Zachman framework [Za87, SZ92, Za01] concentrate on IT only.[7]

3.3.2 Analysis of EA Management Books

Due to the limited availability of contributions dedicated to the application of EA Management in the context of M&A, we analyzed thirteen recent English and German EA Management books published between 2005 and 2011. These books are consulted frequently by EA practitioners willing to apply EA methods and models in real-world situations, such as M&A. Table 3.2 structures the analyzed EA Management books according to author, citation key, year, and type of work. Furthermore, it indicates on which pages the topic of M&A is addressed and, if applicable, the specific M&A process phase the author refers to. The symbol "-" indicates that the topic is not covered by the respective source.

Five EA Management books, Bernard [Be05], Johnson and Ekstedt [JE07], Niemann [Ni08], Schekkerman [Sc08a], Wagter et al. [Wa05] do not bring up M&A at all. A second group of books refers to M&A but does not explicitly dwell on this topic. Land et al. [La08] mention M&A as one driver for change, while Hanschke [Ha09c] provides a definition of the term as part of her book's glossary.

Two books speak of the PMI phase as an application domain for EA Management and list corresponding tasks [En08, Ke06]. Engels et al. [En08] list consolidation of business processes and the application landscape as EA Management tasks. Additionally, they mention M&A as a reason for data redundancies. Keller [Ke06] considers application and infrastructure consolidation as EA Management tasks during the PMI phase and proposes patterns for application consolidation including influence factors and risks. In addition to integration, Ross et al. [RWR06] mention knowledge transfer and provision of standardized best practices as relevant EA Management

[7] In contrast, we included TOGAF as a basis for the research in this thesis because of the business focus and the high practical relevance (see section 3.3.3). Mappings between both frameworks are available [Sa04].

Table 3.2: M&A in EA Management - EA Management Books

Publication			Basic Info		M&A	M&A Phases		
Author	Title	Cit.	Type	Year	mentioned	Pl.	Tr.	PMI
van den Berg, M.; van Steenbergen, M.	Building an Enterprise Architecture Practice: Tools, Tips, Best Practices, Ready-to-Use Insights	BS10	Academic	2010	p. 4, 25, 27, 37, 50, 134, 137	X	X	X
Bernard, S. A.	An Introduction to Enterprise Architecture	Be05	Academic	2005	-			
Engels et al.	Quasar Enterprise: Anwendungslandschaften serviceorientiert gestalten	En08	Practitioner	2008	p. 84, 85, 86, 169, 232, 277			X
Hanschke, I.	Strategic IT Management: A Toolkit for Enterprise Architecture Management	Ha09c	Practitioner	2009	p. 328			
Johnson, P.; Ekstedt, M.	Enterprise Architecture: Models and Analyses for Information Systems Decision Making	JE07	Academic	2007	-			
Keller, W.	IT-Unternehmensarchitektur. Von der Geschäftsstrategie zur optimalen IT-Unterstützung	Ke06	Practitioner	2006	p. 98			X
Land et al.	Enterprise Architecture: Creating Value by Informed Governance	La08	Academic	2008	p. 6			
Lankhorst, M.	Enterprise Architecture at Work: Modelling, Communication and Analysis	La05a	Academic	2005	p. 108-110			X
Niemann, K.	From Enterprise Architecture to IT Governance: Elements of Effective IT Management	Ni08	Partitionier	2006	-			
Ross et al.	Enterprise Architecture As Strategy: Creating a Foundation for Business Execution	RWR06	Academic	2006	p. 176-181			X
Schekkerman, J.	Enterprise Architecture Good Practices Guide: How to Manage the Enterprise Architecture Practice	Sc08a	Academic	2008	-			
Schwarzer et al.	Enterprise Architecture Management: Verstehen - Planen - Umsetzen	Sc09	Partitionier	2009	p. 85, 86	X		X
Wagter et. al.	Dynamic Enterprise Architecture: How to Make It Work	Wa05	Academic	2005	-			

tasks. The authors describe the effects of M&A on the enterprise's foundation for execution and the influence of different architecture maturity levels at the acquiring company and seller side. They propose architectural approaches like unification, replication, coordination that can be applied in M&A situation. Additionally, the authors illustrate these strategies by means of three case studies (UPS, CEMEX, and 7eleven Japan).

In addition to the Post-Merger Phase, Schwarzer [Sc09] also refers to the Pre-Merger Phase, in which EA Management provides information about necessary measures that have to be prepared and implemented. The author points out that IT plays an important role during M&A since it provides the basis for the future integration of the business processes. Furthermore, she emphasizes that EA Management helps to consolidate the IT organization and the IT landscape in the PMI phase by as-is and target architecture planning. The work of Lankhorst et al. [La05a] focuses on EA modeling. The authors name modeling of processes, organizational structure, business functions, IT, applications, and services, as well as the creation of a common understanding among stakeholders and application consolidation as EA Management tasks during M&A. The authors include a PMI example from the insurance industry to demonstrate the applicability of the presented EA models.

Berg and Steenbergen [BS10] refer to M&A, including all phases, as one application domain for EA Management. Based on a fictional M&A example from the banking industry, the authors motivate the importance of EA Management and the implementation of an EA framework. The researchers propose EA Management in order to achieve synergies between both companies being one key goal of M&A. The EA framework can be applied to map the architectural landscape, detect overlaps, and identify what needs to be changed and what needs to continue. As concrete tasks, they mention the homogenization of infrastructure and business processes and the support of standardization.

In summary, five authors do not bring up M&A at all, while eight publications at least mention the topic. However, these EA Management books do not elaborate on M&A in detail. If M&A is addressed, authors dedicate a maximum of five pages to this topic. Most contributions are limited to the Post-Merger Phase. EA tasks mentioned are mostly focused on IT consolidation and integration work as well as support of communication and modeling. The authors do not provide concrete EA artifacts explicitly addressing the challenges of M&A. With regards to empirical means, the authors stick to fictional examples or case studies.

3.3.3 Analysis of EA Management Frameworks

Due to their high practical relevance and continually increasing awareness amongst practitioners and academia, EA Management frameworks are a valuable source to analyze their potential and develop contributions of EA Management in the context of M&A. EA Management frameworks collect and consolidate best practices and lessons learned from practice and make them available in a generalized manner.

Over the past years, several authors worked on structuring and comparing different EA Management frameworks. Matthes [Ma11] published a compendium on available EA Management frameworks, comprising more than fifty different approaches. The author aims to support the selection of an EA framework that optimally supports individual goals. Besides the market overview, Matthes developed an evaluation scheme and elaborated on more than thirty frameworks in detail. Focus of the analysis are the meta model, the architecture model, and the process model. Additionally, the author provides background information such as history, developer/author group, tool support, and access to concept documentation. Schekermann [Sc06] also gives a comprehensive overview about the major available EA frameworks. Minoli [Mi08] focuses his work on TOGAF and Zachman.

Figure 3.1 shows the result of a study on the use of EA frameworks by practitioners. Obviously, TOGAF in its current version 9 and former version 8, as well as Zachman are still the most relevant EA Management frameworks[8].

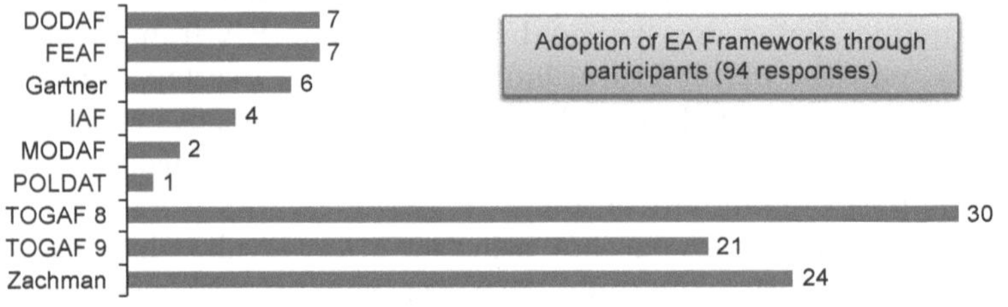

Figure 3.1: Practical Relevance of EA Frameworks [VP09]

While frameworks such as Zachman only classify the descriptions of an EA, TOGAF also provides elements to establish a sustainable architecture function in an organization and proposes a process to manage the evolution of EA Management. BEAMS provides a collection of detailed artifacts supporting the development of an EA function. Thus, it may complement TOGAF or other frameworks [BES09]. Therefore, these three representative EA Management frameworks are included in this section:

- The Open Group Architecture Framework (TOGAF) as today's international standard among practitioners
- Zachman as the "classic framework", still highly relevant in practice
- Building Blocks of Enterprise Architecture Management (BEAMS) as a relatively new academic approach, complementing TOGAF with more detailed artifacts

The Open Group Architecture Framework (TOGAF)

TOGAF became an industry standard framework for EA Management and is used by architecture practitioners worldwide. Being an open standard,

[8] In a second study conducted in 2007, TOGAF was rated as the most relevant EA framework (selected by 33% of participants). The Zachman framework was rated on second position with 22% [Fe07].

it is freely available to use[9]. TOGAF is supported by an open committee. It is a proven method and a result of long term practice. TOGAF uses a standard taxonomy for business, information, and technology modeling, and has a business focus in the architecture development [BMP10]. Additionally, the framework is supported by many EA Management tools.

Initial work on TOGAF in the form of a structured collection of requirements was started in 1994 and the first version was published in 1995. From 1995 to 2001, TOGAF was refined and improved continually, still with a technical focus. Version 7, published in 2001, contained a first statement on TOGAF's positioning regarding the EA concept. TOGAF version 8, published in 2002, was the first real EA Management framework, therefore called "enterprise edition". Since this time, the practical relevance of the framework continually increased. Therefore, the number of enterprises adopting the framework and architects achieving TOGAF certification has been rising constantly over the last decade.

The current TOGAF version 9 was published in 2009 including a broad range of revisions to the TOGAF specification in order to improve usability, focus on holistic enterprise change and increase consistency of work results. Thereby, TOGAF 9 continues its evolution from an IT architecture framework to an holistic EA framework. As TOGAF has grown in depth and maturity it has become a framework for managing business transformation towards a target operating model. Therefore, it promises to be the right framework to evaluate the applicability of EAM for the context of an M&A.

Figure 3.2 shows the structure of TOGAF 9. The structure of the seven elements of the EA framework follows the proven idea of modular chapters in the specification (comparable to the ITIL books). In the following, a brief description of each element is given.

- Architecture Capability Framework:
  The establishment and operation of the EA Capability in the form of an institutionalized architecture function within an enterprise requires appropriate organization structures, processes, roles, responsibilities, and skills. The Architecture Capability Framework provides a set of supporting reference materials. However, although this chapter contains a number of guidelines to support key activities, the Architecture Capability Framework

[9] The specification [Th09] is published and maintained by the Open Group's Architecture Forum (website: `www.opengroup.org/architecture`). It is formed by representatives from more than 300 enterprises (retrieved 2009). The members comprise client organizations (including multinational organizations, small and medium enterprises (SME), public sector organizations) and suppliers of products and services that span all sectors of the economy.

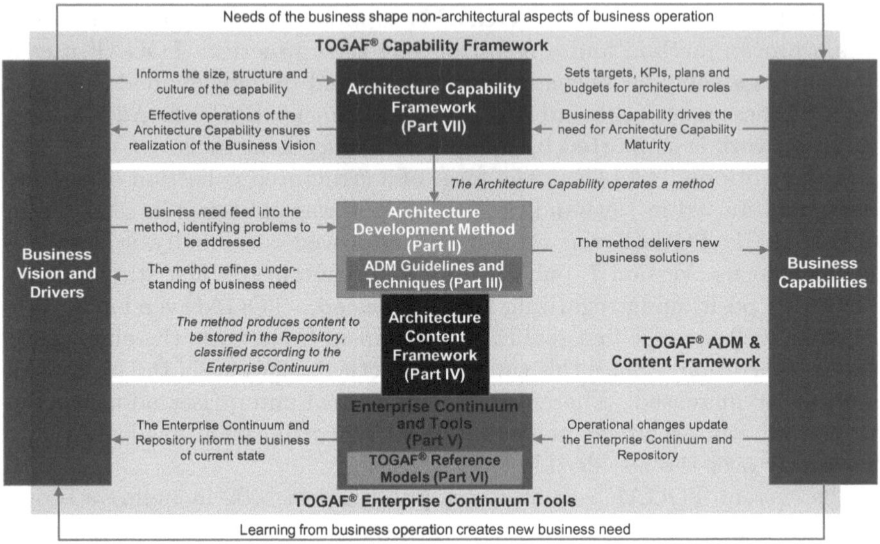

Figure 3.2: TOGAF 9 Structure [Th09]

in its current form is not intended to be a comprehensive template for operating an EA capability.

- Architecture Development Method (ADM):
  The Architecture Development Method (ADM) describes a phase-based approach for the development of architectures. It describes a process for the implementation of requirements in solutions in conformity with the architecture. The process consists of ten phases. As the ADM is iterative, it is possible to return to previous phases within an ADM run. The description of the ADM is generic and can be used independently from a certain industry. It may, but does not need, to be adapted to specific requirements. Moreover, the ADM is designed to run several times, with different scopes and degree of detail. Thus, it requires a clear scope for each phase and run.
- ADM Guidelines and Techniques:
  The chapter ADM Guidelines and Techniques contains guidelines for adapting the ADM process and techniques for architecture development that may be used during the phases of the ADM.
- Architecture Content Framework:
  The Architecture Content Framework provides a structural model for the

elements of the EA. The content meta model defines and categorizes the various building blocks of the architecture and describes their relationships to one another. It allows to consistently define, structure, and present the major artifacts created during architecture work. The content framework allows TOGAF 9 to be used as a stand-alone EA framework[10].

- Enterprise Continuum and Tools:
  The enterprise continuum serves as a table of contents for relevant information from diverse sources on the basis of the content meta model language. It structures the information and its evolution from generic to concrete, specific contents. The architecture repository represents the underlying database.
- TOGAF Reference Models:
  Architecture reference models help to categorize and represent architecture building blocks. TOGAF 9 includes two reference models for the technology architecture, the Technical Reference Model (TRM) and the Integrated Information Infrastructure Reference Model (III-RM).

The structure of the framework (see figure 3.2) depicts how the single EA framework elements work together. The horizontal chain shows how business strategies are transformed into business capabilities, whereas the vertical chain shows the different EA elements needed to facilitate this transformation. The vertical sequence describes the means and methods used to enable this transformation. The business strategy & vision defines the requirements for the EA capability and drives its design. The EA capability operates a process to transform business requirements into business solutions, the architecture development method (ADM). In order to do so, methods (ADM guidelines and techniques) are needed. The operation of the architecture development method requires structured information. The structure is defined in the architecture content framework (meta model). All information is stored in a structured database (enterprise continuum and repository).

TOGAF structures its fundamental EA model in four domains[11] which can be considered separately from one another as well as in their overall context as shown in figure 3.3.

The business architecture includes elements like a product or service strategy, organization, processes, business functions, or locations. The data architecture comprises for example business objects, business data, as well as their types and resources. The application architecture describes IT support

[10] Other content frameworks (such as the Zachman Framework, see section 3.3.3) can be used in conjunction with TOGAF. In these cases, the content framework is used as a reference for TOGAF content to be mapped to other frameworks.

[11] often labeled as "architecture layers" by practitioners

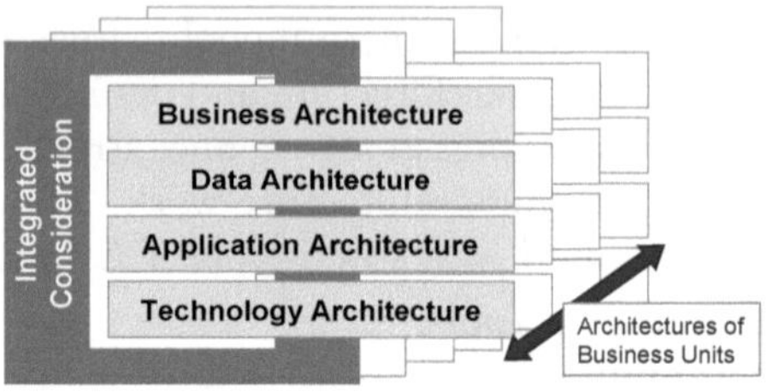

Figure 3.3: TOGAF EA Model (following [Th09])

of business functions, and information flows for instance. The technology architecture includes elements like platforms, components, and technical elements.

In all, TOGAF represents a comprehensive framework, including all elements needed to support business transformation with an EA Management approach. However, given the purpose of being a general framework, TOGAF does not explicitly address specific use-cases like M&A. Nevertheless, the framework may serve as a valuable foundation for developing EA Management concepts for planning and implementation of M&A. Since TOGAF includes many different elements, relevant parts of the chosen framework have to be selected and explicitly tailored to the specific needs. Additionally, the research findings from this work may be integrated into the existing body of knowledge represented in an EA Management framework.

Zachman Framework

The initial Zachman Framework [Za87], introduced in 1987 by the IBM researcher John A. Zachman as "a framework for information systems architecture", was the first EA framework. In his paper, Zachman refers to principles of classical architecture and applies them to his framework for information systems. Since then, it has been slightly renamed, as well as constantly extended and refined [SZ92, Za96, Za11]. In the meantime, it was published as a 3D model on the ZIFA website[12]. The Zachman Framework is method neutral, focusing on the content of the architecture.

The Zachman Framework, as shown in figure 3.4, is a matrix consisting of six rows and six columns, forming 36 cells. To cover the entire organization, the idea of Zachman's framework is to describe the EA from different viewpoints (representing different roles), regarding several aspects at each

[12] The Zachman Institute for Framework Advancement (ZIFA) website: `www.zifa.com`

	Data (What?)	Function (How?)	Network (Where?)	People (Who?)	Time (When?)	Motivation (Why?)
Objectives/Scope (Contextual)	List of things (entities) important to the business	List of processes (functions) the business performs	List of locations in which the business operates	List of organizations important to the business	List of events significant to the business	List of business goals / strategy
Enterprise Model (Conceptual)	e.g. semantic model	e.g. business process model	e.g. business logistics system	e.g. workflow model	e.g. master schedule	e.g. business plan
System Model (Logical)	e.g. logical data model	e.g. application architecture	e.g. distributed system architecture	e.g. human interface architecture	e.g. processing structure	e.g. business rule model
Technology Model (Physical)	e.g. physical data model	e.g. system design	e.g. technology architecture	e.g. presentation architecture	e.g. control structure	e.g. rule design
Detailed Representations (Out-of-context)	e.g. data definition	e.g. program	e.g. network architecture	e.g. security architecture	e.g. timing definition	e.g. rule specification
Functioning Enterprise	e.g. data	e.g. function	e.g. network	e.g. organization	e.g. schedule	e.g. strategy

Figure 3.4: Zachman Framework (simplified, following [Za11])

stage, resulting in a whole range of documents (e.g. diagrams, charts, models etc.), using uniform vocabulary and a given set of rules. The six rows represent different architectural views on the system during the development process:

- Scope (contextual): The senior executive's view, representing the organization's boundaries and connections to the environment.
- Business model (conceptual): Description of models and architectures used by owners of business processes.
- System model (logical): Description of models and architectures used by engineers, architects and those who determine between what is functionally desirable and what is technically possible.
- Technology model (physical): Description of models and architectures used by technicians, engineers and designers who create the actual product.
- Detailed representations (out-of-context perspective): Description of the final product or parts included in it (e.g. software components).
- Functioning enterprise (real world): Representation of the actual deployed or running elements, data, and people of the organization. It is the underlying of all the abstract perspectives above.

Each view can be examined concerning data (what?), functions (how?), network (where?), people (who?), time (when?) and motivation (why?), meaning different types of abstraction.

Similar to TOGAF, given the purpose of being a general framework, the Zachman Framework does not explicitly address the specific use-case M&A. It does not include any tools and it does not dictate to employ specific methods. The strength of the Zachman Framework is to provide a way of thinking about the enterprise in an organized way. It can be seen as a checklist to ensure, that all aspects (every view at every stage) of the EA have been covered. Looking at the views from top to bottom, they move the focus from business to technology. Thereby, it offers a simple and straightforward approach to address the complexity of information systems which could also help during M&A.

Building Blocks of Enterprise Architecture Management (BEAMS)

The aim of the Building Blocks of Enterprise Architecture Management (BEAMS) approach is to support organizations in setting up an individual EA Management function [Bu11]. The central concept of BEAMS are "method building blocks (MBB)", representing *"reusable, problem-independent design prescriptions applicable in a defined context"* [BMS11] which are organized in its method base. Furthermore, BEAMS offers techniques to select and configure MBBs, as well as to support the customization and integration of the selected MBBs into a comprehensive EA Management function for an individual organization.

Figure 3.5 shows the "EA Management activity framework" along the activities "develop & describe", "communicate & enact", and "analyze & evaluate". The additional activity "configure & adapt" is a meta-activity representing the design of the organization-specific EA Management function (development method) and the administration method to continually maintain and evolve the method base.

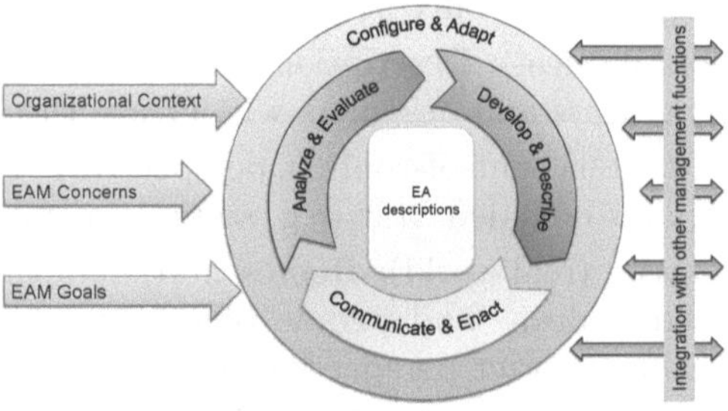

Figure 3.5: BEAMS EA Management Activity Framework [BMS11]

To support the modeling and representation of information, BEAMS does also comprise a set of "viewpoint building blocks (VBB)" and "information building blocks (IBB)". Earlier, Matthes et al. have developed an EA model consisting of architecture layers and cross-cutting aspects [LMW05, Ma08a]. In BEAMS, it has been enhanced with abstraction layers [BMS11]. Cross-cutting aspects (left side, vertical) cover concepts that are not a part of the static EA structure, but may be linked to any element in a layer in different ways (e.g. linking goals or KPIs, defining a project scope, or linking standards to EA concepts). Architectural layers comprise the company's EA structure, ranging from business & organization level, over application & information level to infrastructure & data level. Abstraction layers complement the architectural layers by describing the EA concepts on the corresponding architectural layer on a logical level. Hence, they focus on the functions provided, whereas details of the actual realization are hidden. Figure 3.6 shows the latest version.

Figure 3.6: BEAMS EA Model (following [BMS11])

Likewise to both other EA Frameworks, BEAMS does not offer a concrete solution for applying EA Management in M&A. It does not contain MBBs, VBBs or IBBs that explicitly address M&A. Comparable to TOGAF, some of the EA Management activities, architecture viewpoints and information objects can be applied in the context of M&A. In this case, they need to be tailored to the specific needs of the M&A context.

3.4 Expert Survey on EA Management and M&A

After elaborating on the application of EA Management in M&A from a literature point of view, this section presents the results of a survey conducted among EA Management practitioners. In analogy to the literature analysis, the survey addressed how EA Management is contributing to M&A today, as well as the practitioner's expectations regarding its future role. Subsequently, survey setup and conduction are described and main results are presented.

For the survey setup we followed the questionnaire design process suggested by Frazer and Lawley [FL00]. Aiming at a high return rate and completeness of the answers, the survey was limited to one page, containing 15 concise questions. The distributed sheet was subdivided into three main parts: the participant's background, questions about the company's EA Management, and questions referring to M&A. The full set of questions can be found in appendix A.

The survey was conducted at three European EA Management conferences between February and May 2011. We selected these conferences on purpose as their audience represents a homogeneous sample of EA practitioners in Europe. However, the survey sample cannot be considered to be formally representative [Ma08b]. As shown in table 3.3, overall 44 of 135 participants returned the completed survey, resulting in a response rate of 33%.

Table 3.3: Conferences and Return Rates

Conference Name	Location and Date	Surveys Issued	Surveys Returned
EAM Forum	Frankfurt, Germany (February 2011)	50	14 (28%)
The Open Group Architecture Practitioners Conference	London, UK (May 2011)	50	16 (32%)
EAMKON 2011	Stuttgart, Germany (May 2011)	35	14 (40%)

Participant Background Information: The first set of questions addressed the company's industry sector and the individual role of the survey participant in its organization. From their industry background, the participants represent a homogeneous group. Regarding their roles, the majority of participants follow an EA Management profession. Figure 3.7 shows the resulting distribution to industries and roles. In the right diagram, domain architect subsumes different roles that focus on one architecture domain (e.g. business, application, and technology). In both diagrams, all responses mentioned only once have been assigned to the category "other".

EA Management: The second set of questions addressed the company's EA Management practice in terms of experience, business architecture management, and the role of business architecture models such as business capability models.

As participants of an EA practitioners conference may be experts with long-term experience, as well as beginners who want to learn about EA Management, we asked the survey participants about their experience. 32.5% have been working in EA Management for more than 5 years, 51.2% between 1 and 5 years, and 14.0% for less than 1 year (remaining 2.3% not speci-

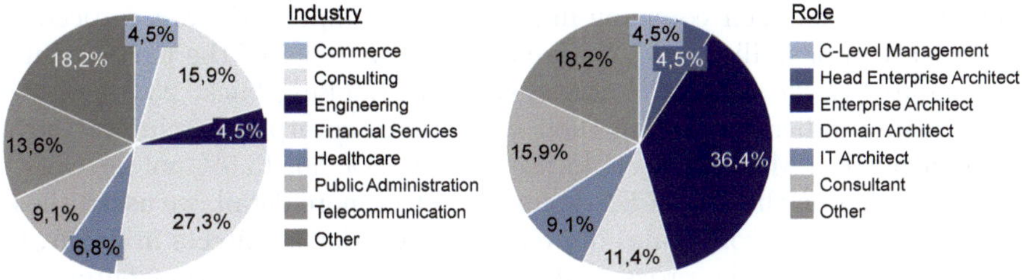

Figure 3.7: Expert Survey: Participant Industry and Role

fied). That implies that a large percentage of participants (83.7%) possesses practical experiences in EA Management.

With three questions, we addressed the current state of business architecture management. As depicted in figure 3.8, the majority of enterprise architects (88.4%) do actively collaborate with their counterparts on the business side. A large share (77.5%) does use architecture models and viewpoints in business architecture work. 41.8% of the participants use business capability models for business architecture work. These findings reconfirm the commonly agreed statement that business architecture management is an integral part of EA Management and enterprise architects have to collaborate with the business side in order to be successful. The same applies for the usage of architecture models and viewpoints. Only a small group of architects works with their counterparts without using visualizations.

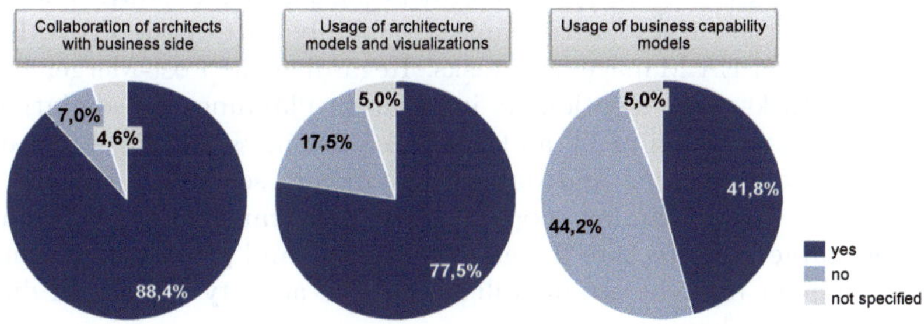

Figure 3.8: Expert Survey: Business Architecture Management

Mergers and Acquisitions: With this group of questions, we addressed the relevance of M&A and the current role of EA Management during M&A. With respect to the overall relevance of M&A, 63.6% of the participant's companies have been involved in M&A in the past, while 56.8% expect M&A

to be relevant for their company in future. The support of M&A projects is seen as a responsibility for EA Management in 29.6% of the participant's companies (47.7% no, 22.7% not specified). Looking back, 23.3% of the participants indicated that in their companies, enterprise architects have been engaged in M&A projects in the past (62.8% no, 13.9% not specified).

Elaborating on the role of EA Management in more detail, we asked those participants whose companies did engage enterprise architects in M&A, to indicate the respective process phase. Figure 3.9 depicts that enterprise architects today mainly contribute to the Post-Merger Phase with minor involvement in the Merger-Planning and Transaction Phase. This situation is reflected in current EA Management literature, where the majority of publications refer to the Post-Merger Phase, while only a small number mentions earlier process phases.

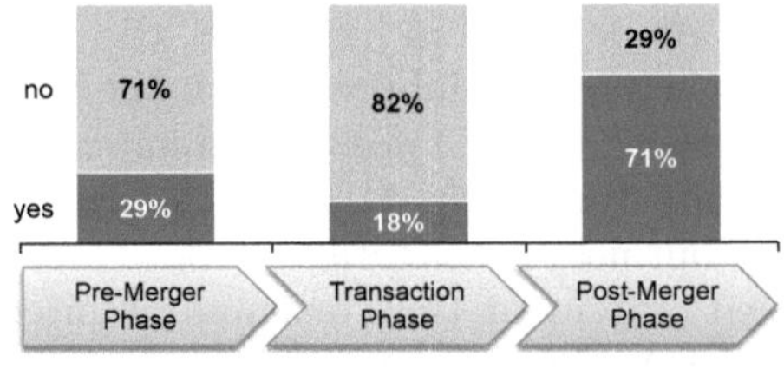

Figure 3.9: Expert Survey: EA Management support per M&A Phase

In the survey, we offered an additional free text field to collect those tasks which are assigned to enterprise architects during M&A today. The tasks mentioned by the survey participants are mainly part of the Post-Merger Phase or general EA Management tasks. Regarding the Post-Merger Phase, subsequent tasks were mentioned: integration planning, consolidation or respectively integration of IT and processes, business and IT integration, migration of applications and data, and software selection. General EA Management tasks included scoping, providing transparency, IT master planning, target architecture design, governance, and project management. One participant brought up due diligence as an activity performed during the Transaction Phase.

Complementary, we offered a free text field to find out how enterprise architects could support M&A projects in the future. Some of the tasks mentioned here as future EA Management responsibilities have also been stated as tasks performed today, namely: due diligence, target architecture design, consolidation of IT and processes, providing transparency, and project management. In addition, the participants mentioned the review of the as-is architecture of the target enterprise and support of C-level management (e.g. CIO, CTO) in decision making (e.g. by pointing out costs of integration), which are part of the Pre-Merger Phase. Furthermore, they proposed the following general EA Management tasks: development of integration scenarios, preparation of a business capability roadmap, dependency analysis, providing a consolidated information base, and mapping of business and IT capabilities.

Similarly to the survey participants, literature considers consolidation of organization and business process, applications, and infrastructure, dependency and redundancy analysis, identification of focus areas (scoping) and measures required, and as-is and target-architecture planning as task which should be performed in the course of the Post-Merger Phase (see section 3.3). Likewise, standardization of best-practices as well as knowledge transfer are considered as being general EA tasks from both, literature and participants. As discussed above, current EA Management literature only lists these tasks without elaborating on them in detail. Additionally, literature proposes EA modeling and the creation of a common understanding. Both tasks were not mentioned by the participants. In turn, participants considered governance, project management, due diligence, application and data migration, preparation of business capability roadmap, and support of management decision making as essential EA tasks during M&A. However, these activities are not addressed by examined EA Management literature.

Finally, we approached the participants with the question of the value of EA Management in M&A straightforward. We asked for their opinion on the potential of EA Management to contribute to the success of M&A as a special type of enterprise transformation. In retrospective, 60.0% of the survey participants stated that EA Management would have made an M&A in their company more successful, while only a very small percentage of 2.5% did not see any value in applying EA Management (37.5% not specified). These figures show that practitioners see a real value of EA Management in the context of M&A. Certainly this outcome is biased, as the majority of participants (61.4%) were enterprise architects who work in this management discipline. The literature analyzed above does not explicitly confirm that the application of EA Management improves the success rate of M&A.

3.5 Architecture Viewpoints and Views

Architecture viewpoints and views are an important concept and typical work products in EA Management. They are mostly graphical, but also textual representations of information, based on the overall EA model of the company. Knowing, that the complete EA model is a large and sometimes complex information base, architecture viewpoints and views are a means to present extracts of the overall EA that are meaningful to individual stakeholders.

In this thesis, we propose capability maps as a starting point for the application of EA Management methods and models in the context of M&A. Formally speaking, the capability maps are one type of architecture viewpoints. In other words, we develop a set of architecture viewpoints that refer to business capabilities to foster communication and a common understanding during the M&A process.

3.5.1 Basic Concept and Definitions

In accordance with the general definitions for EA Management, we adhere to the concepts and definitions applied in TOGAF [Th09]. TOGAF introduces only minor adaptions from the more formal definitions contained in ISO 42010:2007 [In07]. Therefore, it provides an understandable basis, while staying conform with the standard.

The ISO standard [In07] shown in figure 3.10 and TOGAF [Th09] describe the concept in a generic manner. Depending on their concerns, stakeholders have various information requirements with respect to the EA. Stakeholders are people who have a special interest in a system, e.g. users, developers, or managers. Concerns are the interests that stakeholders have in a system. These can relate to its functionality, its development, or its operation (e.g. response times or security). The architecture descriptions show how the contained systems are implemented so that they fulfill their mission. A system is a collection of components which together model a specific function or group of functions. An architecture describes the fundamental structure of a system consisting of its individual building blocks and their relationships to one another and to their environment. In addition, there is a description of principles which control design and evolution. An architecture description is a collection of artifacts which represent an architecture. Viewpoints are the key elements for defining various types of architecture description. Views show stakeholders selected information from the architecture descriptions, which show specific information from a specific viewpoint. Thereby, a viewpoint defines the perspective from which a view is generated. A viewpoint, like a template, defines the information which should be contained in a view and the description method for describing and analyzing the information. A view is the representation of an excerpt from the system from the viewpoint

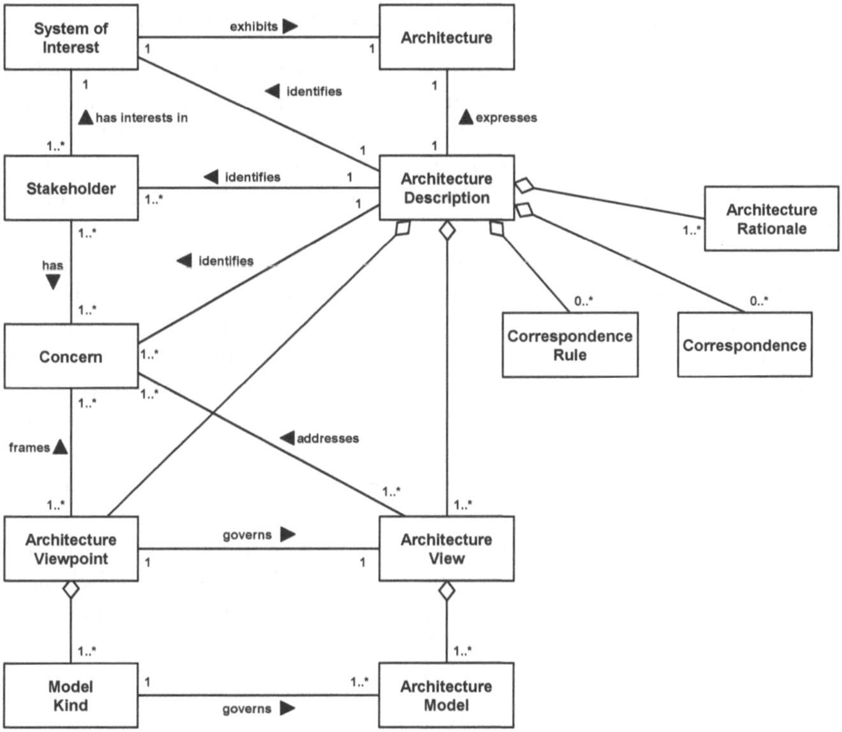

Figure 3.10: Basic Architectural Concepts acc. to ISO 42010:2007 [In07]

of a specific stakeholder. It utilizes the specific concerns a stakeholder has for the system. As a rule, a view consists of architecture models and can be created by using various tools. The differentiation between viewpoints and views is often misunderstood. Viewpoints are generic and can be reused. A view is always specific to the architecture for which it was generated.

Transferring this concept to the research presented in this thesis means: The stakeholder groups and their concerns during the M&A process are represented by the participating management dimensions (see section 2.6). We focus on business capabilities as a leading element of the architecture. The capability maps presented in chapter 7 are one type of architecture viewpoint and therefore part of the architecture description. During the evaluation of our work, we also provide some example views (see figures 8.6, 8.7, 8.8, and 8.9) which are instances of the developed architecture viewpoints.

3.5.2 Method: How to define a viewpoint or view

In theory, and respectively according to ISO 42010:2007 [In07], each enterprise has access to an existing library of viewpoints. Consequently, an appropriate viewpoint could be selected from this library, according to the stakeholders and concerns that need to be covered by views. The enterprise would then be able to generate views of the EA by using the selected viewpoints as templates.

In everyday architecture work, situations in which a view is needed and no appropriate viewpoint has been predefined are common. In this case, TOGAF [Th09] offers two possible approaches. First, the enterprise develops a new viewpoint that covers the current need, and then generates a view from it (ISO 42010:2007 recommended practice). Second, the enterprise can create an ad-hoc view for a specific system and later consider whether a generalized form of the implicit viewpoint should be defined explicitly and saved in a library, so that it can be reused. This is one way to establish a library of viewpoints initially.

To the knowledge of the author, no formal set of architecture viewpoints covering the relevant stakeholder concerns in M&A exist. Nevertheless, the identification of reusable viewpoints with business capabilities is one goal of our literature analysis (see section 4.5).

4 Towards a Theoretical Foundation for Business Capabilities

4.1 Introduction and Overview

Business capabilities are a key element of a modern EA management approach. They are the core component of a business architecture and essential for communication between business and IT [BMP10, SCA10]. There is an enormous interest among academics and practitioners reflected in a growing number of publications on definition, use cases, and experiences from case studies. The concept and application of business capabilities is addressed by numerous publications originating from different sources, for example analyst reports, conference proceedings, consultants, from EA practitioners as well as from academics. Furthermore, they have been addressed in many presentations, workshops, and discussions during EA practitioner conferences (e.g. [Ne10, Th11]).

However, due to the innovative character of business capability approaches, many issues have not been subject to structured research yet. This chapter gives a structured overview on publications and an analysis of business capability literature and related work. Starting from a general view on a business model, it provides an overview on the underlying theories from strategic management that shaped the current understanding of business capabilities in EA Management. Furthermore, this chapter introduces the theoretic foundation for the business capability concept applied in this thesis. At the same time, the theoretic foundation represents a major contribution to the body of knowledge.

The literature analysis for capability resources has been conducted according to the proven guidelines of Webster and Watson [WW02] in order to provide the baseline of existing knowledge and identify existing gaps. Focusing on business capabilities, an evaluation structure is set up to compare the different approaches. In the following the basic understanding, concepts for modeling, concepts for visualization, and potential use cases for business capabilities are analyzed. The related literature is structured into four groups. The sequence does not strictly follow their time line. The related concepts are presented in an order that leads from the general context to concrete elements of a business capability definition.

1. The context for business capabilities is provided by the overall business model of an enterprise which is addressed in section 4.2.
2. The theoretical foundation for business capabilities roots back to theories of strategic management (section 4.3), comprising
   - Porter's strategic management theory (section 4.3.1),
   - the resource-based view (RBV) (section 4.3.2),
   - the concept of core competencies (section 4.3.3),
   - the concept of core capabilities (section 4.3.4),
   - as well as other related concepts (section 4.3.5).
3. The paradigm of capability-based planning (section 4.4) builds on these theories and focuses on the methodology to design and implement capabilities.
4. The status-quo of business capabilities in EA Management (section 4.5) is addressed by an analysis of
   - EA Management books (section 4.5.1),
   - EA Management frameworks (section 4.5.2),
   - literature explicitly addressing business capabilities in EA Management (section 4.5.3),
   - and the strongly related concepts of domains (section 4.5.5) and business entities (section 4.5.6) in EA Management.

4.2 Business Model

According to Osterwalder and Pigneur, a *"business model"* describes *"the rationale of how an organization creates, delivers, and captures value"* [OP10]. In other words, it describes how an enterprise earns money by buying and selling goods or services. The purpose of a model in general is to describe and understand how things work. It addresses the complexity in the real world by working with simplified representations of a particular thing or phenomenon. Therefore, the business model helps to understand where an enterprise's inputs come from and to which customers they are sold, including how they are processed internally and how the enterprise interacts with its environment. Based on a comprehensive literature study Osterwalder states, that a business model has to comprise four essential elements [Os04]. In the "product" area, it has to describe the business activity the company is in as well as the products and value propositions offered to the market. Regarding the "customer interface", it should comprise a description of the company's target customers, how products and services are delivered, and how strong customer relationships are established. The area of "infrastructure management" should address how the company performs efficiently in its internal structure and within external relationships. The business model is completed with the area of "financial aspects", which should comprise the company's revenue model, its cost structure, and the business model's sustainability.

As a business model describes the approach of how a company earns money, it has to be differentiated from an EA. In opposite to an EA, it does not aim at describing the entire enterprise or parts of it in detail. EA Management provides the planning structure (the EA model) and architectural thinking needed to develop and establish the appropriate business capabilities needed to implement a business model [RWR06]. In the EA model, the business model is part of the business architecture layer, together with elements such as the business strategy and business processes. Additional architecture layers (data, applications, and infrastructure) describe single elements of the business model in more detail, for example the key resources (e.g. technologies).

Osterwalder and Pigneur [Os04, OP10] developed a comprehensive approach to business model generation. The central element in their concept is a basic structure and common language for describing, discussing, and designing a business model, called the "business model canvas". It builds on the four elements of a business model mentioned above. Additional to this leading structure, the authors describe typical business model patterns and provide techniques for business model design. Furthermore, they address four strategy areas. These include the environment analysis and evaluation of influencing external forces from an outside-in perspective, the evaluation of business models from an inside-out perspective, the application of the business model canvas with the blue ocean strategy approach[13], as well as

[13] The blue ocean strategy approach has been introduced by Kim and Mauborgne in 2005 [KM05]. The authors illustrate a strategic approach to generate growth and profits by creating new demands in an uncontested market space (the so-called "blue ocean") than by directly competing with other enterprises for known customers in an existing industry.

the management of multiple business models as an integration, autonomy, or separation approach.

The business model canvas depicted in figure 4.1 consists in nine building blocks: customer segments, value proposition, channels, customer relationships, revenue streams, key resources, key activities, key partnerships, and cost structure [OP10]. The combination and design of these nine elements characterizes a business model.

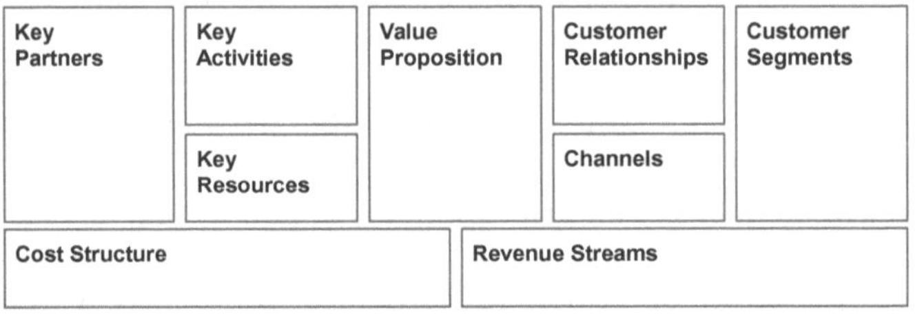

Figure 4.1: Business Model Canvas [OP10]

An enterprise serves one or more "customer segments" (CS). Thereby, it seeks to solve customer problems and satisfy customer needs with "value propositions" (VP). These are delivered to customers through "channels" (CH) which include communication, distribution, and sales channels. "Customer relationships" (CR) are established and maintained with each "customer segment" (CS). "Value propositions" (VP) successfully offered to customers result in "revenue streams" (R$). "Key resources" (KR) are the assets required to offer and deliver the previously described elements by performing a set of "key activities" (KA). Some activities are outsourced and some resources are received from outside the enterprise through "key partnerships" (KP). The combination of the single business model elements results in the "cost structure" (C$).

From a business capability perspective, the "key resources" (KR) and "key activities" (KA) building blocks are especially relevant. Therefore, both concepts are presented in more detail in the following. Where needed, other elements of the business model are referenced as context during the M&A process. In this case, the terminology of the business model canvas is applied.

Key Resources (KR): The building block "key resources" describes *"the most important assets required to make a business model work"* [OP10]. Key resources are needed for the creation of the value proposition as well as for offering the value proposition to customers. These assets can be tangible or intangible. According to Osterwalder and Pigneur, they can be categorized into four groups: physical, financial, intellectual, and human resources. In the business model canvas, key resources can be enterprise-internal (e.g. owned or rented) or obtained from external (via key partners). The concrete set of key resources depends on the type of business model a company selects.

Key Activities (KA): The building block "key activities" describes *"the most important things a company must do to make a business model work"* [OP10]. Like key resources, they are needed for the creation of the value proposition (e.g. supply chain management) as well as for offering the value proposition to customers (e.g. market access or customer relationship management). Key activities are also dependent on the type of business model. According to Osterwalder and Pigneur, they can be categorized into three groups. Production activities (e.g. for a manufacturer) refer to the design, construction, and delivery of a product or service. Problem solving activities (e.g. in a service organization) refer to the creation of solutions to customer problems. Platform/network-related activities (e.g. at a trading platform provider) comprise management of the platform resource, provisioning to customers, as well as promotion of the platform.

4.3 Business Capabilities in Strategic Management

The research domain of strategic management is another potential source for concepts, methods and models relevant to research on business capabilities. Related literature from strategic management can be identified by following the path of contributions over time. The documentation and analysis of business strategies has evolved over the last 30 years, always following the goal to achieve competitive advantage [Co94]. While there is broad agreement about what strategy is, there have been controversial discussions about the process and content of strategic management in the past [Dr02]. Over time, the level of analysis has deepened from an explanation of observed profitability differences between companies, over an understanding of the internal differences that account for profit differences in a certain industry, to the examination of dynamic routines that produce heterogeneous firms [Co94]. This work does not elaborate on the differences between the single approaches to strategic management. However, as the resulting body of knowledge is relevant to the concept of business capabilities and capability-based planning, the following concepts are investigated regarding their basic idea, concepts for modeling, concepts for visualization, and potential relations to business capabilities:

- Porter's strategic management theory has intensively influenced the research domain and is still highly relevant to researchers and practitioners.
- The "resource-based view (RBV)", routing back to Penrose [Pe59], focuses on the enterprise-internal resources as a potential for competitive advantage.
- Prahalad and Hamel's [HP96, PH90] concept of "core competencies" focuses on the enterprise-internal potential for competitive advantage.
- The concept of "core capabilities" is a concept closely related to competencies.
- The concepts of "organizational capabilities", "dynamic capabilities", and "distinctive capabilities" are building on the above theories and might also provide links to business capabilities.

Noteworthy, the publications evaluated in the respective categories tend to use the terms "competence" and "capability" implicitly as synonyms (e.g. [Li06][14]). However, we did not find an explicit statement on the relationship between competences and capabilities. Therefore, it is assumed that due to their analogies, the concepts are compatible to a certain degree. Consequently, both can be a source for the business capability research.

4.3.1 Porter's Strategic Management Theory

Porter was one of the most influential authors in the domain of strategic management and competition [An92]. With his work on five-forces analysis, generic business strategies, the value chain model, as well as strategic groups and clusters, he provided a starting point for a lot of research and many valuable contributions [Po79, Po85, Po87, Po96][15].

Most of Porter's contributions to research in strategic management are related to the concept of "competitive advantage". Actually, Porter did not present a formal conceptual definition for the term [Ho00a]. A detailed discussion about divergent definitions for competitive advantage and matching examples can be found in [RKK03]. For this thesis, the basic understanding is that a company possesses a competitive advantage, if it sustains profits that exceed the average in its industry. Or in other words, a competitive advantage enables a company to outperform its competitors. Matching this

[14] The same applies to German literature, where "Kompetenz" and "Fähigkeit" are sometimes implicitly used as synonyms (e.g. [SG10]).

[15] More recently published in [Po04a, Po04b, Po08].

definition, according to Porter, a *"competitive strategy"* is *"the search for a favorable competitive position in an industry"* [Po04a] in order to *"establish a profitable and sustainable position against the forces that determine industry competition"* [Po04a]. The following theories more or less explicitly refer to the concept of competitive advantage, describing means and concepts to reach and maintain a strong position in a competitive market.

4.3.2 Resource-Based View (RBV)

The resource-based view (RBV) focuses on the internal organization of an enterprise. It can be seen as a complement to the above mentioned approaches to strategy which focus on industry structure and strategic positioning within that structure as determinants of competitive advantage. The idea is to identify the key things an enterprise does better than its competitors. Supporters of the RBV assume, that an enterprise's competitive advantage is derived from its ability to assemble and exploit an appropriate combination of resources, which can be tangible and intangible assets [Pe59, We84]. According to the concept of RBV, competitive advantage and long-term performance differences between companies arise from asymmetric resource allocation with different productivity [AS93, Ba91, We84]. Routing back to Penrose [Pe59], the most relevant contributions have been published (in chronological order) by Prahalad and Hamel [PH90], Rumelt [Ru91], Barney [Ba91], Grant [Gr91], and Peteraf [Pe93].

According to Caves, a *"resource"* can be defined as *"those (tangible and intangible) assets which are tied semipermanently to the firm"* [Ca80]. Examples of resources are brand names, in-house knowledge of technology, employment of skilled personnel, trade contacts, machinery, efficient procedures, and capital. In other words, resources can be seen as the inputs enabling a company to conduct its business activities. Thereby, a resource can be anything that could be considered a strength or weakness of a company [We84]. Resources can be categorizes as tangible (e.g. physical resources, financial resources, and human resources) and intangible (e.g. intellectual resources and reputation). Wernerfelt [We84] states that intangible asset (such as reputation) can only be strategic if it is valuable, rare, imperfectly imitable, and non-substitutable.

Amit and Schoemaker [AS93] state that the resource-based view (RBV) can be seen as complementary to Porter's concepts of competitive advantage and strategic positioning (see section 4.3.1). In analogy to the market-oriented concepts of entry barriers and growth/share matrices, the concepts of resource position barrier and resource/product matrices can be applied to identify new strategic options emerging from the resource perspective [We84].

4.3.3 Core Competencies

Prahalad and Hamel define *"core competencies"* as *"the collective learning in the organization, especially how to coordinate diverse production skills and integrate multiple streams of technologies"* [PH90]. Similar to the resource-based view, they assume that the enterprise-internal assets are the source for competitive advantage. They state that in the long run, companies are competitive if they have the ability to build up core competencies that generate unanticipated products, at lower cost and faster than their competitors and that top executives are judged on their ability to identify, cultivate, and exploit core competencies that enable growth [HP96, PH90]. Therefore, competitive advantage of an enterprise in the long term does not arise from its current products and its current organizational structure, but from its core competencies. Furthermore, the authors propose the following characteristics for a core competence:

- Core competencies consolidate corporate-wide technologies and production skills into competencies that empower individual businesses to adapt quickly to changing opportunities.
- A core competence is about harmonizing streams of technology, it is also about the organization of work and the delivery of value.
- Core competence is communication, involvement, and a deep commitment to working across organizational boundaries. It involves many levels of people and all functions.
- A core competence does not diminish with use. Unlike physical assets, which deteriorate over time, competencies are enhanced as they are applied and shared.
- Core competencies need to be nurtured and protected, as knowledge fades if it is not used.
- Competencies are the glue that binds existing businesses and also the engine for new business development.

In Prahalad and Hamel's model ("The Roots of Competitiveness"), competencies are the foundation for core products that enable business units to provide end products to consumers. In their tree analogy visualization, core competencies represent the root system that provide nourishment, sustenance, and stability for the whole enterprise [PH90].

Several authors emphasize the need to assess the strategic relevance of capabilities [Ba10, TGS09]. Knowing the differences in strategic relevance helps to allocate the right level of resources to the further development and refinement of the appropriate capabilities. The concept of core competencies provides the theoretical foundation for authors elaborating on the characteristics of competencies, as well as methods and criteria to identify core competencies. Thompson, Strickland and Gamble [TGS09] define a so-called *"distinctive competence"* as an activity valuable for being competitive, meaning that a company performs better than its rivals. They further state, that a core competence only becomes the basis for competitive advantage if it rises to the level of a distinctive competence. Barney's [Ba91, Ba10] "VRIO framework" for evaluation of competences proposes a set of questions addressing four criteria:

- Value: Does the availability of the competence provide an additional value in the sense of a competitive advantage for the enterprise?
- Rareness: How are available competences distributed among competitors in the market? Are they rare? Does a competitive advantage arise from being the only one who possess it?
- Imitability: How costly is an imitation or acquisition of the competence for a competitor? How long would it take to duplicate the competence?
- Organization: Is the enterprise organized properly to further develop and retain the resource in the long run?

Figure 4.2 shows the basic "competence mapping framework" that can be helpful in management of an enterprise's competencies [SG10]. It depicts the relationship between the market value and the current state of development for the enterprise's competences.

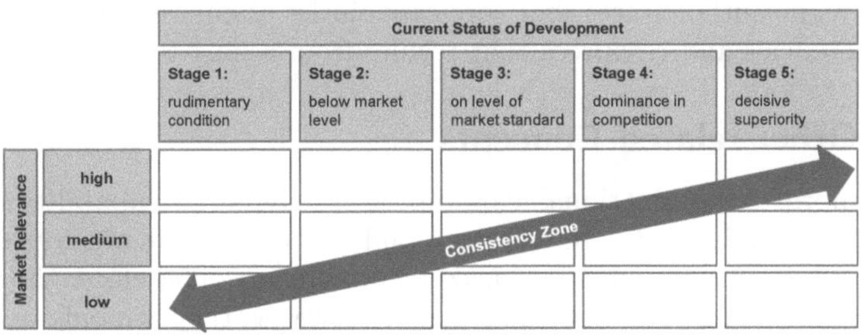

Figure 4.2: Competence Mapping, following [SG10]

The market relevance can be determined by rating the four VRIO characteristics (value, rareness, imitability, and organization). The result can be low, medium, or high. The current status of development for a competence can be only in rudimentary condition (stage 1), below market level (stage 2), on level of market standard (stage 3), dominance in competition (stage 4), or decisive superiority (stage 5). The gray diagonal space marks the consistency zone, where all competences should be located in the target situation. Competences with a low market relevance can be of rudimentary condition, while competencies with a high market relevance should be at least dominant in relation to competitors.

4.3.4 Core Capabilities

Lindstädt [Li06] defines *"core capabilities"*[16] as an enterprise-internal bundle of competencies and resources that are a source of sustainable competitive advantage. According to this definition, "core capabilities" are closely related to "core competencies" and "core resources". The concepts share the same fundamental question of optimally combining enterprise-internal tangible and intangible resources in order to be successful in competition. In order to be rated as a core capability, the authors propose two criteria:

1. Sustainable strategic value:
   The capability provides a substantial competitive advantage by providing a unique selling proposition (USP) and/or generate cost advantages against the competitors. This value has to be sustainable over time.
2. Resistance to duplication[17]:
   The capability can not be directly or indirectly acquired by competitors on the market and it is inimitable.

Moreover, the author states that core capabilities often are a complex bundle of competencies and resources that results from a long-term development.

4.3.5 Other related Concepts

Furthermore, "organizational capabilities", "dynamic capabilities", and "distinctive capabilities" are concepts building on the theories of resource-based view, core competencies, or core capabilities. Therefore, they might also provide links to business capabilities. However, they are only addressed shortly in the following.

[16] Since this is a German publication, the author uses the term "Kernfähigkeiten".
[17] German translation: "faktormarktresistent"

Organizational Capabilities

The concept of organizational capabilities builds on the concept of the RBV of an enterprise. In this theory, organizational capabilities are considered as the fundamental source of sustained competitive advantage [Gr91]. However, some authors argue that the competitive advantage realized through a certain organizational capability is not always sustainable. For example, Collis [Co94] states that a position of competitive advantage based on organizational capabilities is vulnerable to competitor's actions on a number of dimensions, in particularly the case of being superseded by a better capability.

There is no mutually agreed definition for the concept of "organizational capabilities". Therefore, Collis [Co94] performed an analysis of available definitions and classified them into three categories described subsequently.

Category One addresses capabilities that *"reflect an enterprise's ability to perform the basic functional activities of the firm, such as plant lay-out, distribution logistics, and marketing campaigns, more efficiently than competitors"* [Co94]. It is based on the following definitions for a capability:

- Amit and Schoemaker: *"developed in functional areas, e.g. brand management"* [AS93]
- Stalk et al.: *"a set of business processes strategically understood"* [SES92]
- Treacy and Wiersema: *"one of three value disciplines-operational excellence, customer intimacy, or product leadership"* [TW93]

Category Two focuses on capabilities as providing *"dynamic improvement to the activities of the firm"* [Co94], describing them as follows:

- Amit and Schoemaker: *"repeated process or product innovations, manufacturing flexibility, responsiveness to market trends, and short development cycles"* [AS93]
- Teece et al.: *"the ability of an organization to learn, adapt, change and renew over time"* [TPS97]
- Hayes and Pisano: *"enabling a firm to switch gears-from, for example, rapid product development to low cost-relatively quickly and with minimal resources"* [HP94]

Category Three is closely related to these dynamic improvements, but *"comprises the more metaphysical strategic insights that enable firms to recognize the intrinsic value of other resources or to develop novel strategies before competitors"* [Co94]. Thereby, a capability is referred to as:

- Barney: those organizational characteristics that *"enable an organization to conceive, choose and implement strategies"* [Ba92]

- Henderson and Cockburn *"the organizational abilities to deploy the firm's resources and to develop new ones"* [HC94]

All definitions can be subsumed in the larger set of all resources (including physical and intangible assets) that are recognized as possible sources of competitive advantage. Therefore, he proposes to define an *"organizational capability"* as *"the socially complex routines that determine the efficiency with which firms physically transform inputs into outputs"* [Co94]. According to Collis [Co94], the proposed definition contains two important elements:

1. Organizational capabilities are embedded in a company's routines, which are a product of the organization as an entire system.
2. Organizational capabilities transform physical inputs into outputs inside the "black box" of the company.

Thereby, he captures both, capabilities as a direct improvement to efficiency (e.g. continuous improvement in manufacturing process) as well as the ability to find new options to create business value and competitive advantage.

Focusing on knowledge as the strategically most important resource of an enterprise, Grant states that *"knowledge resides in specialized form among individual organizational members, [and therefore] the essence of organizational capability is the integration of individuals' specialized knowledge"* [Gr91]. In other words, an organizational capability integrates multiple knowledge bases.

Dynamic Capabilities

The dynamic-capabilities approach (DCA) has emerged as another important framework in strategic management seeking to explain why companies are different [Pa03]. Building on the concept of the RBV of an enterprise, the idea of dynamic capabilities focuses on adaptation and change by building, integrating, or reconfiguring resources in order to achieve competitive advantage [EM00, TPS97]. The resource-based theory as a whole is understood in dynamic terms.

Eisenhardt and Martin [EM00] state that the RBV of an enterprise reaches its limit in high-velocity markets. The authors confirm that the source for long-term competitive advantage lies in resource configurations in moderately dynamic markets, while the strategic imperative in high-velocity markets moves from leverage of resources to dynamic change of capabilities. Therefore, they define *"dynamic capabilities"* as *"organizational routines of strategic nature through which firms obtain new configurations of resources when markets emerge, collide, divide, evolve and die"* [EM00].

Helfat and Peteraf [HP03] introduce a new concept to dynamic resource-based theory, called the "capability lifecycle", proposing main stages of the capability lifecycle in order to provide a common language and structure for the evolution of capabilities over time. In their model, the capability lifecycle describes recognizable stages, such as growth, maturity, and decline, whereas a capability may also pass through multiple stages of transformation before it faces an ultimate decline. The capability lifecycle is described along three initial stages [HP03]:

- The founding stage starts once a group of individuals organizes around an objective requiring or centrally involving the creation of a capability. It has two general requirements:
    1. An organized group or team has some type of leadership and is capable of joint action.
    2. A central objective, the achievement of which entails the creation of a new capability.
- The development stage begins after the team has organized itself around the objective of developing a particular capability. During this stage, the capability develops through search by the team for viable alternatives for capability development, combined with accumulation of experience over time.
- The maturity stage entails capability maintenance. This involves exercising the capability, which refreshes the organizational memory. If exercised regularly, the capability becomes more deeply embedded in the memory structure of the organization. Routines may become more habitual, requiring less and less conscious thought. Over time, the ability of the team to recall the development path may fade and the capability may become more tacit in nature.

Additionally, the authors describe six alternative phases following the basic lifecycle ("six Rs of capability transformation"). Thereby they reflect the case in which the lifecycles of capabilities extends beyond that of the firms and industries in which they originated, or if their lifecycle extends beyond the products to which they originally applied.

Winter defines *"dynamic capabilities"* as *"those that operate to extend, modify or create ordinary capabilities"* [Wi03]. The author integrates research on knowledge management with the concept of dynamic capabilities. Based on a literature review, he demonstrates how dynamic capabilities can be seen as composed of concrete and well-known knowledge management activities, namely: knowledge creation, acquisition, capture, assembly, sharing, integration, leverage, and exploitation.

Distinctive Capabilities

Another concept in the domain of strategic management are "distinctive capabilities" Kay [Ka93] coined this term, arguing that businesses performing superior derive their strength from a distinctive structure of relationships with their employees, customers, and suppliers. Thereby, continuity and stability in these relationships is essential for flexibility and cooperative responses to change.

According to Kay [Ka93], there are three so-called "distinctive capabilities" which a company can possess to create added value and achieve competitive advantage through relationships:

- Architecture, the structure of relational contacts within or around the organization with employees and with customers and suppliers.
- Reputation, which is built up through customer experiences, quality signals, demonstrations and free trials, warranty, guarantee, word of mouth, and association with other brands.
- Innovation that is translated to competitive advantage successfully.

Actually, Kay's distinctive capabilities have many similarities to the core competency concept (see section 4.3.3).

4.4 Capability-based Planning

The discipline of "capability-based planning"[18] originates from defense planning and transformation of military forces. Today it is an established methodology in governance agencies, for example in the American and Canadian Department of Defense (DoD). Even though several contributions clearly focus on the defense industry and do not claim to be of general relevance, they provide ideas and concepts that can be equally transferred into other industries. The main concepts included in today's EA Management frameworks (e.g. TOGAF) root back to approaches that have been developed by these governance agencies and related research institutes. The following examples illustrate, how the concepts coming from the defense planning discipline can be transferred to a general EA Management approach.

Davis [Da02] provides a profound overview about the topic of capability-based planning, its history in defense planning, and how it is applied today. In his work, the author provides a review of existing concepts and extends them

[18] It has to be noted, that the majority of military-related publications use the term "capabilities-based planning". However, this is replaced with "capability-based planning" to ensure consistency in this work.

with a so-called "analytic architecture for capability-based planning, mission-system analysis, and transformation". According to the author, *"capability-based planning"* is *"planning, under uncertainty, to provide capabilities suitable for a wide range of modern-day challenges and circumstances while working within an economic framework that necessitates choice"* [Da02]. The definition especially addresses the value of business capabilities as a stable structure providing a basis for planning under uncertainty and within a changing environment. The presented capability-based planning approach consists in three key elements:

1. A conceptual framework for planning under uncertainty that emphases flexibility, robustness, and adaptivity of capabilities,
2. An analytical framework that comprises
   - understanding capability needs,
   - assessing capability options (at mission or operation level),
   - and choosing capability levels and choosing among capability options in the context of an integrative portfolio framework that considers other internal factors, risks, and economic limitations.
3. A solution framework that emphasizes building blocks as modular solution modules.

Other publications provide examples for contributions focusing on single aspect or use case of capability-based planning in the military. Kossakowski [Ko05c] presents a methodology that improves communication of a commander's strategic vision in terms of needed content and clarity. According to the author, capability-based planning enhances the quality of information available to decision makers. This is achieved by adding structure to the formulated vision and subsequently decomposing the vision into actionable capabilities. From our experience, this challenge does equally apply to every business organization. Therefore, the presented methodology may be transferred to the business context. As a second example, Caudle [Ca05] elaborates on experiences and challenges of adopting a capability-based planning approach at the Department of Homeland Security (DHS) to define and implement homeland security measures intended to improve preparedness for national catastrophes, including terrorist attacks.

4.5 Business Capabilities in EA Management

The majority of analyzed EA Management literature has been selected from recent EA Management literature reviews [ARW08, Ka08, Sc08b, SW09] and our research group's EA Management literature database [BS11, My11]. A complementary online search has been conducted to identify additional resources, especially those explicitly addressing business capabilities. Thereby, the following key words have been applied: "business capability", "business capabilities" combined with "EA", "EAM", and "enterprise architecture". In a second step, the search was expanded with the terms "capability", "capability model", and "capability management". In the German-speaking EA community, the term "Geschäftsfähigkeit" is used as an agreed translation for business capability [Jo10]. Additional research with this keyword provided several additional publications issued by academics, consultants, and practitioners, which address different fields of application for business capabilities.

The related work analyzed in the following is grouped into

- EA Management books (section 4.5.1),
- EA Management frameworks (section 4.5.2),
- and literature explicitly addressing business capabilities in EA Management (section 4.5.3).

Additionally, we give a short summary of use cases for business capabilities in EA Management (section 4.5.4) and elaborate on the strongly related concepts of domains (section 4.5.5) and business entities (section 4.5.6).

4.5.1 EA Management Books

The EA Management books introduced in section 3.1 are of little benefit regarding the topic of business capabilities. The majority of EA Management books published between 2005 and 2010, e.g. [Be05, En08, Ke06, Ni08] implicitly or explicitly address business capabilities or similar architecture elements. But they neither include business capabilities explicitly in the EA model, nor provide concrete methods for using them. However, one of the EA Management books addresses business capabilities explicitly. Ross, Weill and Robertson [RWR06] apply business capabilities as an instrument for business and IT planning in their book "Enterprise Architecture as Strategy". But the authors seem to presume a common understanding of business capabilities and thus do not provide an explicit definition.

4.5.2 EA Management Frameworks

As mentioned in section 3.3.3, EA frameworks are widely used by EA Management practitioners. Therefore, in the following the three EA frameworks selected as a foundation for this thesis are evaluated regarding their contributions on business capabilities.

In all, TOGAF offers plenty of material to approach the concept of business capabilities. They have been integrated in many elements of the framework. Therefore, the specification offers many starting points in terms of definitions, artifacts, methods and examples. However, it is obvious that there is still some consolidation and streamlining work to do. The authors of BEAMS do not present an explicit definition, but they integrated business capabilities in relevant elements of the framework. Zachman's framework does not explicitly relate to the concept of business capabilities.

TOGAF

A general overview on TOGAF is given in section 3.3.3. Reflecting the relevance of business capabilities among EA Management practitioners, they have been integrated into several parts of the TOGAF standard in version 9 [Th09]. The specification comprises a set of theoretical definitions and practical examples for the topic of business capabilities. In parallel to EA Management, TOGAF assumes the existence of a management framework called *"Business Capability Management (Business Direction and Planning)"*, which *"determines what business capabilities are required to deliver business value including the definition of return on investment and the requisite control/performance measures"* [Th09]. Correspondingly, the authors state that business planning at the strategy level gives directions to EA Management. The mission of EA Management is then to structure, and validate the business planning by means of the EA model. A whole chapter of the specification[19] is dedicated to capability-based planning which is described as *"one of many popular techniques for business planning "* [Th09]. It comprises a method for planning, engineering, and delivery of strategic business capabilities to the enterprise.

TOGAF defines a *"capability"* as *"an ability that an organization, person, or system possesses. Capabilities are typically expressed in general and high-level terms and typically require a combination of organization, people, processes, and technology to achieve. For example, marketing, customer contact, or outbound telemarketing"* [Th09]. A capability can be documented in more detail by describing its dimensions. Based on experiences of the Canadian Department of National Defense (see section 4.4), TOGAF suggests three dimensions: people (training and professional development), process

[19] see TOGAF 9 specification, chapter 32 [Th09]

(concepts, business processes, information management), and material (infrastructure, information technology, equipment). These dimensions may be changed or adapted.

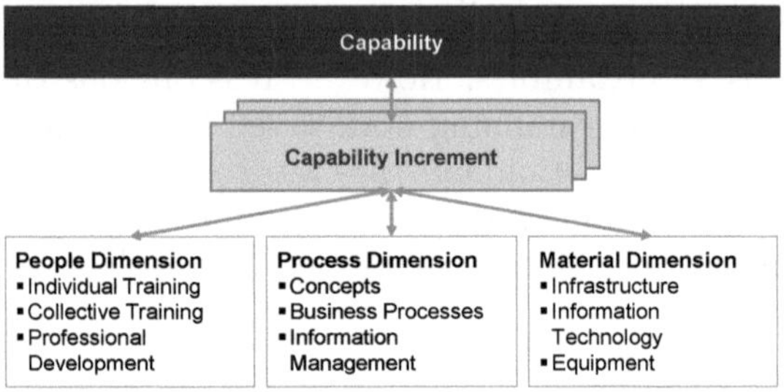

Figure 4.3: Capability Dimensions and Increments [Th09]

Over time, a capability is evolved stepwise along increments that reflect distinct quality stages. In this context, a *"capability increment"* is *"the output from a business change initiative that delivers an increase in performance for a particular capability of the enterprise"* [Th09]. Figure 4.3 shows the concept of capability dimensions and increments.

An additional visualization, the so-called "Capability Increment Radar Diagram" (see figure 4.4) is a suggestion to describe a development plan for a capability.

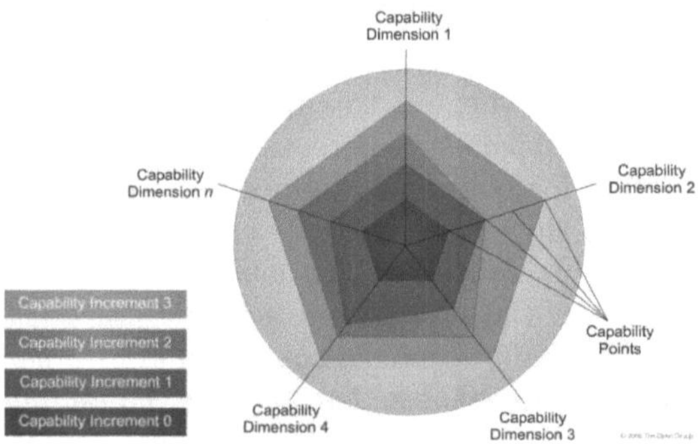

Figure 4.4: Capability Increments Radar [Th09]

The idea is to communicate the potentially complex incremental evolution of a capability to its stakeholders by selecting the aspects of capability (dimensions) that are important to the stakeholder community and indicate lines radiating from the center to show how the gap from as-is to target state is reduced over time.

Furthermore, TOGAF differentiates between vertical and horizontal capabilities. Vertical capabilities have a non-overlapping representation of a certain ability or function, such as human resources management, finance, or customer relationship management. Horizontal capabilities span across the vertical capability structure and represent business capabilities that require co-ordination and alignment across single functional areas. One example is "Sarbanes-Oxley Compliance", which is relevant to large group of business capabilities in different functional areas across the enterprise.

Additionally, TOGAF describes the *"architecture capability"* or in other words an organization's capability to conduct EA Management. According to the authors, the TOGAF documentation itself shows the structure and content of an architecture capability within an enterprise (see section 3.3.3, figure 3.2). The "Architecture Capability Framework" contains a set of reference material (e.g. organization structures, processes, roles, responsibilities, and skills) to support the establishment of the architecture capability.

Business capabilities are not explicitly presented in the basic TOGAF EA model (see section 3.3.3, figure 3.3). But the EA model is part of a comprehensive EA meta model[20] which is structured according to the TOGAF architecture development method (ADM) and defines a set of entities for each phase. In this more detailed documentation, TOGAF states that *"business architecture artifacts capture architectural models of business operation, looking specifically at factors that motivate the enterprise, how the enterprise is organizationally structured, and also what functional capabilities the enterprise has"* [Th09]. Hence, business capabilities are clearly defined as part of the business architecture. At the same time, the graphical representation of the meta model shows capabilities in section "Architecture Realization / Opportunities, Solutions, and Migration Planning". The artifacts in this section focus on change roadmaps, transition architectures and implementation governance.

In the documentation of the detailed meta model, capabilities are referenced from multiple perspectives. In general, TOGAF describes architectures with modular *"building blocks"*, which are *"a (potentially re-usable) component of business, IT, or architectural capability that can be combined with other building blocks to deliver architectures and solutions"* [Th09]. In this context, *"Architecture Building Blocks (ABB)"* describe the "required capability and shape the specification" [Th09], while *"Solution Building Blocks*

[20] "TOGAF Content Metamodel", see TOGAF 9 specification, chapter 34 [Th09]

(SBB)" represent *"components that will be used to implement the required capability"* [Th09].

The TOGAF EA meta model describes a set of entities. Noteworthy, capabilities are not a core entity, but part of the overall list of entities[21]. In this context, a *"business capability"*, is defined as *"a business-focused outcome that is delivered by the completion of one or more work packages. Using a capability-based planning approach, change activities can be sequenced and grouped in order to provide continuous and incremental business value"* [Th09]. Three other entities explicitly reference to capabilities:

- Business Service: *"Supports business capabilities through an explicitly defined interface and is explicitly governed by an organization."* [Th09]
- Function: *"Delivers business capabilities closely aligned to an organization, but not explicitly governed by the organization."* [Th09] or *"Is used to describe a unit of business capability at all levels of granularity, encapsulating terms such as value chain, process area, capability, business function, etc."* [Th09]
- Service: *"An element of behavior that provides specific functionality in response to requests from actors or other services. A service delivers or supports business capabilities, has an explicitly defined interface, and is explicitly governed. Services are defined for business, information systems, and platforms."* [Th09]
- Platform Service: *"A technical capability required to provide enabling infrastructure that supports the delivery of applications."* [Th09]

Additionally, the meta model describes key attributes[22] of entities and key relationships[23] between entities. Two attributes are proposed for a capability: *"business value"*, to describe *"how this capability provides value to the enterprise"* and *"increments"*, to list *"possible maturity/quality levels for the capability"* [Th09]. TOGAF suggests to reference the *"capability delivered"* as one attribute of a *"work package"* which describes *"the contribution this work package makes to capability delivery"* [Th09].

Throughout the architecture development method (ADM), the TOGAF specification references capabilities. For example in the first phase (Phase A, Architecture Vision), one objective is to *"develop a high-level aspirational vision of the capabilities and business value to be delivered as a result of the proposed EA"* [Th09]. The resulting architecture vision *"describes how the new capability will meet the business goals and strategic objectives and*

[21] "Content Metamodel Entities", see TOGAF 9 specification, chapter 34.5 [Th09]
[22] "Content Metamodel Attributes", see TOGAF 9 specification, chapter 34.6 [Th09]
[23] "Metamodel Relationships", see TOGAF 9 specification, chapter 34.7 [Th09]

address the stakeholder concerns when implemented" [Th09]. The development of the architecture vision is supported with a "business scenarios" method *"for identifying and articulating the business requirements implied in new business capability to address key business drivers, and the implied architecture requirements* [Th09].

TOGAF also describes artifacts (catalogs, matrices, and diagrams) that may be created along the phases of the ADM[24]. Table 4.1 lists the business architecture artifacts which reference capabilities. Noteworthy, TOGAF does also use the term capability in artifacts for the description of technical architecture elements and communication infrastructure.

Table 4.1: TOGAF Business Architecture Artifacts

Artifact	Description (Excerpt)
Business Service/ Function Catalog	The catalog can be used to identify capabilities of an organization and to understand the level that governance is applied to the functions of an organization. This functional decomposition can be used to identify new capabilities required to support business change or may be used to determine the scope of change initiatives, applications, or technology components.
Business Footprint Diagram	Describes the links between business goals, organizational units, business functions, and services, and maps these functions to the technical components delivering the required capability.
Functional Decomposition Diagram	Shows on a single page the capabilities of an organization that are relevant to the consideration of an architecture. By examining the capabilities of an organization from a functional perspective, it is possible to quickly develop models of what the organization does without being dragged into extended debate on how the organization does it. Diagram is the basis to layer heat-maps to show scope and decisions. For example, the capabilities to be implemented in different phases of a change program.
Business Use-Case Diagram	Displays the relationships between consumers and providers of business services. Business services are consumed by actors or other business services and the Business Use-Case diagram provides added richness in describing business capability by illustrating how and when that capability is used.

TOGAF also defines a so-called *"capability architecture"*. The first definition[25], *"a highly detailed description of the architectural approach to realize a particular solution or solution aspect"* [Th09] does not really fit into the capability concept as described above. Therefore, it is not taken into account in this thesis. In the second definition[26] it is defined as a concept to *"show in a more detailed fashion how the enterprise can support a particular unit of capability. Capability Architectures are used to provide an overview of current capability, target capability, and capability increments and allow for individual work packages and projects to be grouped within managed portfolios and programs"* [Th09].

[24] "Architectural Artifacts by ADM Phase", see TOGAF 9 specification, chapter 35.6 [Th09]

[25] "Definitions", see TOGAF 9 specification, chapter 3 [Th09]

[26] "Architecture Landscape", see TOGAF 9 specification, chapter 41.2 [Th09]

BEAMS

The most recent BEAMS EA model [BMS11] (see figure 3.6) comprises an abstraction layer for the "business & organization level". It is named *"business capability layer"* and *"describes the entire organization from a customer perspective, i.e. describes the offerings that an organization makes to its customers"* [BMS11]. Additionally, the following questions targeting this layer of the EA are proposed:

- What products and services are offered by the organization?
- Which business interactions are initiated by the organization's customers or by the organization itself?
- Which agreements make prescriptions on the organization's level of service and product offering?

Obviously, these questions are not limited to the business capabilities itself, but also addressing the product portfolio and interactions with the business environment. A definition for a business capability is not provided. The underlying "business & organization level" contains elements like "business event", "business function", "business process", "business transaction", "organizational unit" and "product". Some relationships between these elements are specified, but none of them is related to business capabilities.

The BEAMS method base contains four MBBs that reference capabilities. They are listed in table 4.2.

Table 4.2: BEAMS MBBs

MBB	Description (Excerpt)
Control adherence to business capabilities	The EA description of interest is reviewed if it still fits to the business capabilities by the enterprise architect. As a result, gaps are identified including missing as well as unnecessary architecture elements.
Ensure information consistency	This building block ensures consistency of the gathered information and the architectural description developed. The consistency clerk tries to resolve inconsistencies or contradictions between the different fragments of the description, e.g. if one gathered information piece indicates that IT support is provided for a certain capability, while another one indicates that no IT support exists.
Develop planned states of the EA	Besides a top-down planning planned states of EA can be derived from ongoing projects and project proposals. Organizations have to decide which projects best align with their intended target state and architectural principles. To get an overview on the projects' impact and effect on the overall architecture, the enterprise architect derives planned states based on the available projects. A change project might be initiated by the demand for a new and innovative capability ("change the business").
Develop target state based on business strategy	This building block describes the development of the target state of an EA in respect to the business strategy. Therefore, the business strategy will be used by the strategy board to derive the business capabilities. Based on the business capabilities the capability experts derive target state descriptions in respect to the capability under consideration. Finally, a holistic target state of the EA is consolidated based on the developed capabilities.

VBBs in BEAMS are documented in a generic manner. Therefore, no reference is made to business capabilities. We identified three references to capabilities in the collection of IBBs that refer to "EA related goals", namely "foster innovation", "improve project execution" and "improve capability provision". These IBBs are formulated more as a goal of EA Management than as a building block of the information model. Additionally, BEAMS defines the role of *"capability experts"* as *"a group of persons with special knowledge. They develop the target state and architectural principles for each capability"* [BMS11].

Zachman

Zachman's framework (see figure 3.4) does not explicitly relate to the concept of business capabilities. With the growing importance of business capabilities in EA Management, discussions started about if and how they are represented in the Zachman framework (e.g. [Ma09]). On the business layer, Zachman refers to entities as things important to the business from a data/information point of view and includes processes the business performs from a functional perspective. Thus, the functional view clearly focuses on the "how", not on the "what" as a capability-oriented approach would do. However, Brits, Botha and Herselman state that the construction of business capabilities is closely related to the cells of the Zachman framework as *"all of these abstractions of the organization or cells of the Zachman framework could be used collectively to compile business capabilities that aim to fulfill organizational goals"* [BBH07]. According to our understanding, the cells of the Zachman framework describe single dimensions that together provide a capability to the organization.

4.5.3 Business Capability Literature

A few authors released dedicated publications for the topic of business capabilities. Despite the wide acceptance and usage in practitioner's work, academic literature explicitly dealing with business capabilities in the context of EA is still limited [Ke09a]. Furthermore, no structured overview on available resources is available. Table 4.3 gives an overview on the business capability resources identified during our literature study. The structure of the table is as follows:

- Publication: identification of document by author, title, and reference to bibliography

- Basic info: characterization of document in terms of publication type, author background (academic, practitioner), and year of publication
- Visualization: listing of visualizations for business capabilities
- Relationships: information about relationships of business capabilities to other elements in the EA model (columns "B" business, "D" data, "A" application, and "T" technology architecture layer)
- Use cases: listing of use cases for business capabilities

Barroero, Motta and Pignatelli state, that the *"current TOGAF version recognizes the business component requirements but misses how to bridge those requirements with a data, application and technology architecture"* [BMP10]. The authors propose an extension to TOGAF to link business changes to data, application and technology architecture. The authors introduce business capabilities according to TOGAF. According to their definition, business capabilities are *"a key concept within business architecture domain [..], that are delivered by business components (BC). A BC is a business unit that encompasses a coherent set of activities, supported by assets including people, processes and technology."*In the course of their work, they implicitly use business capabilities and business components as synonyms. The authors strongly refer to sources from IBM Business Component Modeling [Ch05, EN07, Po05] and Microsoft [Ho06, HT06]. The authors understand business capabilities as a vertical concept, that spans across the different architecture domains (see figures 3.3 and 3.6). They provide a list of nine business component diagrams and matrices ("Business Component Map Diagram", "Business Component Collaboration Diagram", "Business Component Sequence Diagram", "Business Service Consumption/Production Matrix", "Business Component/Business Process Matrix", "Business Service Dependencies Matrix", "Business Component/Information Matrix", and "Business Service/Data Entity Lifecycle Matrix") and two examples ("Business Component Map" and "Business Component Collaboration Diagram").

Brits, Botha and Herselman [BBH07] introduce a conceptual framework for business capability modeling consisting of a matrix for analysis and feedback loops for development. Their work includes a listing of definitions for different types of capabilities and a broad compilation of relevant approaches from strategic thinking, innovation to operations, and information modeling discipline. The authors distinguish between four types of capabilities ("functional capabilities", "integral capabilities", "strategic capabilities", and "dynamic capabilities"), collected from related work from several sources (online, related literature). Additionally, they provide a set of definitions for the different types of capabilities, but do not aggregate an own definition.

Table 4.3: Capability Literature Overview

Publication			Basic Info		Visualization	Relationships				Use Cases
Author	Title	Citation	Type, Author Group	Year		B	D	A	T	
Barroero, T.; Motta, G.; Pignatelli, G.	Business Capabilities Centric Enterprise Architecture	BMP10	Book Chapter, Academics	2010	Business Component Map, Business Component, Collaboration Diagram	X	X	X	X	Business Development, Demand Management, Sourcing Decisions
Brits, J.-P.; Botha, G.; Herselman, M.	Conceptual Framework for Modeling Business Capabilities	BBH07	Conference Proceedings, Academics/ Practitioners	2007		X	X	X	X	Business Planning, Innovation, Knowledge Management,
Keller, W.	Using Capabilities in Enterprise Architecture Management	Ke09a	White Paper, Practitioner	2009	Business Capability Map, Heat Map	X		X	X	Application Portfolio Management, Business/IT Communication, Decision Support, Demand Management, Investment Planning Outsourcing
Klinkmüller, C.; Ludwig, A.; Franczyk, B.; Kluge, R.	Visualising Business Capabilities in the Context of Business Analysis	Kl10	Book Section, Academics	2010	Business Capability Map, 3D Sphere Capability Model	X	X	X	X	Business Analysis, Business Modelling, Decision Support, Dependency Analysis, IT Solution Selection, Outsourcing, SOA Modelling
König, W.; Beimborn, D.; Martin, S. F.; Homann, U.	Capability Map : Eine alternative Darstellungsweise für Unternehmensprozesse aus ressourcenorientierter Sicht	Kö05b	Book Chapter, Academics	2005	Capability Map	X		X	X	Business Analysis, Business Process Analysis, Business Process Design, Change Management, Decision Support, Outsourcing
Pulvermueller, E.; Ludwig, A.; Belter, R.; Zyskowski, D.; Heindl, U.; Nguyen, X. T.	A Capability Oriented Management Approach for Business Integration	Pu07	Conference Proceedings, Academics	2007	Capability Map	X	X	X	X	Dependency Analysis, Service Management
Scott, J.; Cullen, A.; An, M.	The Anatomy Of A Capability Map	SCA10	White Paper, Analysts	2010	Capability Map	X				Business Architecture Management

Regarding a capability's relationship, they mention knowledge, processes, as well as strategy in terms of vision, mission, and drivers. According to the authors, the paper represents only a short overview on the research conducted by this group. Thus, not all aspects are explicitly covered in the article. However, no additional publications have been made available to public since then.

In 2009, Keller [Ke09a] published a whitepaper on capabilities in EA Management. The author identifies the need to establish a common understanding of the terms "capability" and "capability model". Therefore, he explains the basic idea of "capability modeling" and "business capability management" and provides a set of definitions from several sources like dictionary, internet (Wikipedia), analysts, and consultants, but does not aggregate an own definition. Instead, he states that from a practitioners point of view, the available definitions are precise enough to be applied, being aware of academic's objections. Based on this foundation, the author provides a set of examples using the pattern format[27] to document examples, problem statement, forces, solution, variants, consequences, related patterns, and known uses. Two patterns address the use of capabilities in EA Management ("heat mapping", "footprinting"), the third one suggests an approach to develop an enterprise's capability model by combining different reference models ("mix the models"). Additionally, he provides two examples for visualizations ("business capability map" and "heat map").

Klinkmüller et al. [Kl10] identify the need for visualization of business capabilities in the context of business analysis. They summarize existing concepts for business capabilities and business analysis. Additionally, they provide an information model for business capabilities derived from characteristics, attributes needed for business analysis, as well as from horizontal and vertical relationships to other entities. It is shown in figure 4.5.

Across the document, Klinkmüller et al. formulate three definition-like statements: *"Business capabilities reflect the structure of a business and abstract from processes, resources and people that are required to provide the capability."*, *"Business capabilities represent potentials of an organization and outline what an organization is able to accomplish."*, and *"Business capabilities are connected with a role model of provider and consumer and specific business capability instances can be compared on the basis of their*

[27] The pattern format is a basic concept which is a major foundation for BEAMS (see section 3.3.3). A more detailed description of the pattern idea is provided by Ernst, who defines an *"EA Management pattern"* as *"a proven practice-based, general, reusable solution to a common problem in EA Management, for a given context, identifying driving forces, denoting known usages, and consequences"* [Er09].

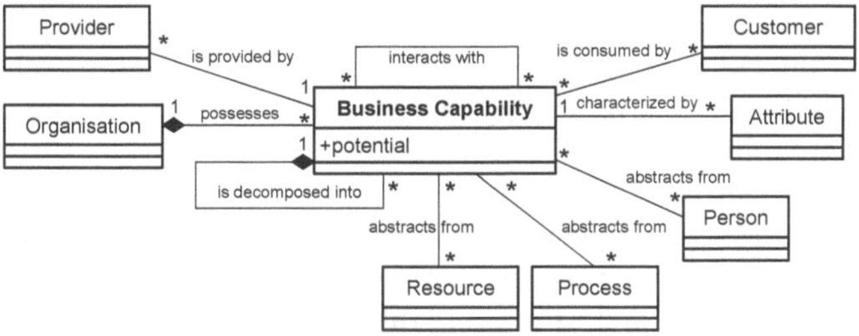

Figure 4.5: Business Capability Information Model [Kl10]

attributes.”. The authors mention relationships of business capabilities to processes and organization on business architecture level. The presented method for “business analysis based on business capabilities” builds on a business capability map. The architecture viewpoint is not described in detail, but the authors refer to a tool to support the creation of a business capability map [KHK09]. Based on this foundation, the authors introduce a three-dimensional visualization (“three-dimensional sphere capability model”) which illustrates vertical (logical composition) and horizontal (dependencies) relations between business capabilities.

König et al. [Kö05b] introduce the “capability map” as a theory-based approach for modeling and analysis of business processes. Their work builds on two management theories, the resource-based view (RBV) [Pe59, We84] and the competence-based view (CBV) [EM00, PH90] on the enterprise, and focuses on the development of a framework to identify and model business capabilities. In their work, a capability is understood as an enterprises potential to apply tangible and intangible as well as intellectual resources, in order to execute a certain business function.[28] Business capabilities can exist on different hierarchical levels. They mention relationships of business capabilities to business processes and organization on business architecture level. Additionally, a business capability encapsulates and abstracts from resources like manpower, technologies and work flows.[29] The authors introduce the capability map as a visualization for business capabilities that can be applied on different hierarchical levels. The practical applicability and potential benefits are illustrated with examples from the

[28] German original: *“Unter dem Begriff „Capability“ ist das Leistungsvermögen eines Unternehmens zu verstehen, materielle und immaterielle sowie intellektuelle Ressourcen einzusetzen, um eine gewisse Geschäftsfunktion auszuführen.”*

[29] German original: *“Eine Capability kapselt und abstrahiert Ressourcen wie Arbeitskraft, Technologien und Arbeitsflüsse.”*

banking industry. In order to do so, they depict several examples at three levels of a generic capability map, some of them including relationships between capabilities. Finally, a screen shot from a prototype software-supported capability cockpit is shown.

Pulvermueller et al. [Pu07] introduce a capability-oriented approach to configuration and management of service-oriented architectures (SOA) in dynamically changing business environments. According to the authors, services are generally regarded as interoperable building blocks for constructing, integrating, and merging applications. The authors argue, that existing SOA approaches often focus on solving technical integration problems, while an integration of a business-level perspective is missing. This results in problems regarding business and management support, insufficient mappings between business and technical solutions from a vertical perspective, and limited support of complex and dynamic environments from a horizontal perspective. They state, that business capability orientation is a necessary element to complete current solutions. Therefore, they propose to extend existing service-oriented solutions with a management level called "capability layer". The authors do not provide a distinct definition. In their approach, *"any resource and its relevant (business) attributes are encapsulated in a resource-specific capability"*. Thus, *"all resources of a dynamic business environment are represented by an associated capability which in turn is an aggregation of the resource's offered functional and nonfunctional characteristics"*. Regarding visualization, they motivate the application of capability maps on a management level.

From an analysts perspective, Scott et al. [SCA10] position business capabilities as an essential part of business architecture models. The authors remark, that it is a relatively new concept in EA Management. Therefore, no industry standard models or frameworks exist, which guide architects during the development of a capability map. The paper represents a collection of practical experiences and hints for the construction of a capability map. They present three approaches for the development of a capability map. In each case, the capabilities are derived from an existing description of the enterprise, the organizational structure, its value streams, or the services that are provided to clients. The authors refer to a series of interviews and state that a three level model of capability maps is a typical representation today. For each of these levels, they emphasize the importance of an adequate level of granularity of the capabilities, but also remark that there is no general right granularity. The capability map has to provide enough detail to connect stakeholders from different disciplines, while too much detail will only be understood by experts in one area.

According to the authors, a good capability map has to follow:

1. represent stable business functions,
2. identify unique business functions,
3. abstract from organizational and process models,
4. allow extension to specific implementations,
5. and capture the business interest.

Furthermore, a capability description should include the capability name, a short description, supporting human resources (meaning a reference to roles), relevant high-level processes, supporting technologies (on a logical level), supporting information, and operational metrics.

Several of the above authors provide references to related literature from the following research domains:

- Service-Oriented Enterprise (e.g. [Ch05]),
- Service-Oriented Architectures (SOA), often referring to technical capabilities and web services (e.g. [Ho06]),
- and Business Component Modeling, often referring to application component development (e.g. [Mc99]).

The same applies to a group of publications we found in the Microsoft Developer Network (MSDN)[30] community, e.g. [Co07, Ho06, MT06]. Some of the resources presented above reference back to these documents. However, most of them are commercial publications describing consultancy services or examples from Microsoft's capability library. Therefore, they do not provide additional depth of information valuable for related work. Furthermore, likewise to our prior literature studies, the online search identified a group of commercial publications describing consultancy service offerings or EA Management tool capabilities, e.g. [Al11b, Be09b, BG09, Br03, FH09, Ku06].

4.5.4 Business Capability Use Cases in EA Management

The literature analysis revealed a set of use cases for business capabilities in EA Management. Today, they are applied in the following EA Management tasks: application portfolio management, business analysis, business development, business planning, business/IT communication, business process analysis, change management, decision support, demand/requirement management, dependency analysis, investment planning, IT solution selection, outsourcing, and SOA modeling. These tasks include architecture description (e.g. as-is landscape, SOA modeling), architecture analysis (e.g. business

[30] The MSDN website: `http://msdn.microsoft.com/en-us/`

strategy support, dependencies between elements, identification of functional redundancies, data quality analysis, business process analysis), architecture planning (e.g. investment, target architecture, SOA modeling), preparation of decisions (e.g. sourcing, selection of solutions or technologies), as well as communication and visualization activities (e.g. demand management, change management). The EA frameworks did also reveal some use cases for business capabilities. In TOGAF they are labeled methods or steps in the ADM phases, while BEAMS uses the concept of MBBs.

The majority of the use cases mentioned above are not limited to the structure of business capabilities or the attributes of a single capability. In addition, they depend on the availability of information about relations to other elements of the EA. For example, the capability-based documentation of the as-is landscape requires knowledge about the relation between a business capability and applications which is represented in an enterprise's EA model [BMP10].

4.5.5 Domain Concept

Some of the EA Management books (e.g. [En08]) mention the concept of domains (or synonymously IT domains or application domains) originating from an IT application context. In this approach, domains are used to group components of an application landscape depending on functional aspects. Especially publications with a background in Service Oriented Architecture (SOA) build on the concept of domains, for example in service design or visualization of the service landscape [En08, He07a]. Additional use cases mentioned for the domain concept are support of communication, definition of responsibilities, contextual clustering, and reduction of complexity [En08, He07a]. In 2008, Aier et al. [ARW08] published their work on EA literature and a survey on the common EA practice. One of Aier's findings from an empirical survey among EA practitioners is a list of typical elements of an EA model. It does not contain business capabilities, but "application domains" have been rated as important among the participants.

According to Aier and Winter, *"domains"* are *"groups of applications (and hence groups of enterprise services) which support coherent business processes, or use coherent software systems, or use coherent information objects and therefore form a designated integration area"* [AW09]. In their article, the authors describe how enterprise services (which link software components and process activities) are aggregated to applications and subsequently into domains for planning/design and communication purposes. As an alternative to top-down design approaches for the construction of enterprise services, applications and domains, the authors propose an alternative bottom-up approach for the identification of domains.

Transferring the domain concept on the business architecture level, TOGAF defines a *"business domain"* as *"a grouping of coherent business functions and activities (in the context of a business sector) over which meaningful responsibility can be taken"* [Th09]. Again, the concept of domains is applied to group elements on a certain layer. This is confirmed by Scott et al. [SCA10] who state that business capabilities can be grouped in domains.

Regarding the relationship between domains and business capabilities, Keller [Ke09a] states that a company's top-level capabilities are nothing else than the top-level domains of the EA. In line, Barroero, Motta and Pignatelli [BMP10] confirms that in the given context, elements grouped by domains are called business capabilities which are used in the creation of value and can be supported by IT. Therefore, the concept of domains, if applied on the business architecture level, can be integrated into a business capability approach. Thereby, business domains relate to level one (top-level) business capabilities.

Summarizing the characteristics mentioned in the different publications, business domains

- are a non-overlapping structure,
- group elements of similar functionality,
- and concentrate responsibilities for grouped objects (e.g. in the dimension of data ownership).

The elements grouped within one domain have

- a higher degree of interdependency than objects in different domains,
- a close thematic linkage and similar frequency of change,
- a high dependency on each other,
- and a similarity in their structure.

4.5.6 Business Entity Concept

A comprehensive business architecture layer is not limited to business capabilities. According to TOGAF, the "business architecture" comprises *"the business strategy, governance, organization, and key business processes information, as well as the interaction between these concepts"* [Th09]. As information is an important aspect when working with business capabilities, the concept of business entities is introduced shortly in the following. Business entities represent a complementary concept to business capabilities.

While business capabilities focus on the enterprise's ability to perform activities from a functional perspective, for example conduct "customer management" or "direct sales", business entities are the corresponding elements of the business architecture that represent the information needed to implement a business model. In other words, a business entity represents the information necessary to deliver the business capabilities of a company. Similar to business capabilities, they have to be comprehensive for business stakeholders and should be defined in a business language. At the same time, they need to be rigorous enough to be used as a requirement basis for development of concrete data models, e.g. for a specific application. Examples are a "customer contract" or a "sales offer". The combination of both concepts provides a common terminology for business and IT stakeholders.

Consequently, business entities should also be considered as a part of the business architecture since they reflect the business point of view on the information and are associated with business capabilities which are a part of this layer too. Currently, comparable architecture elements are often modeled as an element of lower architecture layers (see section 3.3.3: TOGAF EA model, figure 3.3 and sebis EA model, figure 3.6). TOGAF differentiates between logical and physical data assets as well as data management resources [Th09]. Nevertheless, information is not explicitly represented in the business architecture, but part of the information systems architecture. The same applies to BEAMS, representing information only in the application architecture level [BMS11].

We analyzed additional literature in order to elaborate on two aspects. First, we identified publications contributing to the concept of business entities, for example with a definition or visualizations. Second, we investigated literature on the relation of business capabilities and business entities in the EA model. Regarding the concept of business entities, we performed an additional literature search for the terms "information architecture", "business entities", "business information", and "business data". It resulted in the finding that available literature sources do not include a definition of the business entities in the sense considered here.

Noteworthy, Evernden and Evernden [EE03] give a comprehensive overview on information architecture and its development over time. While the first generation in the 1980s focused on developing standalone applications, the second generation around the 1990s applied these ideas at an enterprise level across multiple applications. The current, third generation, focuses on business information rather than technology. Additionally, the authors motivate the need for structuring information by means of a map and the need for a business-oriented language to describe the relevant entities. Furthermore, several publications on business process modeling (BPM) and information systems modeling (ISM) motivate the need to take an informational perspective into consideration (e.g. [Gi01, Wh04]). The modeled elements itself either refer to systems architecture or represent granular entities that are used for business process analysis. The same applies for analyzed literature on information architecture is related to data structures in a system (e.g. information grouping and applied terminology) [Ba05] or the interaction between system and user [To02].

4.6 Definitions and Theoretical Foundation for Thesis

4.6.1 Integration of Related Work

Contributions from recent publications explicitly addressing business capabilities in EA Management (section 4.5) detail on single aspects of the capability map, the characteristics of a business capability, or methods for planning its lifecycle along the capability increments. Having examined these different areas of related literature, the findings have to be composed into a theoretical foundation for the concept of business capabilities. Figure 4.6 gives a condensed overview on the different levels of analysis from the business model to the single dimensions of an individual business capability. Additionally, it depicts the relationships between the single models and elements discussed above.

The business model (section 4.2) provides the context to gain an understanding about the overall value creation approach of the enterprise. Business capabilities refer to the area of key activities. Key activities of a company have been addressed in strategic management theory, for example with the concept of core competencies (section 4.3.3), the concept of core capabilities (section 4.3.4), and other related concepts (section 4.3.5). Key resources are the main subject of the resource-based view (RBV) (section 4.3.2).

The EA Management discipline requires a complete and non-overlapping view on the enterprise's business capabilities. Like the business model, it builds on the activity and resource related theories from strategic management. Therefore, the viewpoint of a capability map provides a more detailed view on the area of key activities. It has to be mentioned, that the business model does not need a complete representation of the capabilities. While the business model elaborates on a small number of very important key activities, the business capability map has to provide a complete picture in

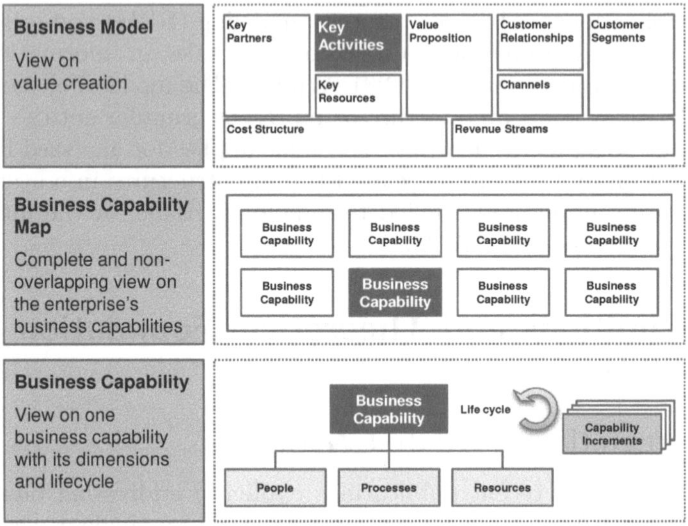

Figure 4.6: Business Capability Context

order to facilitate consistency in planning. Consequently, the capability map breaks down the key activities but may also have additional elements.

The view on a single business capability with its dimensions and its life cycle provides a more detailed view needed for the design and implementation of capabilities. The paradigm of capability-based planning (section 4.4) builds on these theories and focuses on the methodology to design, implement, and further develop capabilities. It provides additional anchor points for the development of capability-based methods for visualization, planning, and controlling.

Our research focuses on business capability maps and how they can be applied during the M&A process. Nevertheless, it is important to establish a linkage of the capability map to the level of the business model and to allow a drill-down to the level of a single capability.

4.6.2 Definition and Concept Details

Concluding from the analysis of related work it has been shown that a business capability is a stable component of the business architecture describing "what" an enterprise does, while a business model describes "why", and business processes describe "how" activities are performed. Consequently, in the EA model, a business capability is an element of the business architecture layer [BMP10, BMS11, Th09]. In this thesis, the focus is laid on vertical capabilities. Unless otherwise noted, business capability refers to this perspective.

Based on the analyzed literature, a *"business capability"* can be defined as follows.

> **Definition: Business Capability**
> A functional building block of the business architecture that supports the business model and the business strategy. It defines the organization's capacity to successfully perform a unique business activity.

Additionally, a business capability has the following characteristics:

- Stability:
  Business capabilities are independent from the organizational model, technologies, and vendor solutions. They represent stable, highly cohesive, logical groups of functionality.
- Abstraction:
  Business capabilities encapsulate and abstract from any explicit resource, business process or IT.
- Horizontal structure:
  Business capabilities provide a complete and non-overlapping functional decomposition of the enterprise.
- Vertical hierarchy:
  Business capabilities can be broken down into more granular business capabilities (e.g. level one to three with an increasing level of detail) and are related to each other in a hierarchical relationship, providing a complete and non-overlapping structure on the next level of detail.

A business capability can be further specified by describing its attributes and the different dimensions that together provide the capability. Business capabilities should be defined at least by a unique and comprehensive name and a description. Additional attributes depend on the individual use case. In this work, the following attributes are selected for a business capability:

- Name:
  The unique name of the capability.
- Short description:
  Textual description of the business capability that ensures a common understanding about the business capability among all stakeholders (e.g. business, IT, and finance).

Furthermore, we recommend to start with the capability dimensions as proposed by TOGAF. Additional dimensions depend on the individual use case. For our research, we did not identify any requirement for an adaption:

- People dimension:
  The human element of a capability reflects the knowledge, skills, and experiences of the enterprise's staff gained through individual or collective training and professional development.
- Process dimension:
  The methodological element of a capability comprises concepts, business processes, and information management.
- Material dimension:
  The resource element of a capability reflects the underlying assets, such as infrastructure, information technology, and equipment.

The development of business capabilities over time is described by using capability increments as introduced by TOGAF. Thus, a business capability can be changed by modifying one or more of its dimensions. For example, the people dimension may be improved by establishing a training program. Or the material dimension may be changed by introducing a new technology. Instead of increasing complexity with a detailed maturity model, it is assumed that a new capability increment represents an advancement of a business capability and therefore a better state or respectively a higher quality.

The concept of domains is not applied in this thesis. Domains as high-level functional clusters are nothing else than the top-level capabilities.

The concept of business entities is applied as far as it is needed for the development of capability-based methods that support the M&A process. As available literature did not provide a definition for business entities, we derive a definition and their characteristics from the definition of business capabilities [Fr11]. Accordingly, a *"business entity"* can be defined as follows.

Definition: Business Entity
An information building block of the business which supports the business model and the business strategy. It defines the information needed to successfully perform a unique business activity.

It possesses the following characteristics:

- Stability:
  independent from the organizational model, technologies, and vendor solutions

- Horizontal view:
  complete and non-overlapping representation of the business information needs of the enterprise necessary to realize a given business model
- Vertical view:
  can be broken down into more granular entities
- Encapsulate and abstract from resources

In order to capture the sense of a business entity it is obligatory to formulate its name and description. Examples of business entities are “customer”, “contract”, or “incident”.

4.7 Visualization

4.7.1 Architecture Viewpoint: Capability Map

A popular architecture viewpoint for visualization of business capabilities is a business capability map [Ke09a, Kl10, Kö05]. According to the developed definition, it is a visual representation of the main functions in the enterprise which are necessary to support the company's business model and which reflect the company's strategic direction. Usually, a business capability map is illustrated as a set of capabilities, which can be gradually detailed forming hierarchies. Figure 4.7 shows the architecture viewpoint capability map. Some example capability maps are available in [Ka11, MT06]. The “Group Domain Model” of Deutsche Telekom AG is one of the rare real-world examples published in [SHG10].

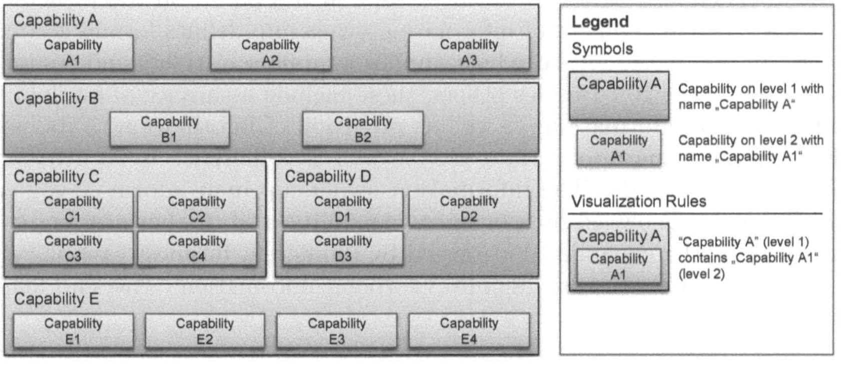

Figure 4.7: Viewpoint Capability Map

4.7.2 Architecture Viewpoint: Business Entity Map

The complementing perspective on information has not been considered in available publications so far. In analogy to the business capability map, a business entity map visualizes the information necessary to deliver the business capabilities. A basic business entity map comprises a set of business entities which gradually detail one another forming hierarchies. Figure 4.8 shows the architecture viewpoint business entity map.

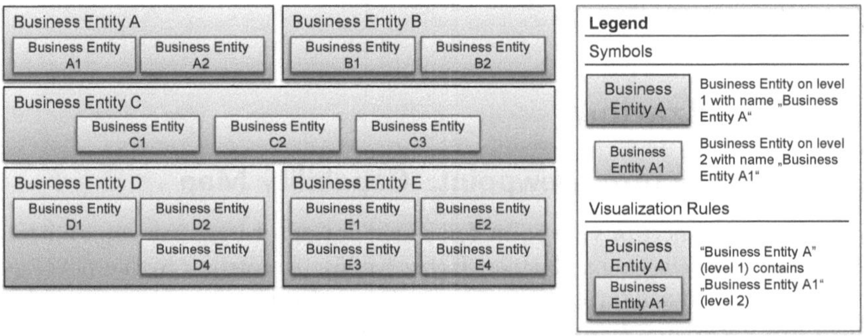

Figure 4.8: Viewpoint Business Entity Map

4.7.3 Architecture Viewpoint: Information Ownership Map

The information ownership map is a viewpoint which visualizes the assignment of business entities to business capabilities based on the ownership principle. The assignment of information ownership defines formal accountability for a business entity, which implies a number of rights and responsibilities [Da09, Da10]. Besides others, these include assurance of availability and quality of information, as well as provision of information to its users while guaranteeing appropriate use, as well as adherence to security and compliance demands. The information ownership map informs if a given business entity is owned by a business capability or if the business entity is only used by the capability but owned by a different business capability.

Figure 4.9 shows the architecture viewpoint information ownership map.

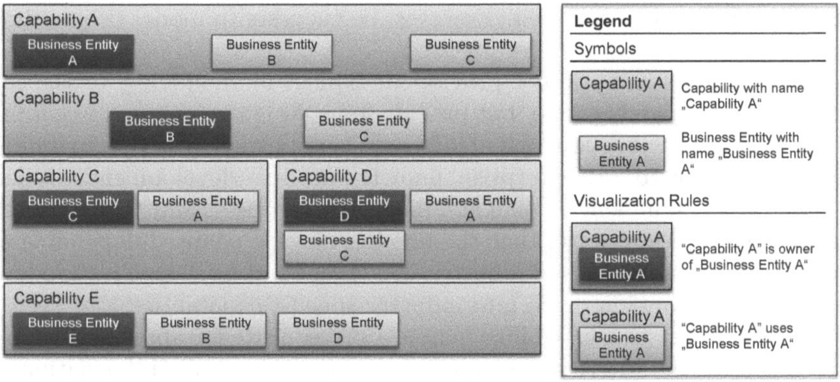

Figure 4.9: Viewpoint Information Ownership Map

4.8 Construction of a Capability Map

As of today, there are no established methods to develop business capability models [SCA10]. Single authors have started to provide hints to capability map construction, but most information remains intellectual property of specialized consultancies or companies that succeeded in design of a comprehensive business capability model.

Aier and Schönherr [AS07] propose a methodology to support service engineering by defining architectural domains in an EA. They present an algorithm-based approach to analyze the information of a basic architecture model (business processes, IT systems, usage of IT systems in processes, and interfaces among IT systems). According to the authors, the algorithm delivers a first clustering (44 clusters in the example case study) that has to be discussed with process and IT owners. The result reveals the current structure of processes and IT systems, but not a targeted future state of the enterprise. Therefore, it represents an option to support the discussion of the model. It does not produce a final version.

Keller [Ke09a] describes a pattern labeled "mix the models" to prepare a basic capability map by mixing an enterprise's capability model from available different available sources. According to the author these sources may be existing models in the enterprise, industry reference models, standard software solution maps, generic maps, as well as maps developed by consultants specialized in a certain industry. After identifying the individual sources, the resulting list of capabilities is used to develop the individual capability map. Keller does not describe how this is done and which design guidelines have to be followed. However, he suggests to model two or three hierarchical levels.

König et al. [Kö05b] do not provide an explicit methodology for the construction of a capability map, but provide some design guidelines. According to the authors, the top level capability map contains five generic capabilities that are relevant to any enterprise, namely “product development”, “client interaction”, “fulfillment”, “plan and manage enterprise”, and “collaboration management”. They state, that the naming may be adapted depending on the individual enterprise and industry. On the second level, the five top-level capabilities are broken down into industry-specific capabilities.

The availability of a capability map is a prerequisite for applying business capabilities in the M&A process. At the same time, public information on how to construct a capability map is missing. Therefore, we present a method for definition of an initial capability map for a company in section 7.6.1.

5 Understanding the Corporate Buyer Scenario

5.1 Corporate Buyer Scenario as Basis for Process Development

We showed that M&A are a very broad topic (see chapter 2). To differentiate between various scenarios, we described different types of M&A and presented the M&A classification scheme in section 2.3 (see figure 2.2). Furthermore, we described the motivation to prepare an organization for upcoming M&A, which is often called "merger readiness" (see section 2.5) and identified the M&A process as a main lever to improve an enterprise's M&A practice (see section 2.6).

The goals of an acquiring company can differ strongly in different scenarios [Ja08]. Companies performing acquisition of strategic capabilities according to a defined external growth strategy have the goal of successful integration of these capabilities into the existing organization [GH08, GS09, LM02]. In opposite, a financial investor willing to exit the company with immediate profits is focused on the (short-term) effects on the stock market. Therefore, this type of investor is not interested in the long-term success of the operational integration of the organization. These different reasons and rationales for M&A activities have an important impact on how the M&A process is executed [An09]. Therefore, they strongly influence the M&A reference process and the selection of necessary steps in the single process phases. For example, the goal of integrating the acquired organization requires activities to estimate integration efforts and the process has to comprise all phases from strategic planning to completion of post-merger integration.

Therefore, the "corporate buyer scenario" is developed to clearly scope the target group for the capability-based approach developed in this thesis. This allows to address the specific requirements of this target group and increase the practical relevance of the research results.

In this thesis, we assume that in a typical corporate buyer scenario an enterprise pursues the goal of sustainable growth with an M&A transaction.

According to this assumption, major parts of the acquired enterprise are integrated, while minor parts may be sold off or decommissioned. Furthermore, the assumed scenario is limited to M&A activities involving the operational merger between previously separate enterprises. It does not include the sole transfer of property, e.g. the acquisition of stock or ownership interests, or acquisition of assets such as individual machines or individual customer contracts. Consequently, efficient integration and holistic optimization are major goals.

The subsequent M&A reference process is described from a corporate buyer's perspective, including planning and performing a merger. The major goal of developing the corporate buyer scenario is to identify the main characteristics that drive the design of the M&A process. This process should help enterprises to improve their M&A practice.

Noteworthy, the establishment of a regular M&A process as part of the M&A practice is more beneficial if the enterprise plans to acquire and integrate target organizations repeatedly. In literature, this is often called a "serial acquirer". Kengelbach et al. [Ke11] for example, rate companies performing at least two acquisitions in every three years as serial acquirers. Based on this definition, serial acquirers count for 60% of all acquisitions. However, we refrain from discussing different definitions or criteria to differentiate serial acquirers from other organizations. According to Laamanen and Keil 2008 [LK08], these organizations execute complex acquisition programs with multiple interrelated acquisitions, often even in parallel. Consequently, the integration of IT along a series of acquisitions represents a challenging task [HY13].

In addition to the information identified during the literature study on the domain of M&A (chapter 2), we included practitioners experiences for the description of the corporate buyer scenario. First, we performed a series of interviews with experts from the German banking industry, focusing on IT transformation during M&A (section 5.2.1). Second, we included findings from a workshop with practitioners from the insurance industry, focusing on the topic of IT integration during PMI (section 5.2.2). Additionally, the elaborated corporate buyer scenario has been discussed during a series of practitioner workshops, which have been performed with an international bank and a group of management consultants working for an international management consultancy.

5.2 Practitioners View: Expert Interviews and Workshops

5.2.1 Findings from IT Expert Interviews

Based on results from the literature analysis for the field of M&A, we conducted a series of 15 expert interviews with industry partners from the German banking industry, who were involved in a merger [FMS10b, FMS11]. Even though we focused this study on the German banking industry, the majority of findings remained industry-neutral.

Our interview partners revealed insights into practical problems, solutions, and pitfalls occurring during the transformation of IT, describing some of the characteristics for the corporate buyer scenario. This section shortly summarizes the key findings of the semi-structured interviews relevant to the development of the M&A process. Additional information on the setup of the study and the questions can be found in appendix B.

Characteristics of a Merger Project: The interviewees confirmed the high complexity and strong external influences of merger projects. They especially stressed the interdependence of the different elements in an enterprise such as organization structure, business processes, application landscape, and infrastructure. Additionally, the interviewees stated, that according to their experience, time as a project constraint was often fixed for immediate measures during the Transaction Phase and the early Post-Merger Phase, e.g. the establishment of a common presence in the market comprising brand, product portfolio, and customer services. Later, during the Post-Merger Phase, additional mid and long-term measures were initiated, for internal integration work between the enterprises, as well as for business and IT optimization. The interviewees also confirmed the importance of a comprehensive stakeholder management and the establishment of adequate communication measures. Furthermore, they emphasized that cultural differences of the merging enterprises have lead to substantial loss in working efficiency.

Key Success Factors: The interviewees confirmed the key success factors identified during our literature study (see section 2.2.3): a clear business vision (committed, explicitly described, and measurable), a high aspiration level with definite directions and common performance indicators, stakeholder management (effective communication and consideration of corporate cultures), an adequate project organization (structures and processes), coordinated and holistic planning of business and IT, consistent decisions for business and IT, knowledge management, risk management, as well as realization of growth and demonstration of early wins. They especially stressed the availability of a clear business vision, a stringent approach with clear decisions, defined roles and rules for collaboration, as well as strong stakeholder management and communications.

Role of IT: There was a mutual consent among our interviewees, that IT is not the main driver for M&A. Additionally to general economies of scope and scale, they pointed out cost reductions on the business side (e.g. rationalization of functional units, consolidation of the branch network) and extensions of the business model (e.g. direct banking) as main motivations for M&A in their organization. Regarding IT, the partners confirmed that the consolidation of application landscapes and infrastructure also provides a remarkable potential for cost reductions. Furthermore, the interview partners also agreed that the progress and quality of IT integration can significantly influence business operations with potential negative implications on customer retention and compliance to law and regulation. Thereby, they confirmed our findings from literature (see section 2.7) that during a merger, IT is the backbone of daily business operations, basis for business process target design, and subject for integration and rationalization. The interviewees considered PMI of IT as one of the most challenging tasks during a merger and stated that IT should be in the scope of planning activities directly from the beginning of the M&A process in order to estimate the feasibility and costs of the integration. According to their experience, today PMI of IT is planned and moved forward by the IT department itself. They also reported about positive experiences from close collaboration between business and IT departments to ensure a clear understanding of the organization's new strategic orientation and the implied consequences for IT.

Metrics and KPIs: One interviewee reported about intensified usage of metrics and KPIs to ensure uninterrupted business operation during the Post-Merger Phase. The majority of interviewees did not make use of metrics to measure the overall integration progress during the transformation. However, several interview partners mentioned the usage of their standard project management KPIs. Instead, the majority of the partners focused on measurement of concrete integration objects, e.g. the fulfillment of nonfunctional requirements of a target application.

Merger Readiness: The interviewees confirmed the need for building and advancement of an M&A competence in the enterprise. Especially representatives from organizations with a communicated growth-oriented business strategy stressed the value of a pro-active establishment of a dedicated M&A

competence team. Several interview partners reported that the maturity of their capability for integrating IT increased with the number of mergers the enterprises has completed in the past. Additionally, all partners made a clear distinction between business and IT related merger competences. Furthermore, they confirmed that the M&A organization needs an adequate knowledge management system to collect and systematically store merger information and past experiences. During the interviews, they mentioned various information sources. According to the experts, both buyer and target enterprise contributed to the IT transformation success by exchanging their respective merger know-how and experiences. This was especially important during the initial steps of the transformation. However, information was mainly collected during ex-post debriefings of experiences, not during ongoing M&A projects.

Knowledge Repository: The interviewees agreed that the collection of know-how gained during past M&A activities is vital for an organization pursuing an external growth strategy. If stored in an adequate knowledge source, the information may ease the successful planning, implementation, and accomplishment of future mergers. For the majority of interview partners, practical experiences have been only implicitly available among the individual team members, resulting in a mutual learning process when working conjointly on the different integration tasks. Two interviewees referred to written textbooks representing a structured collection of the enterprise's past M&A experiences, providing valuable guidance during M&A projects. Besides these examples, no explicit establishment of a shared data source was mentioned during the interviews. The participants stated that due to the high operational workload, no sustainable knowledge repository is implemented and maintained during the integration phase. Instead, they used temporal knowledge exchange solutions (e.g. web portal, wiki solutions) but no efforts were made for sustainability of the knowledge gained.

Terminology: According to the interviewees, a common language is indispensable from a business and IT perspective. Before execution of the transformation, a common terminology for business and IT as well as between different departments must be clarified. Only with a common and shared understanding of the fundamental concepts and their interrelations, the different elements of the merging enterprises (e.g. organization, business processes, IT application landscape, infrastructure) can be integrated.

They reported that terminology is substantiated when detailing the PMI plan. In most cases, dedicated planning sessions were scheduled for the definition of a stable foundation of terms. Single interviewees rated these activities as being of low value, while others especially emphasized their importance. One participant referred to examples of industry-specific regulations as being a valuable source for predefined and well-understood set of terms since those official documents turned out to facilitate the labor-extensive task significantly.

Other (IT-related) Transformation Issues: Additionally, the interviews mentioned the following issues regarding IT transformation.

- IT integration team:
  Outsourcing and off-shoring are not regarded as helpful alternatives to deal with the enormous integration workload. Instead, internal staff originating from the merging companies is supported by consultants who also bring in their experience from past IT transformations.
- Target IT organization:
  Early and clear communication of organizational changes is a key success factor for IT transformation. Thereby, demonstration of future tasks and professional perspectives helps to reduce personal resistance and friction among IT employees.
- Application migration:
  Absorption of the acquired application landscape through the existing one is preferred to best-of-breed, greenfield, and co-existence approach. However, functional adjustments were always implemented to the absorbing landscape. Big bang strategies dominate the migration process, even if they dilute in the course of the integration work.
- Data migration:
  Data migration from decommissioned to target applications represents a major work blocks in IT transformations. Performed mostly on weekends in a big bang style, concrete methods exist in order to speed up the migration process and to reduce risk.
- Workarounds:
  According to the interview partners, workarounds may help to mitigate risks and to fulfill regulatory constraints in the short term. Additional cleanup activities are scheduled to refine the respective solutions.
- Testing:
  Intensive testing of the IT transformation results was rated as important by all interviewees.

5.2.2 Findings from Practitioner Workshop at an Insurance Conference

The following integration challenges have been experienced by the participants in a workshop on successful PMI performed by an international management consultancy. It was hold during a conference on current trends in the insurance industry in November 2009. The aspects mentioned by practitioners widely match to those identified during the literature analysis (see section 2.2.3) and provide additional hints for the definition of a corporate buyer scenario.

Merger Motivations and Merger Type: The workshop participants mentioned the risk of value loss in a merger of equals and assumed a higher success rate for the integration of minor entities into a major organization. They especially promoted market-oriented acquisition strategies, focusing on the customer's view on the resulting merged enterprise. Additionally, the practitioners pointed out missing market knowledge as a risk in conglomerate mergers.

Strategy and Target Picture: The participants identified the need for a mutually agreed target picture, which explicitly describes the transformation strategy and goals.

Governance and Project Organization: The practitioners demanded a clear governance model and an adequate project organization. They especially stressed the need to integrate the right stakeholders and experts in the single steps of the integration process.

Communication, Stakeholder Management, Culture and Human Aspects: The experience of a missing common motivation throughout the enterprise was traced back to the absence of a profound stakeholder management and an adequate communication concept. Overall, human aspects such as the integration of cultures have been identified as currently underrepresented in business transformation. The participants assumed that this is one reason for the appearance of resistance among employees and management and may negatively influence the loyalty of employees.

Business and IT Transformation: According to the participants, the business transformation activities resulting from M&A often exceed the organization's ability to change. Regarding the transformation approach, they preferred quick implementations against discussion of individual benefits. Furthermore, they mentioned the need to preserve experiences from past transformation projects, e.g. methods and criteria for target application selection.

Decision Making: Decision making and the availability of consistent information for valuation of alternatives has been identified as a common challenge among the participants. As a consequence, business cases often turned out to be wrong or calculated too favorably. Due to missing facts and figures, the monitoring of benefit realization remained complicated or impossible.

5.3 Definition of a Corporate Buyer Scenario

5.3.1 Corporate Buyer Classification Scheme

In the following the basic conditions of a corporate buyer scenario are described using the M&A classification scheme introduced in section 2.3. Figure 5.1 visualizes the typical characteristics that are described subsequently. A bold font indicates typical elements.

Attribute	Deal Characteristic			
Transaction Type	Merger		**Acquisition**	
Direction of Integration	**Horizontal**	**Vertical**	Conglomerate	
Distribution of Power	Minor	Equal	**Majority**	**Full Control**
Deal Setting	**Friendly**		Hostile	
Deal Motivation	**Strategic**		Financial	
Other	No exit of investor			

Figure 5.1: M&A Classification Scheme for Corporate Buyer Scenario

Transaction Type: The most relevant case for a corporate buyer scenario is an acquisition of a target entity of minor size. The target entity can be a complete company or a selective part that was separated from the company before. In the given scenario, the corporate buyer fully acquires the target entity. During the M&A process, the acquired entity will be legally integrated into the existing corporate governance and management structures.

Direction of Integration: The direction of integration in the defined corporate buyer scenario can be horizontal or vertical. In the case of horizontal integration, the corporate buyer acquires a company operating in the same market. Regarding vertical integration, both directions are included, a forward acquisition towards the final purchaser facing the customer (e.g. a manufacturer acquiring a distribution network) or backwards in direction of the raw material suppliers (e.g. a manufacturer acquiring a supplier). Both result in a complete integration of the acquired company into the corporate buyer enterprise. The acquisition of a conglomerate organization, offering different products in different markets, predominantly aims at diversification of the enterprise. Therefore, it supports the goal of growth but does not include integration of the core business.

Distribution of Power: The acquired enterprise is of minor size, or at least decision power for integration strategies is on the side of the corporate buyer. Consequently, the special case of a merger of equals is excluded. It is assumed that the majority of existing management positions remain stable and are complemented selectively with representatives from the acquired organization. In this way, the existing management team keeps the overall responsibility across the M&A process, including Pre-Merger Phase, Transaction Phase, and Post-Merger Phase. Additionally, key decision makers, responsible for certain aspects of the merger, remain available throughout the process.

Deal Setting: A friendly deal setting is assumed for the corporate buyer scenario. As the case of a hostile takeover results in additional challenges, for example access to required information for evaluation of the target organization and integration planning. However, an initially hostile transaction may be transferred into a friendly environment.

Deal Motivation: The motivation for the deal is a strategic investment, an acquisition of an enterprise to gain access to certain products, services, or market segments. Therefore, a purely financial investment is excluded. For the corporate buyer, it is a means to establish new internal business capabilities that lead to a competitive advantage through differentiation. The external acquisition complements existing capabilities to use them more efficiently, or even comprise completely new capabilities. M&A transactions can be the result of opportunities (driven by offers) or the result of thorough analysis and planning. In this case, the assumption is made that the deal is derived from the enterprise's strategic plans.

Other: The corporate buyer does not plan an exit as investor, but aims to keep the acquired company. No additional assumptions have been made regarding the payment method, the channel of submission, and the internationality of the transaction.

5.3.2 Transformation Challenges

The findings from the literature study (section 2.2.3), the interviews (section 5.2.1), and the workshop (section 5.2.2) can be aggregated into a list of transformation challenges in a corporate buyer scenario. Table 5.1 shows the result with unique identifiers that will be used during the design phase and referenced during evaluation of the research outcomes.

Table 5.1: Transformation Challenges in a Corporate Buyer Scenario

ID	Transformation Challenge
TC1	Provide a clear business vision - committed, explicitly described, and measurable
TC2	Support high aspiration level with definite directions and common KPIs
TC3	Stakeholder management, effective communication, and corporate cultures
TC4	Establish an adequate project organization (structures and processes)
TC5	Coordinated and holistic planning of business and IT
TC6	Consistent decisions for business and IT
TC7	Establish adequate knowledge management (merger repository)
TC8	Establish adequate risk management
TC9	Realize growth and demonstrate early wins

6 The Corporate Buyer M&A Process (CBMA Process)

6.1 Process Development Approach

For our research, we need a complete M&A process documentation with a balanced level of detail for activities and deliverables along the phases. With this structured representation of work in the M&A discipline we can start to identify anchor points for the application of EA Management and especially for the application of business capabilities. As this kind of M&A process reference model is not available (see section 2.6), we consolidate available approaches into the "Corporate Buyer M&A Process" (CBMA Process). The development of the CBMA Process is based on a set of pre-conditions and basic assumptions which reflect a typical scenario of the corporate buyer organization, as presented in chapter 5. While literature also demands for a clearly structured and detailed process for the management of M&A, practitioners often emphasize the high dynamic and complexity of a merger project. Hence, the CBMA Process aims to balance the requirement of providing a guiding structure for the overall progress and offering adequate degrees of freedom for efficient transformation work.

The CBMA Process details the three phases Pre-Merger, Transaction, and Post-Merger as introduced in section 2.6. A suitable level of detail for this work is to break down the phases into process steps on the next level. These steps are documented with a short textual description, a specification of methods identified during the literature analysis, and resulting deliverables. The structure and different levels of the process follow the idea that

- process phases structure the main process into parts with different context and goals,
- process steps break-down the tasks performed during each process phase,
- each process step results in a concrete deliverable,
- and each deliverable is elaborated by applying a certain method.

Additionally, the process is complemented with a set of management dimensions. Each of them is documented with a textual description. Furthermore, it is specified which process steps are a primary focus and in which a participation of the respective experts and stakeholders is required.

Figure 6.1 gives an overview of the approach for the developed of the CBMA Process. The approach included three elements, initial and extended literature analysis, attendance of an academic training course, and regular practitioner workshops. All of them are described shortly in the following.

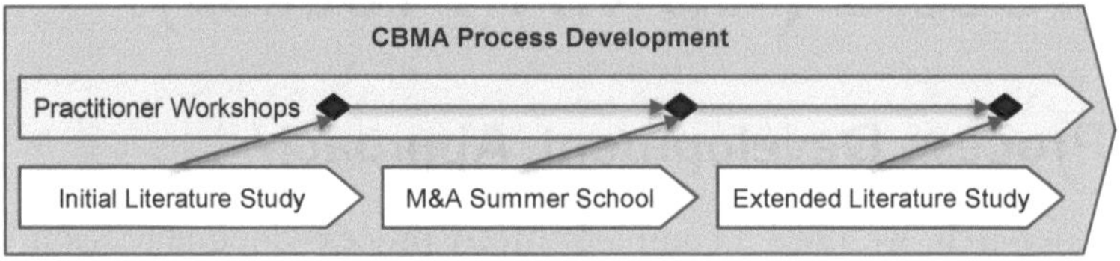

Figure 6.1: Development Approach

Initial Literature Study: The first step of the artifact design was based on the findings from the initial literature study on core M&A resources. The goal was to define the basic structure in terms of process phases, process steps, and management dimensions. Furthermore main activities and deliverables have been identified. The most important group of literature in this phase were M&A handbooks, e.g. [Ja08, KHG06, LM02, Lu02, Pi08b, PP00, Wi06b].

M&A Summer School: Additional insights have been gained by the attendance of an academic training course. This was especially valuable for the Pre-Merger and Transaction Phase, as well as for the strategy, financial, and legal management dimensions. The course offered by the Institute for International Business Law at the University of Münster is delivered by specialist and practitioners of international law and other advisory firms. It aims to combine fundamental and current economic and legal rules with the practical experiences of the lecturers and participants. Especially the sessions on the M&A process, due diligence, and the role of decision makers and managers provided valuable impulses for the overall balancing of the different management dimensions in the process design.

Practitioner Workshops: In parallel to the design activities, a series of practitioner workshops have been performed with representatives of an international bank and a group of management consultants. The discussions of intermediate results of the designed CBMA Process helped to review and refine the process structure in terms of process phases, process steps, main activities and deliverables. During the expert workshops, the proposed process was challenged regarding the identified M&A success factors (see section 2.2.3), the list of IT transformation challenges for the corporate buyer (see section 5.3.1, table 5.1), as well as with personal experiences of the workshop participants.

Extended literature study: Based on the feedback from practitioner workshops and the insights gained during the attendance of the academic training course, an extended literature analysis was performed to refine the process where necessary. The subject of analysis were publications from practitioners and academics (e.g. [ADF01, BC08, Be08, Br90, BU05, HG08, Ho96, Ju99, LM02, Lu03, Me06, Pi08a, St93b]) that elaborate on certain aspects of the process in more detail. While some of them cover the whole process with focus on a certain aspect (or management dimension), others focus on single steps, activities, or deliverables. Examples for the resulting refinements are early integration planning [Ja99], project organization setup and establishing governance structures and processes [Be09a], as well as stakeholder management, communication, and corporate culture [CL04, GSV06]. Penzels handbook [PP00] has been especially useful for the refinement of the management dimensions.

6.2 CBMA Process Structure: Phases and Dimensions

While the overall progress is structured into three major phases, different management domains cluster single activities across all three phases according to classical management disciplines (see section 2.6). As mentioned above, the CBMA Process in this thesis is constructed for the defined corporate buyer scenario, according to a structure that meets the requirements of a balanced depth with process phases, steps, and activities. For each activity it provides methods and deliverables. Figure 6.2 gives an overview on the developed CBMA Process, consisting of the following three phases and eight management dimensions.

6.2.1 CBMA Process Phases

Merger Planning Phase: The Merger-Planning Phase includes strategic planning of corporate M&A activities, environmental analysis, identification of acquisition or merger candidates, and a high level valuation of target scenarios. A detailed documentation of the Merger-Planning Phase is given in section 6.3.

Transaction Phase: The Transaction Phase commences with the initial contact and negotiations between the enterprises involved. This phase includes financial planning, the due diligence, pre-closing integration planning, and corporate valuation. It ends with the official announcement of the merger, contract signing, antitrust clearance and is completed with the final closing which includes the payment. At this time (also called "day 1"), the formerly independent enterprises close their deal and legally become one single company. A detailed documentation of the Transaction Phase is given in section 6.4.

Post-Merger Phase: During the Post-Merger Phase, a post-closing integration plan is worked out to plan and implement the integration of strategy, organization, business processes, systems, administration, operations, culture, and external relationships of the enterprise. Further activities include monitoring of progress, a formal post merger audit, and a possible follow up restructuring. A detailed documentation of the Post-Merger Phase is given in section 6.5.

6.2.2 CBMA Process Management Dimensions

In the following, eight management disciplines are listed and described shortly. They represent a set of perspectives, representing the variety of

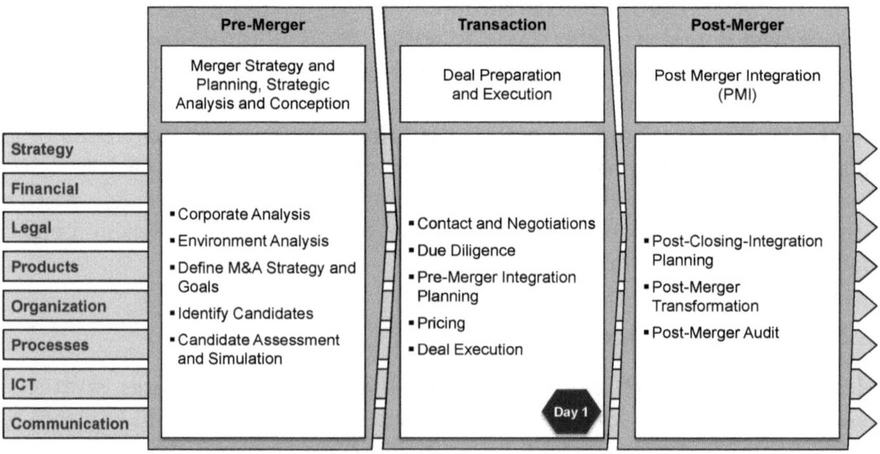

Figure 6.2: Corporate Buyer M&A Process (CBMA Process)

special experts, as well as internal and external stakeholders identified for the corporate buyer scenario.

Strategy: The strategy dimension is driving the overall M&A process along all phases from the beginning of the merger planning [LM02]. It focuses on the definition of the general direction by strategic decisions on the M&A transaction itself, design of the target enterprise, as well as the integration strategy and implementation planning. The decisions and management plans elaborated during the earlier phases are actively managed and controlled during the execution of the transaction and integration work [Me06].

Financial: The financial dimension comprises any monetary valuation, estimation, or calculation activities. These range from early estimations of a potential target enterprise, over valuation of potential target enterprises on the basis of expected assets and risks, to concrete cost estimations for planned integration measures [Ja08, LM02]. During the Post-Merger Phase, it drives the financial controlling of the business transformation, by providing financial information and specification of methods for cost modeling.

Legal: An M&A transaction is performed under a strong influence of external laws and regulations [PF08]. These include besides others financial, fiscal, legal, and political boundary conditions [Ja08]. These laws and regulations are relevant to all phases of the M&A process with different emphasis. They influence the design of the target enterprise and the planning of adequate measures to reach this target picture. Applicable tax and fiscal laws and regulations affect the organizational structure of the enterprise. Relevant employment law limits the availability of efficient measures for staff reduction.

Product: The product dimension focuses on the design of a common target product portfolio [PP00]. This refers to the content, for example the consolidation of the product portfolio, as well as to the organizational aspects, e.g. the definition or reconfirmation of responsibilities. The results of the product dimensions are especially relevant to the organization and process dimensions.

Organization: The target enterprise has to be fully operative as fast as possible [BC08, GS09]. Therefore, in this management dimension different aspects have to be considered from top-level management to the employee level [GS09, Me06]. These include, the establishment of the management and leadership team with a common understanding about the company's future and the definition of an efficient target organization structure. Further aspects are the assignment of important positions, the identification of key staff, ensuring their loyalty, as well as active management of the cultural integration. The planning of the target organization is closely related to the setup of the project teams for the integration work and the establishment of adequate governance mechanisms [GSV06, Lu02]. As soon as measures of staff reduction (e.g. mass dismissal) are included in the transformation plan, the legal aspects become especially important [PF08].

Processes: The predominant aspect of the process dimension is the structural and systematic integration of the target enterprise in terms of daily business operations [GS09]. It includes different levels of processes, the unification of the high-level business process model, representing the enterprise's value chain, as well as the alignment of daily business activities to ensure efficiency. The level of detail for process-related activities increases in the course of the M&A process [Lu02].

Information Technology (IT): The IT dimension is closely related to the process dimension. It has to be continually aligned with the overall integration perspective managed in the strategy dimension [RS99, SJR96]. Uninterrupted business operations demand fast and consistent integration of IT systems [GS09, PP00]. The IT perspective includes the selection of an IT integration strategy, IT transformation planning, integration of business applications, integration of information and data, as well as the implementation of software, hardware, and infrastructure [PP00]. With increasing convergence between information and communication technologies, this management dimension may also include communication technologies. However, in this thesis no differentiation is made between IT and information and communication technology (ICT).

Communication: The communication dimension refers to internal and external distribution of information regarding the M&A activity and includes stakeholder management [Me06, ZH08]. A well-organized communication is key to successful M&A [GSV06, Lu02]. It supports planning, management, controlling/monitoring, and documentation activities. Among others, internal stakeholders include the management team, staff, and employee councils. Examples for external stakeholders are shareholders, the target enterprise, clients, and suppliers. The information distributed comprises facts like the upcoming M&A process steps, milestones, current progress of planning and integration work, as well as motivating elements like incentives, individual explanations, or infotainment [Lu02, ZH08]. The communication dimension during the M&A process is strongly related to corporate communications [ZH08].

Summarizing, figure 6.3 shows the primary focus of each management dimension in the M&A process and indicates areas of participation. The figure transfers the presentation style of Lucks and Meckl [LM02] to the developed structure of the CBMA Process.

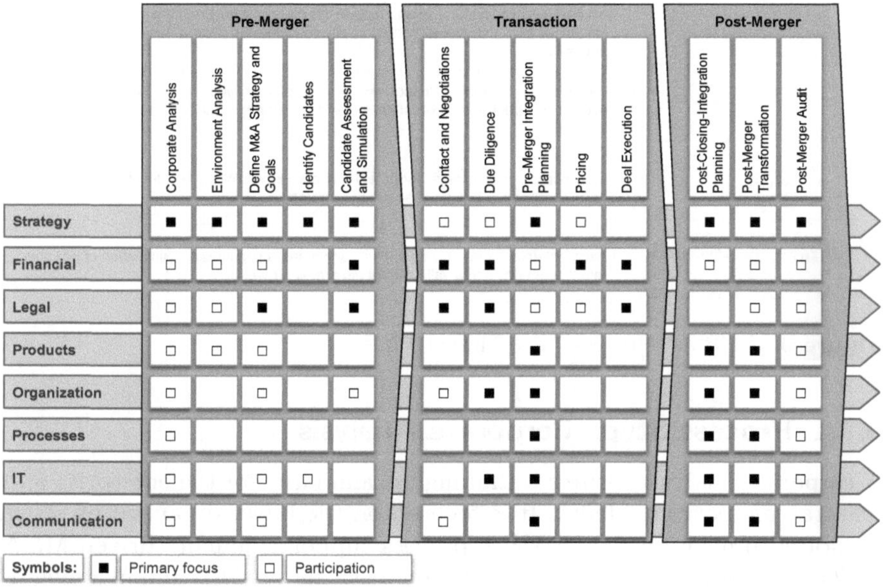

Figure 6.3: CBMA Process Management Dimensions

6.3 Pre-Merger Phase

The first phase of the CBMA Process includes the activities ranging from strategic planning of corporate M&A activities to the preparation of possible transactions [BU05, Ja08, WS06]. It includes a corporate analysis, an environmental analysis, the identification of potential acquisition or merger candidates, and a high-level valuation of target scenarios and their approvability. The phase is concluded with a short list of potential candidates. Figure 6.4 gives an overview of the process steps in the Pre-Merger Phase.

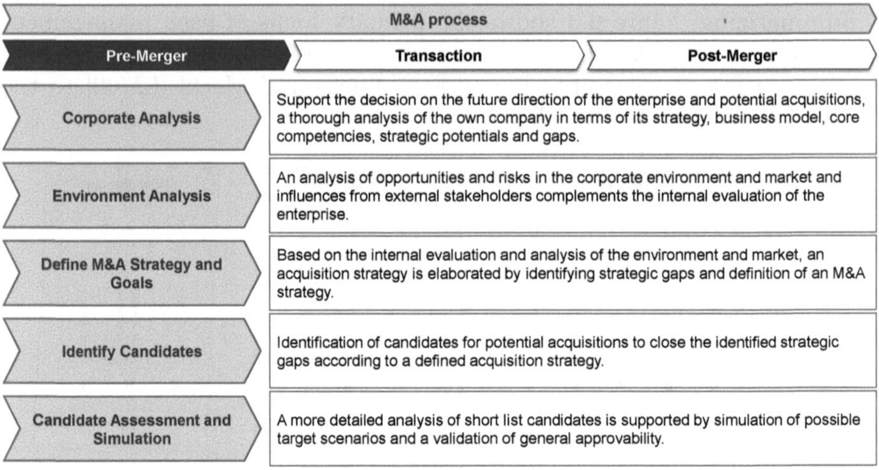

Figure 6.4: CBMA Process - Pre-Merger Phase

6.3.1 Process Step: Corporate Analysis

A corporate analysis ensures a thorough examination of the enterprise and its strategic position [Ja08]. It is focused on the buyer organization itself. As stated in chapter 5, the M&A process supports demand driven M&A activities. Corporate analysis provides the basis for analysis and planning in terms of the buyer organization's strategy, business model, core competencies, strategic potentials, and gaps [Ja08, HW10]. Figure 6.5 gives an overview of the activities, methods, and deliverables of this process step.

Analysis of Company Goals and Business Model: The analysis of the buyer organization's goals and business models ensures that the information on the strategic positioning in terms of corporate strategy and business plan are available in the required formal and structured way. Therefore, both are analyzed and reviewed if necessary. They are documented and confirmed by executive management. The deliverables of this process step are:

- Corporate strategy (reviewed/confirmed):
  Documentation of the corporate strategy in a formal and structured way, including a long-term vision, enterprise mission, goals and objectives, business value drivers, and strategic measures [HW10].
- Business plan (reviewed/confirmed):
  Documentation of the business plan in a formal and structured way, showing how the defined corporate goals and objectives can be reached.

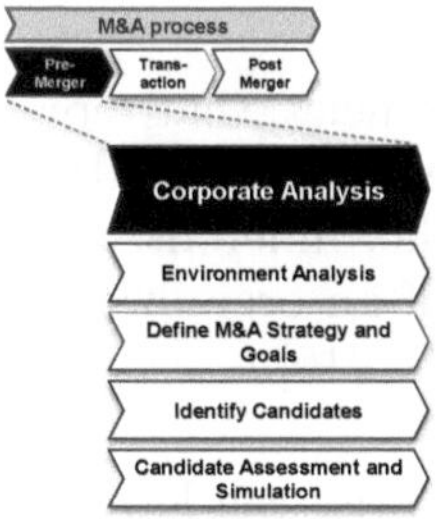

Description		
Support the decision on the future direction of the enterprise and potential acquisitions, a thorough analysis of the own company in terms of its strategy, business model, core competencies, strategic potentials and gaps.		

Activity	Methods	Deliverables
Analysis of company goals and business model	▪ Strategy analysis ▪ Business model analysis	▪ Corporate strategy (reviewed/confirmed) ▪ Business plan (reviewed/confirmed)
Analysis of strategic potentials and gaps	▪ SWOT analysis (focus SW) ▪ Core competency definition ▪ Portfolio analysis ▪ Value Chain analysis ▪ Economies of scale and scope analysis	▪ SWOT profile ▪ Company core competencies ▪ Strategic potentials ▪ Gap List
Transformation self assessment	▪ Readiness assessment ▪ Cultural due diligence ▪ Legal/regulatory analysis	▪ Transformation issues

Figure 6.5: Pre-Merger Phase - Corporate Analysis

Analysis of Strategic Potentials and Gaps: In a next step, the buyer organization is analyzed in more detail in order to identify its strategic potentials and gaps. Typical methods are a SWOT analysis, focusing on the internal side (strengths and weaknesses), portfolio analysis, and value chain analysis [Ja08]. The definition of the organization's core competencies is needed to show, if and how existing capabilities bear the potential to provide the aspired products and access the target market as defined in the business strategy and business model [HP96, HW10, PH90].

The analysis is completed with additional economies of scale and scope analysis. Economies of scale elaborate on possible measures to improve efficiency by unit cost reductions through increased production quantity. Initially, economies of scope have been understood as synergies resulting from a product portfolio extension [PW81]. Today, the term is also used for the case of increased vertical integration[31]. The deliverables of the analysis are:

- SWOT profile (SW part):
  A matrix consisting of the most important factors to the enterprise's future (strategic factors): strengths, weakness, opportunities and threats (SWOT) [HHS03]. Strengths and weakness represent the internal factors.

[31] Both concepts are subject to controversial discussion among economists, also due to their different relevance for certain industries. This discussion is not in the scope of this thesis.

- Company core competencies:
  Documentation of the buyer organization's core competencies, that represent differentiating abilities in a competitive environment [HHS03, HP96, PH90]. Core competencies are combinations of specific, inherent, integrated, and applied knowledge, skills, and attitudes of an organization that build the foundation for strategic plans [HHS03, HW10].
- Strategic potentials:
  Documentation of internal strategic potentials the enterprise can leverage to reach the organization's goals as defined in the corporate strategy.
- Gap list:
  Preliminary collection of gaps that represent missing competencies to reach the organization's goals as defined in the corporate strategy.

Transformation Self Assessment: The self assessment evaluates the readiness of the buyer organization for any M&A activity to follow. Therefore, the ability to manage and perform the business transformation activities is assessed [GS09]. A thorough analysis of the legal and regulatory environment identifies the essential legal and regulatory aspects (for example industry-specific or country-specific) that need to be considered in M&A planning [PF08]. Additionally, the self assessment includes an evaluation of the organization's ability to adapt to changes from a human and cultural perspective, for example by applying a cultural assessment model [CL04]. The findings from the different self assessments are aggregated in the following deliverable:

- Transformation issues:
  A documentation of any identified transformation issue, for example management, cultural, social, legal, and regulatory issues.

6.3.2 Process Step: Environment analysis

The environment analysis complements the internal analysis of the buyer organization with a view on opportunities and risks in the corporate environment [Ja08, WS06]. Additionally, it elaborates on influences from the market and external stakeholders [Ja08, WS06]. Figure 6.6 gives an overview of the activities, methods, and deliverables of this process step.

Analysis of Corporate Environment: The analysis of the corporate environment elaborates on the enterprise's stakeholders from economy, society, and politics [Ja08]. A stakeholder analysis can be combined with games theory methods or the technique of a strategic radar [An75, BN95, Ja08]. A strategic radar is a means for documentation of weak signals in the environ-

Description		
An analysis of opportunities and risks in the corporate environment and market and influences from external stakeholders complements the internal evaluation of the enterprise.		
Activity	**Methods**	**Deliverables**
Analysis of corporate environment	▪ Stakeholder analysis ▪ Games theory ▪ Strategic radar	▪ Environment analysis report
Analysis of industry and market	▪ Industry analysis ▪ Market analysis	▪ Industry and market report
Complete SWOT	▪ SWOT analysis (focus OT)	▪ SWOT profile

Figure 6.6: Pre-Merger Phase - Environment Analysis

ment, that may have a strategic impact on the enterprise. The deliverable of this analysis is:

- Environment analysis report:
  Documentation of findings from the analysis of the corporate environment.

Analysis of Industry and Market: The analysis of the industries and markets relevant to the enterprise completes the information on the environment. It elaborates on key players (e.g. number, size, turnover, financial power), products, product demand, balance of power between supply and demand, industry trends, market life cycle, and market dynamics [Ja08, St93b]. The deliverable of the analysis is:

- Industry and market report:
  Documentation of findings from the analysis of the industry and market

Complete SWOT: The SWOT profile created during the corporate analysis focused on the strengths and weaknesses (SW) of the enterprise. At this stage, it can be completed with the identified opportunities and threats (OT) in the external environment. The deliverable is:

- SWOT profile (completed):
  A matrix consisting of the most important factors to the enterprise's future (strategic factors): strengths, weakness, opportunities and threats (SWOT) [HHS03]. Strengths and weakness are internal factors, opportunities and threats are external factors.

6.3.3 Process Step: Define M&A Strategy and Goals

Based on the internal evaluation and the analysis of the environment, the industry, and market, an M&A strategy is elaborated. The three activities comprise a structured analysis of strategic gaps, a gap assessment regarding their potential to be addressed with an M&A measure, and the formulation of the enterprise's M&A strategy. Figure 6.7 gives an overview of the activities, methods, and deliverables of this process step.

Description		
Based on the internal evaluation and the analysis of the environment, the industry, and market, an M&A strategy is elaborated by identifying strategic gaps and decide on acquisition measure to address each gap.		
Activity	**Methods**	**Deliverables**
Identification of Gaps	▪ Gap Analysis ▪ Strategic Statement Development	▪ Operational Gaps ▪ Strategic Gaps ▪ Strategic Statement
Derive M&A needs and options	▪ Scenario Analysis ▪ Ansoff Product-Market Growth Matrix	▪ M&A Demand
Finalize M&A strategy & goals	▪ n/a	▪ M&A Strategy ▪ Acquisition Goals

Figure 6.7: Pre-Merger Phase - Define M&A Strategy and Goals

Identification of Gaps: A gap analysis identifies deviations of available core competencies and strategic potentials from the aspired goals formulated in the enterprise's business strategy [Ja08]. To ensure a viable planning, these goals have to be verified regarding their practicability considering the identified influences from the environment [Ja08]. To identify gaps relevant to a growth strategy, a distinction is made between strategic and operational gaps. An operational gap can be closed with existing markets and products, while a strategic gap requires an extension of the product portfolio or the development of new markets [Ja08]. As a means to support a gap analysis, the findings from the strategic analysis are organized in the form of a strategic statement [Ja08]. This structure transfers the concept of a balance sheet (assets and liabilities) to the comparison of core competencies of the organization in relation to competitors in the corporate environment [Ja08, Ma87]. The deliverables of the gap review are:

- Operational gaps:
  Documentation of operational gaps
- Strategic gaps:
  Documentation of strategic gaps
- Strategic statement:
  Balance sheet view on core competencies of the enterprise in relation to the corporate environment

Derive M&A Needs and Options: An acquisition is only one of several options to close a strategic gap [Ja08]. Other examples are organic expansion, increased market penetration, and internal innovation [Ja08]. Therefore, an adequate means has to be selected for each strategic gap. The decision on the right course of action can be supported by scenario analysis and sensitivity analysis methods [Ja08, HHS03]. The deliverable is:

- M&A demand:
  Documentation of demand for M&A activities to close strategic gaps

Finalize M&A Strategy and Goals: The M&A demand derived from the strategic analysis is documented in the enterprise's M&A strategy [LM02, Ja08]. The document comprises a description of planned M&A activities and formulated goals to be achieved with these means. The documentation of the M&A strategy can be supported by strategic planning methods and visualizations like Ansoff's product/market growth matrix [An07, HHS03, Ja08]. The deliverables are:

- M&A strategy:
  A documentation of the M&A strategy
- Acquisition goals:
  Formulation of measurable goals to be achieved by implementing the M&A strategy

6.3.4 Process Step: Identify Candidates

In the next step, candidates for potential acquisitions have to be identified to close the identified strategic gaps according to the defined M&A strategy. Therefore, this step comprises the definition of requirements in the form of candidate selection criteria and an analysis of the acquisition environment to identify matching candidates in the market. Figure 6.8 gives an overview of the activities, methods, and deliverables of this process step.

Define Candidate Selection Criteria: In order to structure the candidate selection, all requirements for a potential target candidate are compiled into the acquisition profile [Ja08]. They are collected from deliverables elaborated during the previous process: e.g. strategic radar, strategic statement, or value chain analysis. Additional criteria may assess how good potential candidates match to the organization in terms of strategic fit (e.g. corporate mission), organizational fit (e.g. incentive system), and cultural fit (e.g. aspiration for innovation) [Ja08]. The acquisition profile can be substantiated with concrete scoring models.

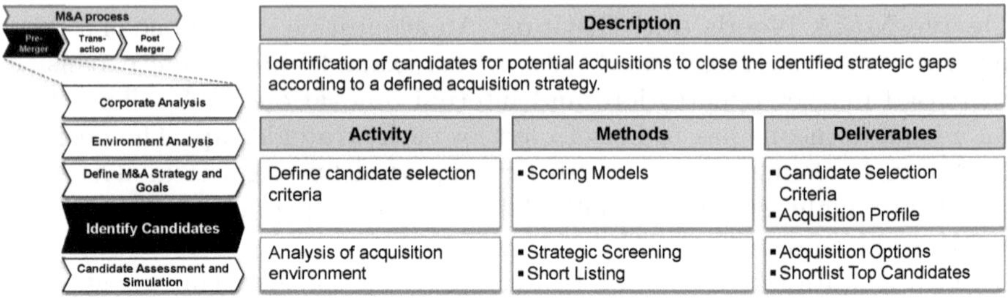

Figure 6.8: Pre-Merger Phase - Identify Candidates

The deliverables are:

- Acquisition profile:
  Requirement profile for potential acquisition candidates
- Candidate selection criteria:
  Additional selection criteria for potential acquisition candidates

Analysis of Acquisition Environment: In the next step, the acquisition environment is evaluated to identify options to close the strategic gaps according to the defined M&A strategy and targets. Possible approaches are country-oriented (regional limitation of candidates), market-oriented (stock market and capital market, but also legislation and social acceptance), and business segment-oriented analysis (industry and products) [Ja08, St93a]. In general, these methods are combined and their results merged into a complete view on the acquisition environment. In the assumed demand-driven scenario (see chapter 5), a strategic screening is required for the identification of potential candidates in the acquisition environment. This has to be done very carefully to avoid negative effects on following negotiations and disclosure of the M&A strategy to competitors [Ja08]. Subsequently, the number of potential candidates is stepwise reduced ("selection funnel") by additional analysis and systematic rating through assessment against acquisition profile and selection criteria [Ja08]. While the number of candidates decreases, the demand for detailed information increases [St93a]. Therefore, this process step concludes by selecting a small number of potential candidates for final consideration which are documented on a short list [LM02, Ja08]. The deliverables of this analysis are:

- Acquisition options:
  A prioritized list of potential candidates
- Shortlist of top candidates:
  A small number of potential candidates, selected for final consideration

6.3.5 Process Step: Candidate Assessment and Simulation

The Pre-Merger Phase is completed with a more detailed analysis of a small number of short list candidates. This is supported by the simulation of possible target scenarios and a validation of general approvability in terms of legal and regulatory restrictions. Figure 6.9 gives an overview of the activities, methods, and deliverables of this process step.

Description		
A more detailed analysis of short list candidates is supported by simulation of possible target scenarios and a validation of general approvability.		
Activity	**Methods**	**Deliverables**
Modeling of the integrated enterprise	▪ Simulation ▪ Organization Design	▪ Integration Scenario (high-level) ▪ Target Governance Model (high-level) ▪ Pre-Closing Integration Plan (high-level draft)
Validation of approvability	▪ n/a	▪ Documentation of Approvability and Risks

Figure 6.9: Pre-Merger Phase - Simulation

Modeling of the Integrated Enterprise: The modeling of the integrated enterprise comprises an evaluation of a potential integration scenario with a small number of short list candidates, the definition of the adequate target governance model, and a first draft of an integration plan. The final result of the completed M&A process is an integrated unit, which combines present and purchased activities in a business segment, e.g. the provision of a product or access to a certain market. This integrated unit should be able to positively contribute to business success [LM02, Lu03].

At an early stage, a simulation of the potential integration allows to consider whether the integrated unit is able to achieve the targeted strategic objectives [LM02, Lu03]. An initial common business plan is drawn up on the basis of the company's own business model, the business model of the potential candidate, as well as the estimated synergies and restructuring costs [Lu03]. Due to the high effort, a simulation will normally be limited to a maximum of top 3 candidates. It builds on the findings from strategic screening, where a rough analysis has been performed for a number of candidates. A target governance model is elaborated on a high level, documenting the aspired corporate structure, an adjusted organizational structure, and the distribution of decision-making power [LM02]. In the assumed scenario (see chapter 5) this will normally result in a legal integration of the acquired unit and an absorption into the existing governance model.

At this stage, a first high-level version of a pre-closing integration plan can be drafted to gather basic integration measures and document risks identified during the Pre-Merger Phase. The deliverables are:

- Integration scenario (high-level):
  Documentation of potential target scenarios for the integration of a target candidate
- Target governance model (high-level):
  Corporate structure, organizational structure and distribution of decision rights
- Pre-closing integration plan (high-level draft):
  Structured collection of basic integration measures and risks

Validation of Approvability: The legal analysis of a potential M&A transaction starts long before signing of a sales agreement. An assessment of approvability ensures that the defined governance model, including the proposed organization structure (e.g. locations) and resulting competition constellation (e.g. number of remaining market players), will be authorized by antitrust and fulfills relevant legal restrictions [LM02, Lu03]. In the case of international M&A activities, the validation of approvability is even more important [BU05, LM02]. The deliverable is:

- Documentation of approvability and risks:
  Documentation of relevant regulatory and legal restrictions, resulting approvability for a potential M&A transaction and remaining risks

6.4 Transaction Phase

The Transaction Phase comprises activities for preparation and execution of a concrete M&A transaction. Figure 6.10 gives an overview of the process steps.

The phase commences with the initial contact and negotiations between the enterprises involved. This phase includes financial planning, due diligence, pre-closing integration planning, and financial valuation. It ends with the official announcement of the merger, contract signing, antitrust clearance and is completed with the final closing which includes the payment. At this time, the so-called "day one", the formerly independent entities close their deal and legally become one single entity. Jansen [Ja08] provides a time line that shows a typical duration of about 38 weeks from initial contact of the target candidate to closing of the deal.

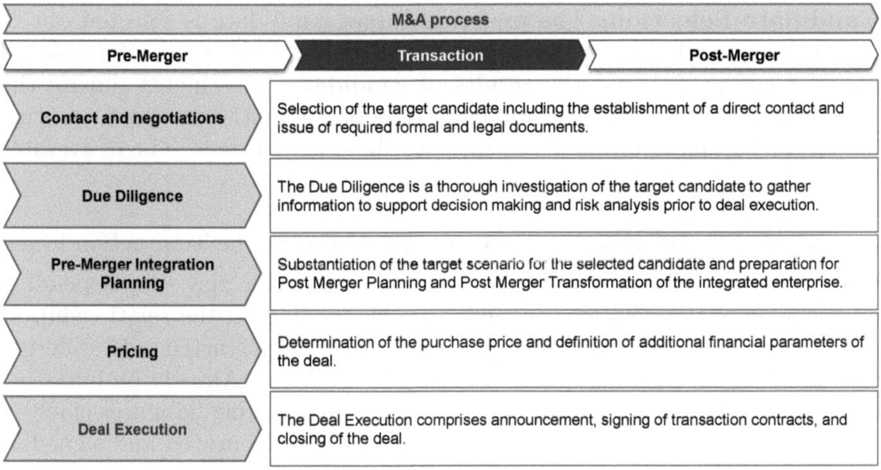

Figure 6.10: CBMA Process - Transaction Phase

6.4.1 Process Step: Contact and Negotiations

In the first process step of the Transaction Phase, the target candidate subject to the transaction is selected out of the shortlist candidates. The direct contact is established and required formal and legal documents are issued. Figure 6.11 gives an overview of the activities, methods, and deliverables of this process step.

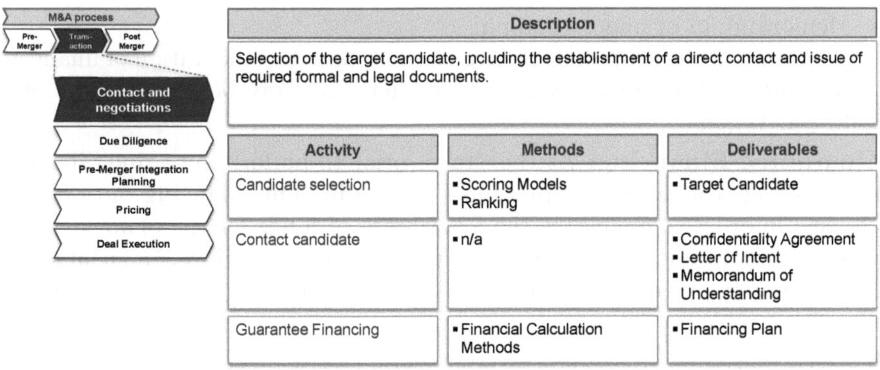

Figure 6.11: Transaction Phase - Contact and Negotiations

Candidate Selection: The preferred target candidate is selected out of the short list, which has been elaborated on the basis of the formulated requirement profile and the results of candidate assessments during the Pre-Merger Phase. If there is still more than one potential candidate, scoring models and ranking mechanisms support the final decision. The deliverable is:

- Target candidate:
  Company or part of company to be acquired during the Transaction Phase

Contact Candidate: The initial contact to the seller may vary depending on the type of the deal (see section 2.3). Depending on the relationship to the target candidate, the establishment of contacts is started with different individuals or at a certain point of time [BU05, Ja08]. Already by initiating contract negotiations, each counterpart incurs far-reaching liabilities [Ja08][32]. Therefore, at this early stage legal documents are elaborated and signed in order to regulate confidentiality (confidentiality agreement), record statements of intent for the transaction and partial results of the negotiations (letter of intent), as well as to define the procedure for negotiations, and document financial, conceptual, legal and tax issues that have already been resolved (memorandum of understanding) [Ja08]. The deliverables are:

- Confidentiality agreement:
  Statement of non-disclosure between the buyer and the seller [Ja08, Pi08a, WS06]
- Letter of intent:
  Statement of intent for the transaction including a documentation of partial results of the negotiation [Ja08, Pi08a, WS06]
- Memorandum of understanding:
  Definition of the procedure for negotiations and documentation of financial, conceptual, legal and tax issues that have already been resolved [Ja08, Pi08a, WS06]

Guarantee Financing: At this stage, prior to performing a due diligence and the negotiation of the purchase price, different financing options are checked in order to guarantee the availability of funds for the planned M&A transaction. Besides internal calculation of financing options, the contact to investment banks and financial advisers is established in this early phase. The deliverable is:

- Financing plan:
  Strategy for financing the planned M&A transaction

[32] This is referred to as the "culpa in contrahendo" pinciple. More detailed information on the legal aspects of the deal can be found in [Ja08, Pi08a] and additional law literature.

6.4.2 Process Step: Due Diligence

A due diligence is a thorough investigation of the target candidate to gather transparent and concise information prior to deal execution [CG98, CL04, Ja08]. It fosters understanding about the target candidate by identification and structured documentation of factors for success and risks in order to improve valuations and contract design, and supports negotiations and decision making. It improves the definition of a reasonable purchase price and design of the legal contracts during the M&A transaction. Regarding the planning and execution of the integration, due diligence information helps to set the right priorities, mitigate risks, and estimate efforts. Figure 6.12 gives an overview of the activities, methods, and deliverables of this process step.

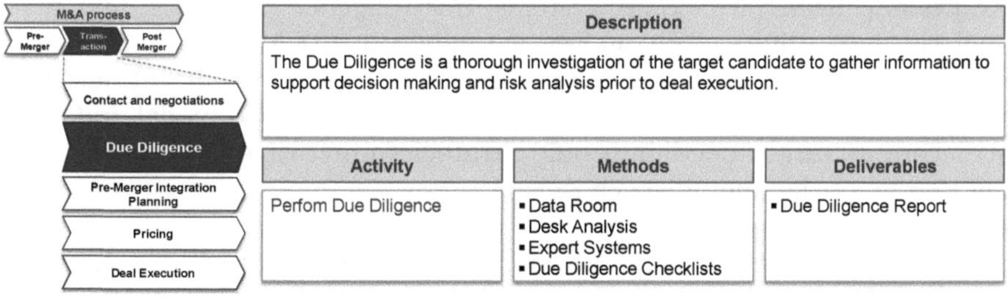

Figure 6.12: Transaction Phase - Due Diligence

Perform Due Diligence: The systematic analysis and valuation covers a range of disciplines. The most common sub-areas are: commercial, financial, legal, tax, human resource, and environmental due diligence [CL04, Ja08, LM02, Pi08a, WS06]. Each of them includes a set of important issues to be covered. Financial due diligence focuses on key drivers that impact profitability. Therefore, it comprises analysis of profit and loss (P&L) statements, balance sheet, cash flows, prospectives, analyst reports, and regulatory filings.

Legal due diligence focuses on the identification of legal chances and risks. They can be identified by an analysis of regulatory filings, tax law, extraordinary contracts, insurance contracts, patents, and licenses. Tax due diligence is strongly related to financial and legal due diligence. It is focused on the identification of potential tax indemnification, tax risks, and impacts on target tax structure. Commercial (or operational) due diligence covers the candidate's strategy, industry, market, and product or service development. Human resource due diligence comprises management risks, staff structure, social schemes, and available industry know-how. IT due diligence covers the application portfolio, data centers, the technology portfolio, IT security, compliance and IT management structures. Traditional due diligence approaches primarily focus on the financial, legal, regulatory, and tax issues. A cultural due diligence analyzes the compatibility of management systems, readiness for transformation, and corporate cultures (e.g. internationality, innovation ability) [CL04][33]. An environmental and political due diligence deals with the ecological and political risks associated with the planned transaction.

The due diligence is usually performed in data rooms which are provided by the target candidate [Ja08, LM02, Pi08a, WS06]. The teams focusing on the different sub-areas have to be synchronized to exchange information on dependencies (e.g. legal and tax aspects) and to avoid double work [Ja08]. Additional means are expert systems, due diligence checklists, and desk analysis [Ja08, Pi08a]. The analysis is conducted with strongly limited time and resources, which demands for a purposeful resource allocation. Key areas of the concrete due diligence depend on the business model, industry, structure of target candidate, and strategic aims within the deal. The deliverable of the due diligence is:

- Due diligence report:
  Summarized documentation of information gathered during due diligence. Detailed information is stored in a repository.

6.4.3 Process Step: Pre-Merger Integration Planning

According to Jansen [Ja99], only one in five M&A transactions includes integration planning activities during merger planning and negotiations. A first high-level integration scenario and a corresponding pre-closing integration plan have been elaborated as part of the candidate assessment and simulation activities during the Pre-Merger Phase. Now, the information collected during the due diligence can be used to substantiate the target scenario for the selected candidate [LM02]. Besides the detailing of the target scenario, the integration itself can be prepared prior to closing by definition of the integration procedure and the development of a communication plan.

[33] Carleton and Lineberry [CL04] see an additional Cultural Due Diligence (CDD) as a mandatory step during a merger to maximize organizational effectiveness and profitability. The goal of CDD is to ascertain cultural alignment or compatibility between the companies. This is achieved by establishing CDD as a parallel process to the traditional financial and legal due diligence. Thereby, potential areas of culture clashes and their level of difficulty can be determined early in the M&A process to prepare effective alignment plans for integration and change management (especially culture and organization) during the Post-Merger Phase.

Figure 6.13 gives an overview of the methods and deliverables of this process step.

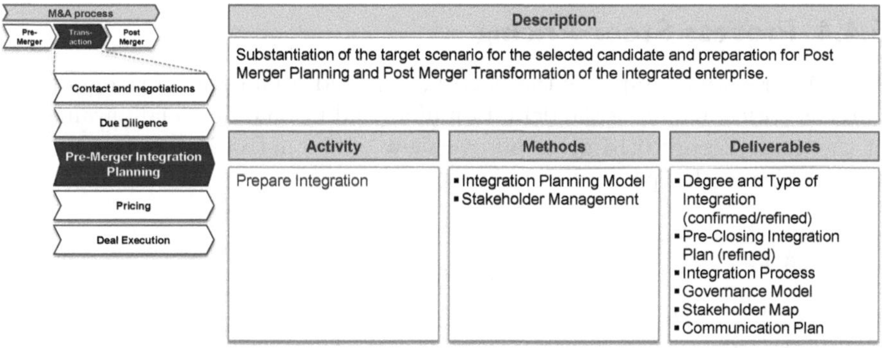

Figure 6.13: Transaction Phase - Pre-Merger Integration Planning

Prepare Integration: The business target picture is thoroughly analyzed in order to derive the strategic requirements, which drive the design of the target enterprise. An integration planning model (e.g. the 7k-model [Kr90]) helps to work out the critical issues of the planned integration in a structured way [Ja08]. At this stage of the transaction, the decisions on the target enterprise and the integration plan get a binding character [LM02]. Thus, the degree and type of integration is finally determined and the milestones for the integration plan can be defined [Ja08, LM02]. Therefore, also the estimation of cost and synergy effects becomes more reliable. With the more detailed view on the target enterprise, the integration process and a matching governance model for the subsequent Post-Merger Phase can be defined [Ja08]. The main rationale behind is to provide a binding working environment and to form a foundation for all subsequent steps performed by the responsible PMI project team. The governance model for integration gives information about the project organization, roles, clear responsibilities, conductive rules for collaboration, reporting, as well as effective escalation paths [Be09a, Ja08]. Besides the formal governance model, the overall project success strongly relies on the management of multidisciplinary stakeholders and the establishment of adequate communication and information activities [BC08, CL04, LM02]. Thus, the stakeholder map is refined and a schedule of communication activities is elaborated. The deliverables is:

- Pre-closing integration plan (refined):
  Confirmed or refined versions of the target enterprise, including degree

and type of integration, integration process, the governance model for integration, a stakeholder map, and a communication plan

6.4.4 Process Step: Pricing

This process step comprises the negotiations and final determination of the purchase price including the definition of any additional financial parameters of the deal. Figure 6.14 gives an overview of the activities, methods, and deliverables of this process step.

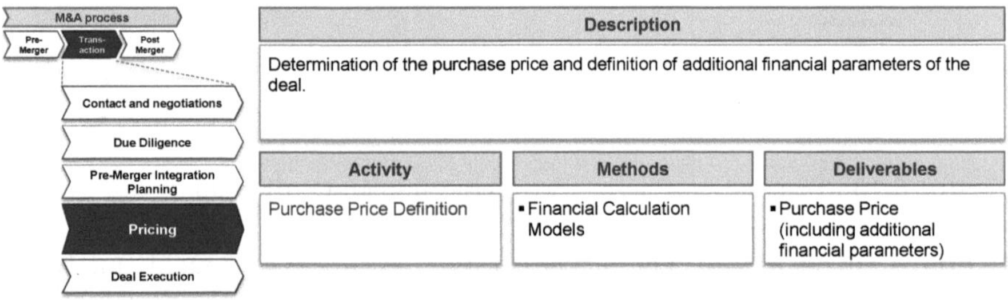

Figure 6.14: Transaction Phase - Pricing

Purchase Price Definition: The definition of the purchase price includes both, the determination of the value of the target candidate, and second, the negotiation of the purchase price that is paid. The value contribution of the M&A transaction is the value of the target candidate plus synergies, minus the purchase price to be paid and transaction costs (see section 2.1.1). Potential synergies and integration costs have been evaluated during the Pre-Merger Phase and have been verified or refined during the due diligence.

The determination of the value of the target candidate is done with the help of financial calculation methods. A structured lineup and illustration of the different valuation methods (e.g. cash flow analysis, net asset value, value of earnings, real options, comparative company approach, or liquidation value) can be found in M&A literature [Ja08, HG08, LM02, WS06] or dedicated books on financial valuation [DS09, EST10, Wi10]. The individual methods adhere to assumptions, leading to different results for the calculated company value. Therefore, buyers tend to select methods leading up to lower results, while sellers prefer methods yielding higher company values. Additionally, both organizations may have different points of opinion regarding other factors (e.g. synergies or integration costs) to be factored into the valuation [BU05, Ja08, HG08, LM02, WS06]. At this point in the process, an agreement on the purchase price is achieved during the negotiation with the target candidate [HG08, Ja08]. Besides the purchase price, additional financial parameters may be defined to regulate matters like payment method, or payment schedule. The deliverables are:

- Target candidate value:
  Subjective value of the target candidate according to the selected valuation method, incorporating synergies and costs
- Purchase price:
  Agreed price to be paid for the target candidate including additional financial parameters of the transaction

6.4.5 Process Step: Deal Execution

The last step in the Transaction Phase executes the transaction. It comprises public and formal announcement, signing of transaction contracts, and closing of the deal. With the completion of this step, the formerly independent entities legally become a single entity (day one) [Ja08]. The details of the legal documents signed differ, depending on the M&A transaction (see section 2.3) in terms of deal type (asset deal vs. share deal), the location of the target candidates headquarters (national vs. crossborder), and the relationship to the target candidate (friendly vs. hostile takeover) [Ja08, LM02, Pi08c]. Figure 6.15 gives an overview of the activities, methods, and deliverables of this process step.

Description		
The Deal Execution comprises announcement, signing of transaction contracts, and closing of the deal.		
Activity	**Methods**	**Deliverables**
Announcement	▪ n/a	▪ Official Announcement ▪ Tentative Agreements
Signing	▪ n/a	▪ Sales Agreement (including Warranties and Guaranties)
Closing	▪ Antitrust Audit	▪ Antitrust Clearance ▪ New Legal Entity (Transfer of Ownership)

Figure 6.15: Transaction Phase - Deal Execution

Announcement: The deal execution itself starts with the announcement of the M&A transaction and the issuing of tentative agreements. The announcement is an official, public declaration of intent for the transaction [BC08].

With the signed tentative agreements both parties enter an obligation to sign the prime contract [Pi08a]. However, at this point single aspects of the deal can still be subject to ongoing negotiations. The deliverables are:

- Announcement:
  Official, public declaration of intent for the transaction
- Tentative agreement:
  Obligation with target candidate to sign the prime contract

Signing: Signing constitutes the end of negotiations and results in the underwriting of the sales agreement as the prime contract for the transaction [Ja08]. The inclusion of warranties and guaranties clearly distributes the liability for risks between buyer and seller and regulates appropriate waiver agreements. [Ja08]. The deliverable is:

- Sales agreement
  Prime contract for takeover of target candidate including warranties and guaranties

Closing: Before the official closing of the transaction, an antitrust audit is performed [BC08, Be08, Ja08, LM02]. Additionally, any required approval from other regulatory authorities is obtained. The acceptance of the transaction has already been analyzed and proceedings have been prepared during the validation of general approvability in terms of legal and regulatory restrictions during the Pre-Merger Phase. At the end of this phase, with the issue of the antitrust approval, the deal is closed and ownership is transferred forming the new legal entity [BC08, Be08, Ja08, LM02].
The deliverables are:

- Antitrust clearance
  Approval from antitrust authorities
- New legal entity
  Resulting legal entity after transfer of ownership

6.5 Post-Merger Phase

The Post-Merger Phase starts immediately after the Transaction Phase has been completed (at day one). It comprises finalization of planning and execution of post merger transformation activities, a post merger audit and the definition of follow-up activities, if needed. Normally, the duration of this process phase is several years and thus much longer than the previous phases. Furthermore, it is common that enterprises have to manage multiple parallel PMI activities resulting from different acquisitions. This is especially relevant for enterprises that regularly apply M&A as an instrument for external growth. Figure 6.16 gives an overview of the process steps in the Post-Merger Phase.

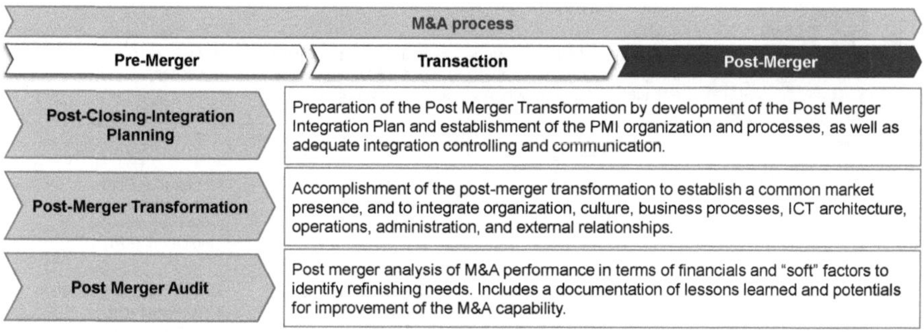

Figure 6.16: CBMA Process - Post-Merger Phase

6.5.1 Process Step: Post-Closing Integration Planning

Post-closing integration planning prepares the post merger transformation by finalization of the post merger integration plan and establishment of the necessary PMI organization and processes, as well as adequate integration controlling and communication. Figure 6.17 gives an overview of the activities, methods, and deliverables of this process step.

Develop PMI Plan: The main measures for the PMI plan have been defined during the pre-merger planning [Lu03, Ja08] (see process step pre-merger integration planning). The finalization includes a review and further detailing of the project plan for the post merger transformation of the enterprise. To make the implementation of the integration plan controllable, the agreed integration goals are documented and their realization can be assessed with a set of defined key performance indicators (KPI). The deliverables of this step are:

- Integration goals:
  Integration goals to be achieved
- PMI plan:
  Project plan for PMI, including the integration process describing the transformation approach

- Key performance indicators (KPI):
  Metrics to measure the performance of the PMI project and the achievement of defined goals

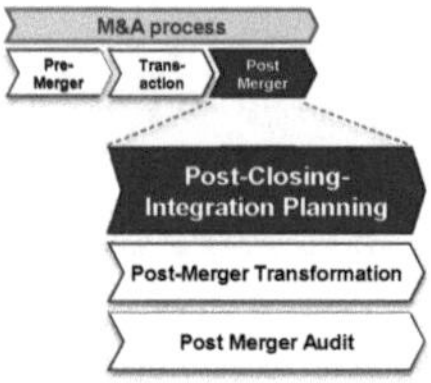

Description
Preparation of the Post Merger Transformation by development of the Post Merger Integration Plan and establishment of the PMI organization and processes, as well as adequate integration controlling and communication.

Activity	Methods	Deliverables
Develop PMI Plan	▪ PMI Reference Process ▪ Roadmap Planning	▪ Integration Plan ▪ Integration Goals ▪ Key Performance Indicators (KPI)
Establish PMI Organization	▪ PMI Project Organization Reference Model ▪ RACI Matrix	▪ PMI Project Organization ▪ PMI Roles and Responsibilities ▪ Integration Controlling Model
Establish Internal and External Communication	▪ Stakeholder Management	▪ Communication Concept

Figure 6.17: Post-Merger Phase - Post-Closing-Integration Planning

Establish PMI Organization: PMI are complex business transformation projects. Due to their broad scope, high complexity, and singularity, PMI is performed in a dedicated project environment [Ja08, Lu02, Lu03]. Like any project, a merger is performed and completed within the interdependent constraints of given scope, time, and costs [Ke09b, Le06]. Additionally, M&A projects are characterized by increased uncertainty and influenced intensively by third parties [Be09a, Lu03], which has to be considered in the PMI project setup. Consequently in order to execute the PMI plan, a binding working environment with appropriate structures, processes and rules has to be established [Be09a, BC08, CL04, Ja08]. Integration controlling comprises activities to monitor changes driven by the PMI project in order to track progress and readjust the PMI plan, if needed. Besides the optimization of the ongoing integration process, any identified lessons learned and potentials for improvement are fed into the post merger audit at a later stage. The deliverables of this step are:

- PMI project organization:
  Organization structure for the PMI project
- PMI roles and responsibilities:
  Defined roles and responsibilities to specify the decision rights and accountabilities in the PMI project organization

- Integration controlling model:
  Structures and procedures for controlling of the integration progress and success

Establish Internal and External Communication: A PMI project includes a large number of stakeholders from multiple disciplines, that have to be managed [PP00]. Therefore, besides the formal governance model, the overall project success strongly relies on the management of multidisciplinary stakeholders and the establishment of adequate communication and information activities [Ja08]. A communication concept for the planned PMI project allows for this communication to be carried out within a planned and managed process. Good communication ensures a high degree of acceptance and sustainability for the decisions made in the course of the PMI project. The deliverable of this step is:

- Communication concept:
  Plan of stakeholder-specific communication activities comprising content, channels, and schedule

6.5.2 Process Step: Post-Merger Transformation

The accomplishment of the post-merger transformation comprises the concrete realization of changes in the enterprise. These include all measures needed for the establishment of a common market presence, the integration of organization, culture, business processes, ICT architecture, operations, administration, as well as external relationships [BU05, Ja08, LM02, PP00]. Figure 6.18 gives an overview of the activities, methods, and deliverables of this process step.

Integration of Strategies: In the assumed scenario (see chapter 5), the common business strategy is defined by including the additional M&A related aspects elaborated during the Pre-Merger Phase. The directions formulated in the general business strategy are then broken down into functional strategies, such as product, market, IT, or HR strategies. The deliverable of this step is:

- Set of common strategies:
  A common business strategy and a matching set of common functional strategies

Integration of Market Presence: As one of the first activities after the official closing of the deal, establishment of a common presence and offering in the market in terms of branding, products, and customer services is established. This activity focuses on the integration of the enterprise from

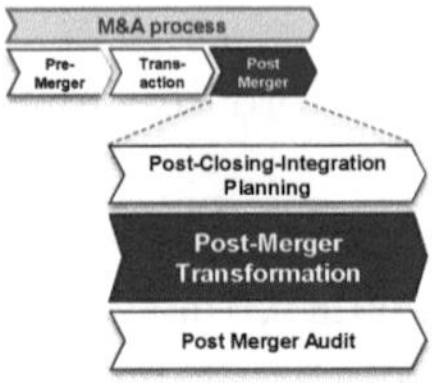

Description
Accomplishment of the post-merger transformation to establish a common market presence, and to **integrate** organization, culture, business processes, ICT architecture, operations, administration, and external relationships.

Activity	Methods	Deliverables
Integration of Strategies	▪ n/a	▪ Set of Common Strategies
Integration of Market Presence	▪ n/a	▪ Common Brand(s) ▪ Common Product Portfolio
Integration of Organization and Culture	▪ Target Architecture Planning (Business)	▪ Common Organizational Structure ▪ Employee Placement ▪ Common Businesses Processes
Integration of Business Information and IT	▪ Target Architecture Planning (IT)	▪ Common Business Information ▪ Integrated IT Architecture
Integration of Infrastructure	▪ Target Architecture Planning (Infrastructure)	▪ Integrated Infrastructure

Figure 6.18: Post-Merger Phase - Post-Merger Transformation

an external point of view. The entire public image of the company is aligned to the defined common product and marketing strategies. The deliverables of this step are:

- Common brands:
  Concerted brand or portfolio of multiple brands represented in the market
- Common product portfolio
  Integrated product portfolio offered to customer segments

Integration of Organization and Culture: After adjusting the external perception, the internal integration of the enterprise is a prerequisite to make the new entity operational and productive. This includes a consolidation of the organization structure, which is typically performed top-down from executives and management level to the operational level. Employees are allocated to positions in the organization structure. In the assumed case of a strategic corporate buyer, the main part of the existing structures will remain stable and new organizational units will be integrated where necessary.

At the same time, the enterprise's business processes are aligned. Even though this activity can be manifold, depending on the concrete business model and the acquired target organization, it can be assumed that the existing process model will remain stable to a great extend in the described buyer scenario. Additionally, a comprehensive plan for the integration of cultures is elaborated and its implementation is started. It has to be noted that the implementation of the cultural integration plan is a lengthy activity that has to continue beyond restructuring measures. The deliverables of this step are:

- Common organizational structure:
  A concerted organization model
- Employee placement:
  Allocation of employees in the organizational structure
- Common business processes:
  A concerted business process model

Integration of Business Information and ICT: In order to support the resulting business processes, relevant information from both source organizations has to be made available. Therefore, the underlying information and communication technologies have to be integrated. Possible integration strategies as well as relevant selection criteria and consequences have been presented in section 2.8. Depending on the overall integration strategy, defined in the PMI plan, an adequate integration strategy can be selected and implemented. The deliverables of this step are:

- Common business information:
  A common business information base, including an integrated knowledge management system
- Integrated ICT architecture:
  Integrated information and communication architecture

Integration of Infrastructure: Finally, the enterprise's infrastructure has to be integrated. This includes for example buildings, networks, data centers, hardware. The deliverable of this step is:

- Integrated infrastructure:
  Integrated physical infrastructure of the enterprise

6.5.3 Process Step: Post-Merger Audit

In the post merger audit, the performance of the transaction and transformation is analyzed in terms of financial, functional and social factors to identify refinishing needs. This step includes a documentation of lessons learned and identified potentials for improvement of the M&A capability.

Control Achievement of Targets: The success controlling activity comprises both, controlling of the procedure as well as its outcomes [Kr06]. A critical reflection of the chosen approach and methods delivers lessons learned and potentials for continual improvement of the M&A capability. The assessment of the integration results against the defined targets is re-

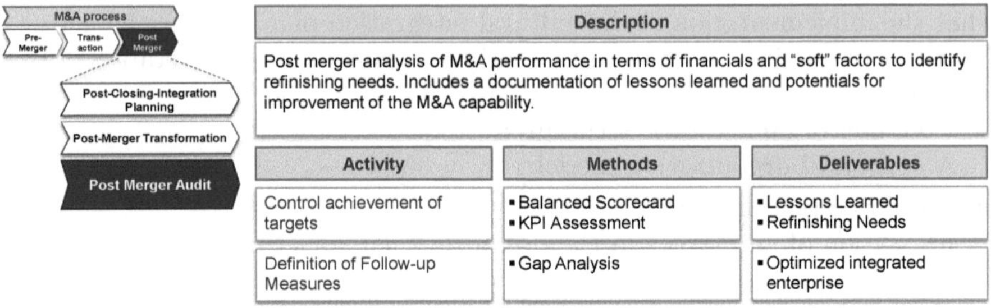

Figure 6.19: Post-Merger Phase - Post-Merger Audit

quired to identify needs for subsequent completion efforts. The deliverables of this step are:

- Lessons learned:
  A collection of lessons learned during the M&A process
- Refinishing needs:
  Remaining minor issues to be solved to complete the integration or optimize interim solutions

Follow-up Restructuring: The post merger audit will result in the definition of follow-up activities according to refinishing needs identified during analysis of achievements. There may be reasons to cluster the execution of follow-up activities from different PMI projects into a greater restructuring and optimization program. The deliverables of this step is:

- Optimized integrated enterprise:
  Resulting target enterprise after complete integration of the acquired entity

7 Applying Business Capabilities in the CBMA Process

7.1 Business Capability Models

7.1.1 Company Business Capability Map (C-BCM)

The Company Business Capability Map (C-BCM) is based on the architecture viewpoint "capability map" as introduced in section 4.7. It is the individual capability map for one company, a complete but non-overlapping decomposition of the individual enterprise by the means of business capabilities. It describes the business capabilities needed to support the defined business model in order to implement the defined business strategy. The Company Capability Map (C-BCM) is the starting point for any of the following capability maps. It can be used on different hierarchical levels. In the subsequent examples, a depth of three levels is assumed.

Today, many companies have a capability model in place. As companies will only implement an M&A process if they expect to execute it repeatedly, the availability of an initial C-BCM is assumed. The development of a C-BCM is a one time effort and an EA Management responsibility. Thus, it should not be part of a regular M&A process. However, if the C-BCM is not available at the initiation of the M&A process (for example in a pilot project or the first execution of the process), an initial version has to be developed. The method for developing a C-BCM is documented separately in section 7.6.1.

7.1.2 Business Capability Map - Color Code (BCM-CC)

Color coding illustrates the value of a business capability attribute (or relationship) by changing the color of the inner area of the rectangle representing the respective business capability in the capability map. Detailed information on different styles of color coding (palette, spectrum, or chroma based), suitable modeling languages for color coded maps and potential tool support can be found in [BMS11]. Figure 7.1 shows an example, as well as the symbols and visualization rules for color coding used in the Business Capability Map - Color Code (BCM-CC) viewpoint.

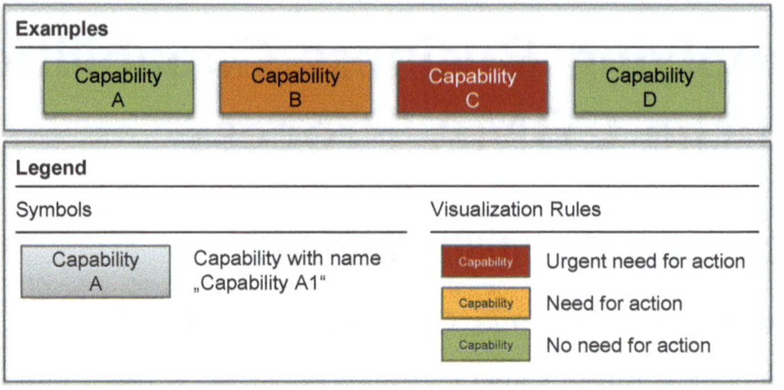

Figure 7.1: Business Capability Map - Color Code (BCM-CC)

7.1.3 Business Capability Map - Border Code (BCM-BC)

Border coding is an additional way of illustrating the value of a business capability attribute (or relationship) by changing the border style of the rectangle representing the respective business capability in the capability map. Figure 7.2 shows an example, as well as the symbols and visualization rules for border coding used in the Business Capability Map - Border Code (BCM-BC) viewpoint.

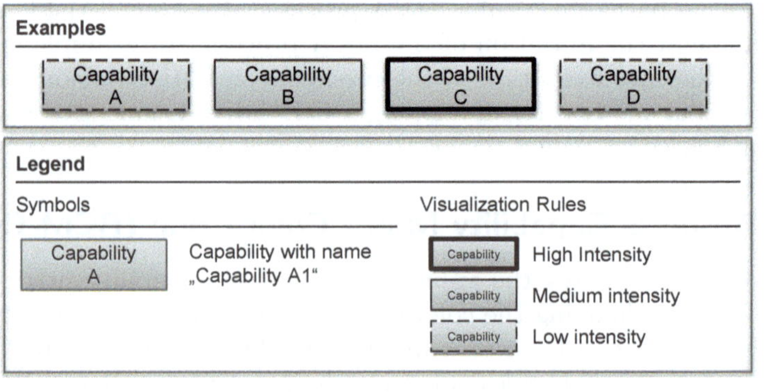

Figure 7.2: Business Capability Map - Border Code (BCM-BC)

The Business Capability Map - Border Code (BCM-BC) uses three different border styles for visualization: dotted line, drawn line, and bold line. The interpretation of the chosen border style depends on the concrete attribute that is visualized. In general, a less distinct texture should indicate less intensity of an attribute or respectively less relevance of the business capability for the aspect that is subject to analysis.

7.1.4 Business Capability Map - Texture Code (BCM-TC)

Texture coding illustrates the value of a business capability attribute (or relationship) by changing the texture of the inner area of the rectangle representing the respective business capability in the capability map. The Business Capability Map - Texture Code (BCM-TC) uses three different textures for visualization: no texture (white color), dotted horizontal lines, and crossed horizontal and vertical lines. The interpretation of the chosen texture depends on the concrete attribute that is visualized. In general, less texture should indicate less intensity of an attribute or respectively less relevance of the business capability for the aspect that is subject to analysis. Figure 7.3 shows an example, as well as the symbols and visualization rules for color coding used in the Business Capability Map - Texture Code (BCM-TC) viewpoint.

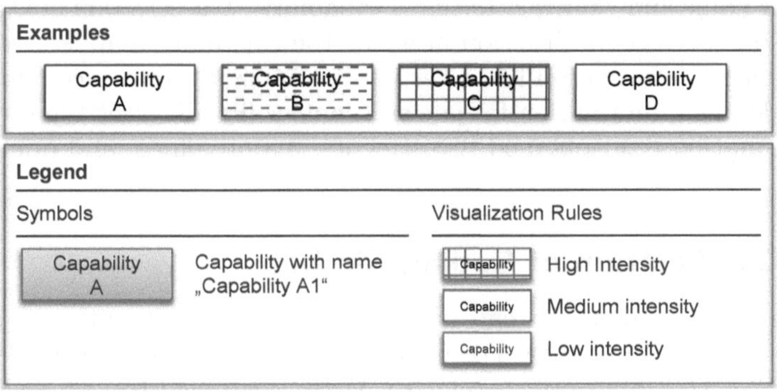

Figure 7.3: Business Capability Map - Texture Code (BCM-TC)

7.1.5 Business Capability Map - Attributes (BCM-A)

Additional to the graphical coding of the business capability map with colors, textures, or border styles, it may be beneficial to depict the concrete value of a business capability attribute as a numerical or text information. Figure 7.4 shows an example, as well as the symbols and visualization rules for visualizing capability attributes as used in the Business Capability Map - Attributes (BCM-A).

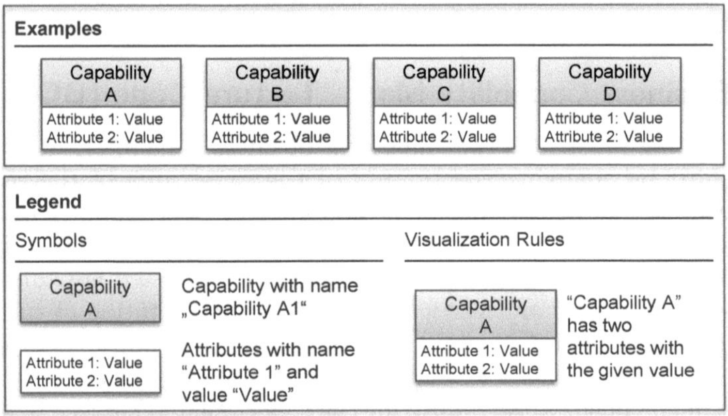

Figure 7.4: Business Capability Map - Attributes (BCM-A)

The BCM-A viewpoint provides the possibility to show a set of attributes with their name and value per business capability. The selection of attributes depends on the specific situation in which the capability map is used. They can be general information like a responsible unit or a reference number, or provide detailed information for one stakeholder like different types of financial information (e.g. planned investments, maintenance, and operational costs).

7.1.6 Combination of Coding Methods

The single coding methods can be combined to visualize different aspects of an analysis in one figure. For example, the simultaneous use of texture code (BCM-TC) and border code (BCM-BC) can lead to new insights by bringing together two views on the business capabilities. Furthermore, coding methods can be used on different levels of the capability maps.

The coding methods chosen for the capability models presented in this chapter have to be taken as suggestions. It is not the intend to limit the possibilities of stakeholder-specific presentations, but to provide tangible examples for the application of business capabilities in the M&A process. Consequently, the selection of a specific coding method does not exclude others in general. However, it is better to use different coding methods for different kind of information and to re-use coding methods for presentation of similar information.

7.2 Identification of Anchor Points for Capability Models

We assume that business capabilities are relevant for several parts of the CBMA Process, however this does not apply to all elements (process steps, activities, methods, deliverables) of the process. Therefore, before elaborating on the concrete application of business capability models, the relevant parts have to be identified. This can be achieved by a structured analysis of the applied methods and the deliverables produced during these activities.

The application of business capabilities in the methods that support single activities in the CBMA Process can be diverse:

- The company capability map can be an input for a method and be used as a reference structure.
- The methods may gather information about the current or aspired future state for one or more business capabilities as an outcome.
- Methods may change the company capability map, thus adding or removing business capabilities as an outcome.
- Business capabilities may also be not relevant for a method.

The deliverables produced during the CBMA Process are the second option for investigation. The relationship between deliverables and the capability map can be twofold:

- The company capability map can be used as a reference structure in deliverables.
- Information contained in the deliverables may be linked to one or more business capabilities to describe current or aspired future state for one or more business capabilities.

In the following, each process step is investigated to identify potential anchor points for the application of business capability models. Following the sequence of the developed CBMA Process, a structured analysis indicates which methods and deliverables may be a relevant anchor point for business capability models. A summary table per process step shows if business capabilities may be used. It specifies which activities may use business capabilities as a reference ("Reference") an which activities may include a review and potentially change the existing business capability model ("Review/Change"). Additionally, it lists which deliverables may use business capabilities as a reference structure ("Reference"), thus providing information that may be illustrated with a business capability model. The table also indicates if business capabilities are not relevant to a method or deliverable ("n/a").

7.3 Pre-Merger Phase

7.3.1 Process Step: Corporate Analysis

The process step corporate analysis provides several anchor points for the application of business capabilities. The Company Business Capability Map (C-BCM) is an input for corporate analysis to be used as a reference structure for the analysis of the strategy and business model. The C-BCM should be a complete but non-overlapping decomposition of the enterprise by the means of business capabilities. During the analysis of the strategy and business model, the C-BCM is reviewed and may be changed to ensure its actuality. The resulting C-BCM should provide the basic structure and terminology for any following activities. While it may change during this process step, its structure should remain stable during the rest of the CBMA Process, where additional information is gathered or respectively gathered information is used to perform certain activities.

A new business strategy may lead to changes in the C-BCM. It may require additional business capabilities, make existing business capabilities obsolete, or change the aspired target state of business capabilities resulting in a different design of business capabilities in terms of their dimensions (people, process, material). Additional business capabilities result in new elements in the C-BCM. Depending on the magnitude of a change, new business capabilities can be located on all levels of the capability map. A new level one capability may result from a new strategic repositioning of the company (e.g. the introduction of a sales partner management) or a major change in the business model (e.g. a universal bank plans to offer insurance services), while changes may result from changed strategic approach to one business capability (e.g. a new strategy for customer management). If existing business capabilities are not relevant for the companies business strategy and the business model, they can be removed from the C-BCM. However, a representation will be required as long as these business capabilities are part of transformation initiatives. For example to plan and control the retirement of existing infrastructure or manage the transition of employees. A different design of business capabilities may be driven from business or technology changes. On the one hand, it may result from a different level of strategic relevance of a certain business capability for the enterprise. On the other hand, a design change can also be triggered by new technology that can lead to more emphasis on the material dimension which includes information and communication technology.

Table 7.1 gives an overview on the methods and deliverables for each activity of this process step and indicates the relevance of business capabilities for each of them.

Table 7.1: Business Capabilities in Corporate Analysis

Activity: Analysis of Company Goals and Business Model	
Method	**Capability Relevance**
Strategy Analysis	Review/Change
Business Model Analysis	Review/Change
Deliverable	**Capability Relevance**
Corporate Strategy (reviewed/confirmed) Reference	Reference
Business Plan (reviewed/confirmed) Reference	Reference
Activity: Analysis of Strategic Potentials and Gaps	
Method	**Capability Relevance**
SWOT Analysis	Reference
Portfolio Analysis	Reference
Value Chain Analysis	Reference
Core Competency Definition	Reference
Economies of Scale and Scope Analysis	Reference
Deliverable	**Capability Relevance**
SWOT Profile	Reference
Company Core Competencies	Reference
Strategic Potentials	Reference
Strategic Gaps	Reference
Activity: Transformation Self Assessment	
Method	**Capability Relevance**
Readiness Assessment	Reference
Cultural Due Diligence	n/a
Legal/Regulatory Analysis	Reference
Deliverable	**Capability Relevance**
Transformation Issues	Reference

During the process step "corporate analysis", three business capability maps can be applied which are based on the Company Capability Map (C-BCM) and make use of different visualization methods: the Strategic Relevance Map (SR-Map), the Capability Condition Map (CC-Map), and the Strategic Gap Map (SG-Map). The three business capability maps, their relationships and the sequence of their usage are described in the following.

The Strategic Relevance Map (SR-Map) may be used to illustrate the strategic relevance of each business capability as a result of the activities "strategy analysis" and "business model analysis". Figure 7.5 gives an example for the visualization of the Strategic Relevance Map (SR-Map) using border coding (BCM-BC). In this example, the coding method is applied to capability level 2.

Strategic relevance indicates the importance of a certain business capability for the overall success of the enterprise, or respectively how important it is for implementing the corporate strategy and the accomplishment of the formulated goals. An appropriate visualization method for the Strategic Relevance Map (SR-Map) is border coding (BCM-BC). In this capability map, the proposed border styles are used as follows:

- bold line: high strategic relevance
- drawn line: medium strategic relevance
- dotted line: low strategic relevance

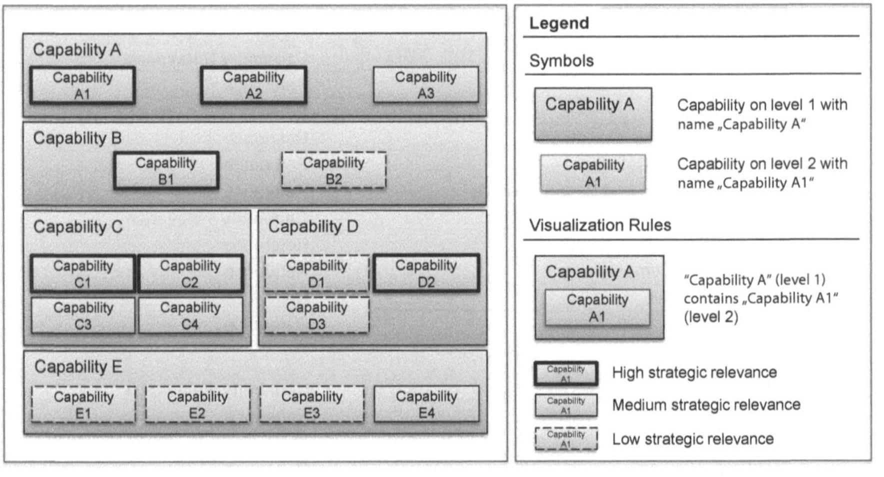

Figure 7.5: Strategic Relevance Map (SR-Map)

There may be different approaches for the determination of the strategic relevance value for each business capability. Ideally, the established valuation method that is already used by strategic management should be reused here. However, if no approach is in place, strategic management theory offers two techniques for evaluation of competencies that can also be used for business capabilities (see section 4.3).

The Capability Condition Map (CC-Map) may be used to illustrate the current condition of each business capability as result of the activity "analysis of strategic potentials and gaps". Figure 7.6 gives an example for the visualization of the Capability Condition Map (CC-Map) using texture coding (BCM-TC). In this example, the coding method is applied to capability level 2. The current condition indicates the actual overall maturity of the single business capability. In this capability map, the proposed textures are as follows:

- crossed horizontal and vertical lines: advanced condition
- dotted horizontal lines: medium condition
- no texture (white color): poor condition

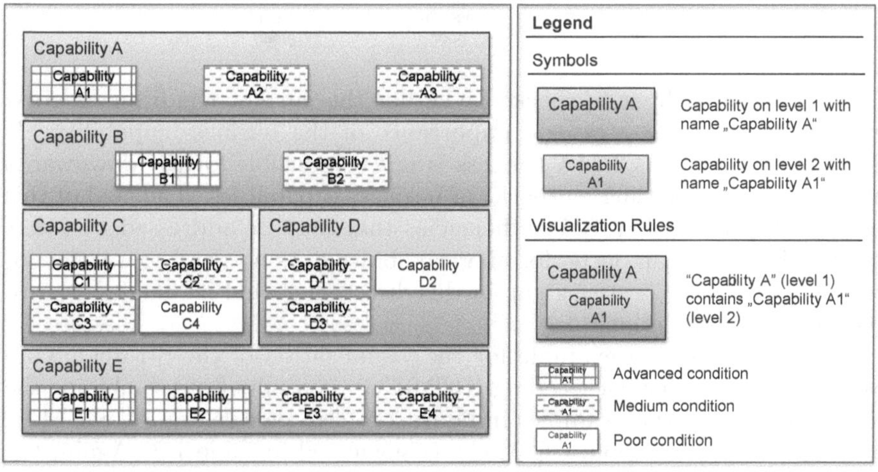

Figure 7.6: Capability Condition Map (CC-Map)

In the next step, the Strategic Gap Map (SG-Map) combines the information about the strategic relevance of each business capability as shown in the Strategic Relevance Map (SR-Map) with the additional information on their current condition illustrated in the Capability Condition Map (CC-Map). An appropriate visualization method for the Strategic Gap Map (SG-Map) is color coding (BCM-CC).

In this capability map, the proposed colors are used as follows:

- red: strong gap
- yellow: medium gap
- green: small or no gap

Table 7.2 is a suggestion on how to combine strategic relevance and current condition to derive strategic gaps.

Table 7.2: Strategic Gap Indicator Determination

Strategic Relevance	Capability Condition	Strategic Gap
high	advanced	green
high	medium	yellow
high	poor	red
medium	advanced	green
medium	medium	green
medium	poor	yellow
low	advanced	green
low	medium	green
low	poor	green

In this approach, it is checked whether the current condition is good enough knowing the strategic importance of the business capability. It is assumed that the CBMA Process is not responsible for the downwards adjustment (dismantling, cutback) of business capabilities. The goal of this process step is to identify insufficiencies that may be addressed by M&A means. Therefore, an outperforming capability does not lead to a yellow or red color. However, a strong gap in this direction should be handed over to the responsible function.

Figure 7.7 gives an example for the visualization of the Strategic Gap Map (SG-Map) using color coding (BCM-CC). It results from combining the information from the examples in figure 7.5 (strategic relevance, SR-Map) and figure 7.6 (condition, CC-Map) as suggested in table 7.2. Again, the coding method is applied to capability level 2.

Business capability models do not provide great benefit to the activity "transformation self assessment" itself. However, the transformation issues identified during the readiness assessment and the legal/regulatory analysis may reference to the business capabilities in the Company Business Capability Map (C-BCM) where applicable. Thereby, they remain more traceable during later process steps, especially during the pre- and post-merger integration planning. The information can be handed over to the responsible project teams that implement the transformation roadmap. How this is achieved, is described in section 7.5.1 (PMI planning).

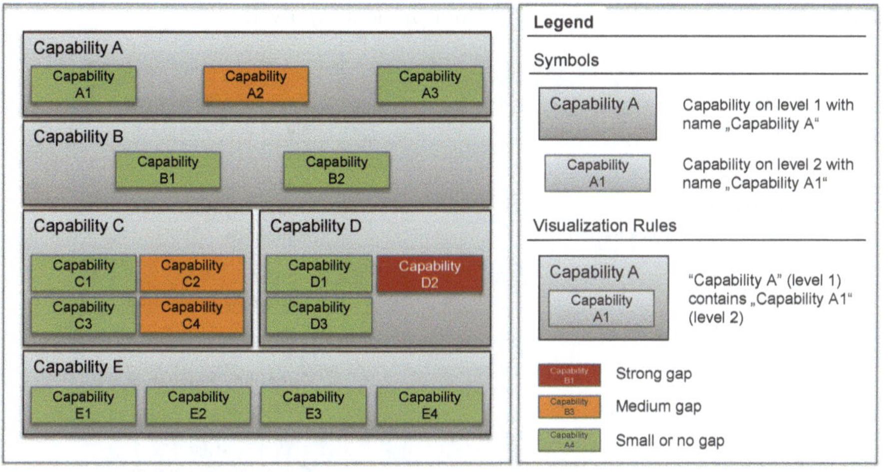

Figure 7.7: Strategic Gap Map (SG-Map)

7.3.2 Process Step: Environment Analysis

The process step "environment analysis" complements the internal analysis of the enterprise with information on the corporate environment, its industry and market, and external opportunities and threats. Nevertheless, the Company Business Capability Map (C-BCM) should be an input for this process step. The C-BCM can be used as a reference structure for the documentation of results.

Table 7.3 gives an overview on the methods and deliverables for each activity of this process step and indicates the relevance of business capabilities for each of them. The deliverable "environment analysis report" as well as the "industry and market report" may be supported by the C-BCM. Where applicable, the findings may reference a certain business capability in order to make results traceable and thus accessible for later process steps. For example, the knowledge about industry trends and their influence on one or more business capabilities.

The Market Strengths Map (MS-Map) shown in figure 7.8 presents the results from the environment analysis by applying the following color codes to the single capabilities:

- black: strong
- grey: weak
- white: unknown / not applicable

Table 7.3: Business Capabilities in Environment Analysis

Activity: Analysis of Corporate Environment	
Method	**Capability Relevance**
Stakeholder Analysis	n/a
Games Theory	n/a
Strategic Radar	n/a
Deliverable	**Capability Relevance**
Environment Analysis Report	Reference
Activity: Analysis of Industry and Market	
Method	**Capability Relevance**
Industry Analysis	n/a
Market Analysis	n/a
Deliverable	**Capability Relevance**
Industry and Market Report	Reference
Activity: Complete SWOT	
Method	**Capability Relevance**
SWOT Analysis (focus on OT)	Reference
Deliverable	**Capability Relevance**
SWOT Profile	Reference

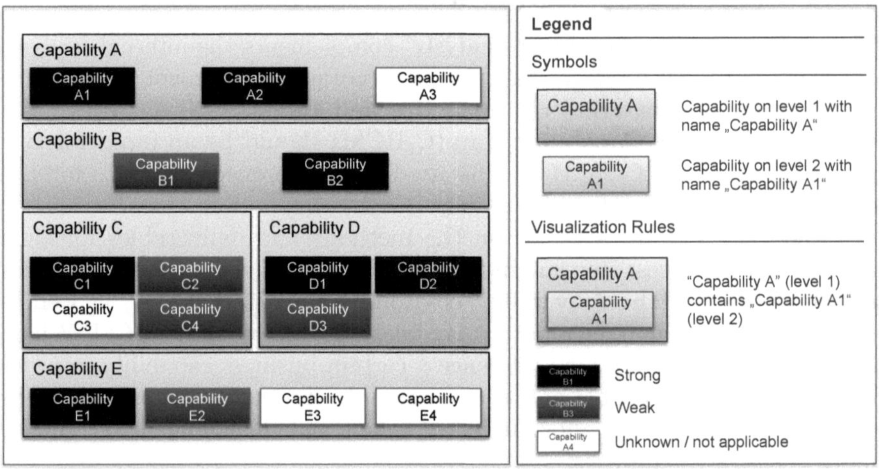

Figure 7.8: Market Strengths Map (MS-Map)

The latter includes capabilities where available information is insufficient for a rating. Thereby, the MS-Map shows the availability of certain capabilities in the corporate environment. On the one hand, it reveals the strengths and weaknesses of the company's competitors in the market. On the other hand, it shows the availability of capabilities which the company may decide to access by an acquisition. At this point in the CBMA Process, the capability map is elaborated for the market as a whole, not for an individual competitor or acquisition target. Therefore, the intensity of analysis should be adapted to the need for market insight.

The next deliverable, the "complete SWOT" can also be linked to the elements of the C-BCM. An opportunity or threat may be relevant to one or more business capabilities and thus should be made available to the responsible stakeholders.

7.3.3 Process Step: Define M&A Strategy and Goals

The process step "define M&A strategy and goals" combines findings from the internal and external analysis of the enterprise. Therefore, the Strategic Gap Map (SG-Map) is one important input. In the course of this process step, it can be refined to an Acquisition Goals Map (AG-Map), which can be integrated into the major deliverables of the company's "M&A strategy" and corresponding "acquisition goals". Table 7.4 gives an overview on the methods and deliverables for each activity of this process step and indicates the relevance of business capabilities for each of them.

The determined acquisition goals in the enterprise's M&A strategy can be structured according to the company capability map. The resulting Acquisition Goals Map (AG-Map) visualizes areas for planned investments with different priorities. In this case, the coloring differentiates between business capabilities that are "M&A investment (priority 1)" (dark blue), capabilities that are "M&A investment (priority 2)" (light blue) and capabilities that are "no investment" areas (white). The example assumes, that all strategic gaps are planned to be closed by an acquisition, while strong gaps are rated as "M&A investment (priority 1)" whereas medium gaps are defined as "M&A investment (priority 2)". Figure 7.9 shows the Acquisition Goals Map (AG-Map).

7.3.4 Process Step: Identify Candidates

In the process step "identify candidates" findings from previous analysis are condensed in order to define requirements in the form of candidate selection criteria. These are the basis for an analysis of the acquisition environment to identify matching candidates in the market.

Table 7.4: Business Capabilities in M&A Strategy and Goals

Activity: Identification of Gaps	
Method	**Capability Relevance**
Gap Analysis	Reference
Strategic Statement Development	n/a
Deliverable	**Capability Relevance**
Operational Gaps	Reference
Strategic Gaps	Reference
Strategic Statement	Reference
Activity: Derive M&A Needs and Options	
Method	**Capability Relevance**
Scenario Analysis	Reference
Ansoff Product-Market Growth Matrix	n/a
Deliverable	**Capability Relevance**
M&A Demand	Reference
Activity: Finalize M&A Strategy and Goals	
Method	**Capability Relevance**
n/a	n/a
Deliverable	**Capability Relevance**
M&A Strategy	Reference
Acquisition Goals	Reference

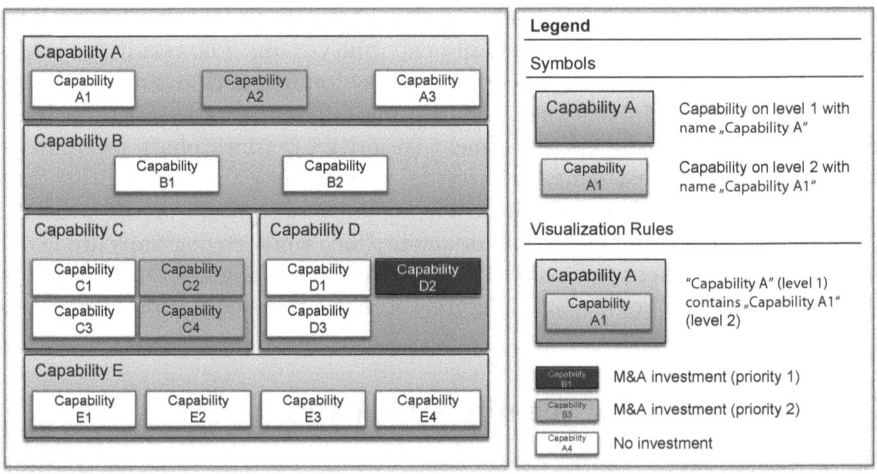

Figure 7.9: Acquisition Goals Map (AG-Map)

Table 7.5 gives an overview on the methods and deliverables for each activity of this process step and indicates the relevance of business capabilities for each of them.

Table 7.5: Business Capabilities in Identify Candidates

Activity: Define Candidate Selection Criteria	
Method	**Capability Relevance**
Scoring Models	n/a
Deliverable	**Capability Relevance**
Candidate Selection Criteria	n/a
Acquisition Profile	Reference
Activity: Analysis of Acquisition Environment	
Method	**Capability Relevance**
Strategic Screening	Reference
Short Listing	n/a
Deliverable	**Capability Relevance**
Acquisition Options	n/a
Top Candidates Shortlist	n/a

As the acquisition of a target organization should close the identified strategic gaps, the formulated acquisition goals are integrated. Therefore, the Acquisition Goals Map (AG-Map) shown in figure 7.9 can be integrated into the candidate profile. Besides the required competencies and products, a typical candidate profile contains information about size, financial prerequisites, or access management [Ja08]. Business capabilities that have been rated with "high relevance" in the AG-Map should be the focus for the screening of the acquisition environment. Therefore, the capability map can also be used as a reference in this activity.

7.3.5 Process Step: Candidate Assessment and Simulation

The final step of the Pre-Merger Phase comprises a more detailed analysis of a small number of short list candidates. Table 7.6 gives an overview on the methods and deliverables for each activity of this process step and indicates the relevance of business capabilities for each of them.

During the assessment of single candidates, capability maps can be used for a high-level simulation of the target enterprise. During the corporate analysis, it has been ensured that the C-BCM includes all relevant business capabilities. Including those currently not available in necessary condition in the enterprise. Therefore, the C-BCM can also be used to assess a candidate.

Table 7.6: Business Capabilities in Candidate Assessment

Activity: Modeling of the Integrated Enterprise	
Method	**Capability Relevance**
Simulation	Reference
Organization Design	n/a
Deliverable	**Capability Relevance**
Integration Scenario	Reference
Target Governance Model	n/a
Pre-Closing Integration Plan	Reference
Activity: Validation of Approvability	
Method	**Capability Relevance**
n/a	n/a
Deliverable	**Capability Relevance**
Documentation of Approvability and Risks	n/a

The Candidate Assessment Map (CA-Map) shown in figure 7.10 is similar to the idea of the Market Strengths Map (MS-Map) (see figure 7.8).

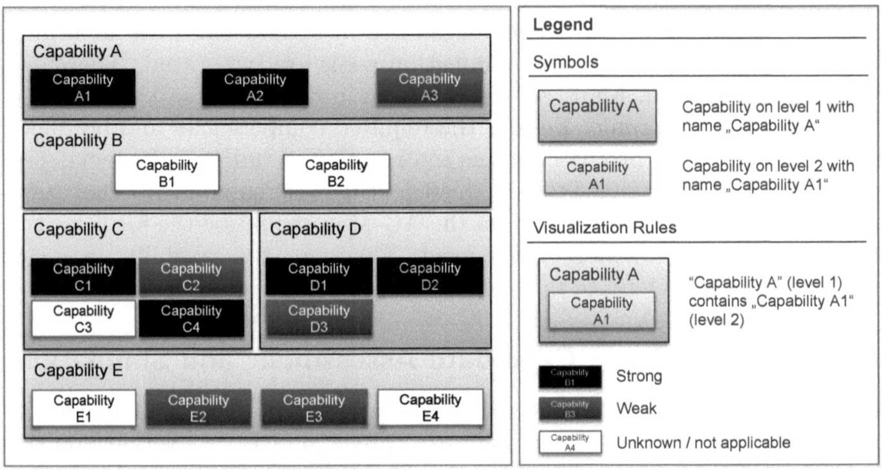

Figure 7.10: Candidate Assessment Map (CA-Map)

Instead of showing the availability of certain capabilities in the corporate environment, it shows the results of the assessment of one candidate by applying color codes to the single capabilities. Again, the coloring differentiates between capabilities that are "strong" (black), capabilities that are "weak" (grey) and capabilities that are "unknown / not applicable" (white), latter including capabilities where available information is insufficient for a rating.

In a second step, the Candidate Assessment Map (CA-Map) can be combined with the elaborated Strategic Gap Map (see figure 7.7) to simulate the contribution of the potential acquisition. The result can be visualized with a Target Enterprise Map (TE-Map) shown in figure 7.11. It applies the same color codes to the single capabilities. Again, the coloring differentiates between capabilities that are "available, in required quality" (green), capabilities that are "available, but not in required quality" (yellow) and capabilities that are "not available" (red).

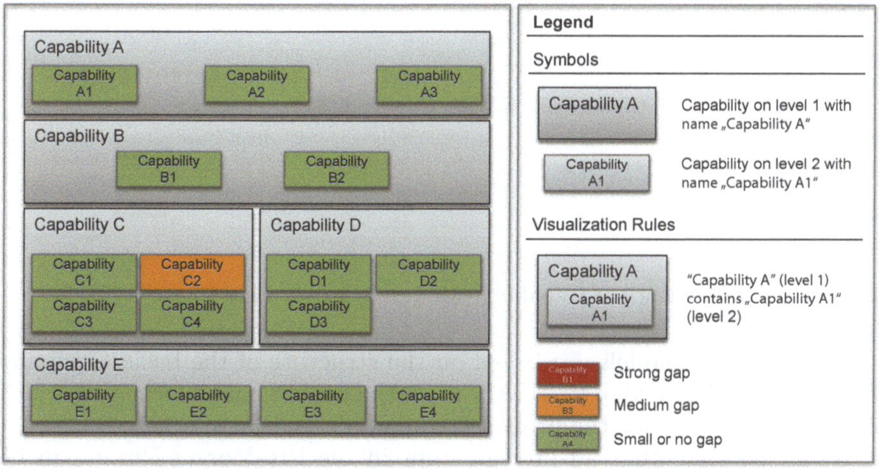

Figure 7.11: Target Enterprise Map (TE-Map)

The optimal outcome would be a map with green color only. This would indicate a perfect match of the candidate to the defined M&A goals. In the presented example, the strong gap in "capability D2" is closed through the strong capability of the target candidate. The medium gaps in "capability A2" and "capability C4" are closed with a complementary strong value of the target candidate. "Capability C2" remains as a medium gap as the acquired capability is also rated medium.

7.3.6 Summary for Pre-Merger Phase

Figure 7.12 illustrates the sequence in which the introduced business capability models, namely Strategic Relevance Map (SR-Map), Capability

Condition Map (CC-Map), Strategic Gap Map (SG-Map), Market Strengths Map (MS-Map), Acquisition Goals Map (AG-Map), Candidate Assessment Map (CA-Map), and Target Enterprise Map (TE-Map) can be used along the process steps in the Pre-Merger Phase.

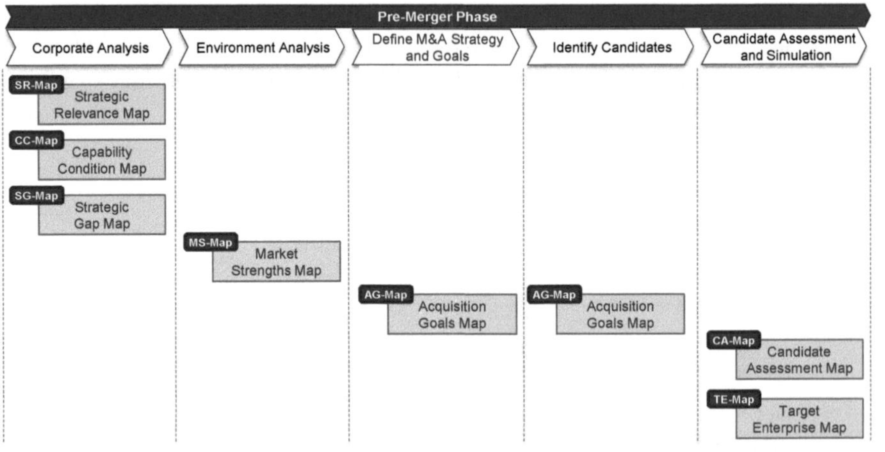

Figure 7.12: Sequence of Capability Models in Pre-Merger Phase

All capability models are based on the structure of the basic Company Business Capability Map (C-BCM) and include additional information which can be visualized with the proposed coding methods.

It can be seen, that all process steps in the Pre-Merger Phase can be supported by capability models. While the first process step "corporate analysis" includes activities that may change the initial Company Business Capability Map (C-BCM), it is used as a reference structure in the methods and deliverables of the remaining process steps. However, as expected not all activities can profit from the availability of the model and the connected information.

Regarding the management dimensions, the emphasis during the Pre-Merger Phase is on strategy, financial, and legal. Additionally, condensed information from a product, organization, process and IT dimension are included. The establishment of the business capability structure enables the integration of the required information across these management dimensions. Especially, the EA Management practice may contribute relevant information on the IT landscape, for example technology information or cost data.

7.4 Transaction Phase

7.4.1 Process Step: Contact and Negotiations

As shown in table 7.7, the process step "contact and negotiations" does not provide anchor points for the application of business capabilities.

Table 7.7: Business Capabilities in Contact and Negotiations

Activity: Candidate Selection	
Method	**Capability Relevance**
Scoring Models	n/a
Ranking	n/a
Deliverable	**Capability Relevance**
Target Candidate	n/a
Activity: Contact Candidate	
Method	**Capability Relevance**
Contact Candidate	n/a
Deliverable	**Capability Relevance**
Confidentiality Agreement	n/a
Letter of Intent	n/a
Memorandum of Understanding	n/a
Activity: Guarantee Financing	
Method	**Capability Relevance**
Financial Calculation Methods	n/a
Deliverable	**Capability Relevance**
Financing Plan	n/a

7.4.2 Process Step: Due Diligence

The process step "due diligence" is the most important step for collecting information on the target enterprise prior to execution of the deal. Table 7.8 gives an overview on the methods and deliverables for each activity of this process step and indicates the relevance of business capabilities for each of them.

The value of a due diligence and the resulting insights is depending on identifying the relevant information in an efficient procedure. Additionally, time constraints are a main challenge during due diligence. Especially access to data rooms is limited. Therefore, it is even more important to focus the analysis on critical aspects. Primarily, these aspects are financial and legal issues but other assets such as IT may also have strong effects on the value of the target enterprise. There are established procedures of conducting a

Table 7.8: Business Capabilities in Due Diligence

Activity: Perform Due Diligence	
Method	**Capability Relevance**
Data Room	Reference
Desk Analysis	Reference
Expert Systems	Reference
Due Diligence Checklists	Reference
Deliverable	**Capability Relevance**
Due Diligence Reports	Reference

due diligence and the presented approach does not aim at replacing them. The capability model can be used twofold in a complementary manner. On the one hand, it can be used as an input. Based on the information gathered during the Pre-Merger Phase, focus areas for information collection during data room sessions or desk analysis can be defined. On the other hand, results from due diligence can be structured according to the capability model to make them available for subsequent activities. If the capability structure has been established in the enterprise's expert systems and due diligence checklists, gathered information from past mergers is available. Additionally, during a series of acquisitions, the single target enterprises can be compared by referencing to the same valuation structure.

The Candidate Assessment Map (CA-Map) (as introduced in section 7.3.5, figure 7.10) can be refined with any information gained during the initial contact and ongoing negotiations. This may result in a new value ("strong" (black) or "weak" (grey)) for a capability or in adding information for capabilities that have been rated "unknown / not applicable" (white) so far. Furthermore, the color coding scale may be extended to more alternatives to enable a more detailed visualization.

In the following two capability models are proposed. First, a Due Diligence Map (DD-Map) that can be used to define core areas for analysis. Figure 7.13 shows an example Due Diligence Map (DD-Map) matching to the examples used during the Pre-Merger Phase. The core areas depend on the defined strategic gaps (Strategic Gap Map (SG-Map), see figure 7.7) and the available information about the target candidate. These information can be a result from the initial assessments (e.g. Candidate Assessment Map (CA-Map), see figure 7.10), additional information gained during ongoing negotiations, or from past merger experiences. For example, redundant capabilities assumed as main cost drivers during a consolidation may be rated as core areas. Additionally, findings from a legal and regulatory due diligence can lead to new focus areas to address identified risks. Furthermore, dependencies to core areas can make additional business capabilities relevant for analysis. A method for the identification of dependencies is provided in section 7.6.2.

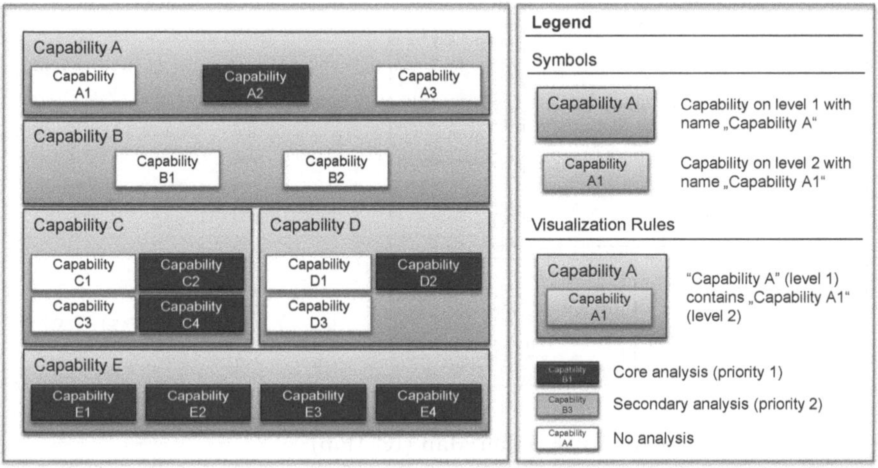

Figure 7.13: Due Diligence Map (DD-Map)

In the presented capability map, the coloring differentiates between business capabilities that are part of the "core analysis (priority 1)" (dark blue), capabilities that are part of "secondary analysis (priority 2)" (light blue) and capabilities that are "no analysis" areas (white). Consequently, the presented Due Diligence Map (DD-Map) assumes that the strategic gaps that should be filled by the planned acquisition are defined as core areas (in the given example "capability A2", "capability C2", "capability C4", and "capability D2"), while "capability E" should be analyzed too, but with lower priority, for example due to expected integration issues.

A second complementary capability map can be used to detail the focus areas defined in the DD-Map to support for analysis and collection of results on capability level 2 or 3. It is assumed that the next level of capabilities is available. In this step, the Business Capability Map - Attributes (BCM-A) viewpoint is useful to present the collected values for a set of defined attributes for each relevant business capability.

Figure 7.14 shows an example Information Collection Map (IC-Map) detailing "capability E". The Due Diligence Map (DD-Map) is substantiated with a group of Information Collection Maps (IC-Map). In the given example, corresponding maps are needed for "capability A2", "capability C2", "capability C4", and "capability D2".

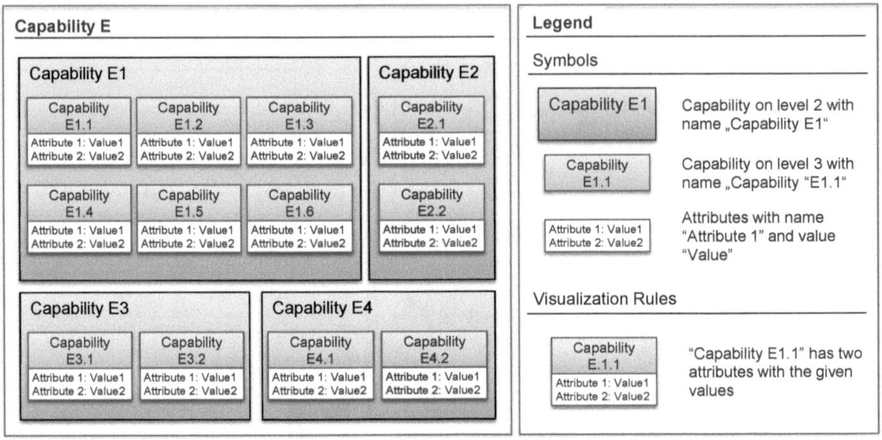

Figure 7.14: Information Collection Map (IC-Map)

The attributes should be defined according to existing due diligence checklists as this approach aims at integrating information from different sources instead of creating a new set of attributes. Example attributes for an assessment of the underlying IT architecture may be technologies, costs, license models, as well as IT staff and skills. Furthermore, one attribute may be used to monitor progress of information collection. Alternatively, the progress can be visualized by additional usage of color coding or border coding methods.

7.4.3 Process Step: Pre-Merger Integration Planning

The main goal of pre-merger integration planning is to substantiate the target scenario for the selected candidate and prepare the planning of the Post-Merger Phase. The information gained during the merger planning has been complemented with information collected during the diligence. Both should now be consolidated to prepare the subsequent transformation activities. Table 7.9 gives an overview on the methods and deliverables for each activity of this process step and indicates the relevance of business capabilities for each of them.

The pre-closing integration plan, as well as the integration process should reference to the Company Business Capability Map (C-BCM). The pre-

Table 7.9: Business Capabilities in Pre-Merger Integration Planning

Activity: Prepare Integration	
Method	**Capability Relevance**
Integration Planning Model	Reference
Stakeholder Management	Reference
Deliverable	**Capability Relevance**
Degree and Type of Integration	n/a
Pre-Closing Integration Plan	Reference
Integration Process	Reference
Governance Model	Reference
Stakeholder Map	n/a
Communication Plan	n/a

closing integration plan should make clear statements on the target state of existing and acquired business capabilities. Depending on the selected type of integration, it defines how business capabilities are integrated, if existing capabilities are replaced and which of the acquired capabilities are subject to decommissioning. The integration process depicts a high-level timeline of the integration steps. Each of these steps should reference to a business capability, describing the capability increment as well as its initial and target state.

The governance model for the subsequent Post-Merger Phase provides a binding working environment for the responsible project teams. As major constituents, the governance model gives information about the project organization, clear responsibilities, conductive rules for collaboration, reporting, as well as effective escalation paths. At this stage of the CBMA Process the definition is still on a high-level, but the structure of the Company Business Capability Map (C-BCM) can be used to support the allocation of responsibilities to single teams in the project organization. For example the PMI project as a whole is managed on program level, whereas a portfolio of projects is defined to work on certain groups of business capabilities. The defined project structure will be reviewed and refined during the post-closing integration planning.

Even though, project teams are not set up prior to closing of the transaction, the early establishment of the capability map as a common structure for the management of relevant information is key to guarantee a common language and efficient communication. Furthermore, the collection of additional information can be started in parallel to the legal and financial finalization of the transaction.

7.4.4 Process Step: Pricing

As shown in table 7.10, the process step pricing does not provide anchor points for the application of business capabilities.

Table 7.10: Business Capabilities in Pricing

Activity: Purchase Price Definition	
Method	**Capability Relevance**
Financial Calculation Methods	n/a
Deliverable	**Capability Relevance**
Purchase Price	n/a

7.4.5 Process Step: Deal Execution

The same applies for the process step deal execution. As shown in table 7.11, it does not provide anchor points for the application of business capabilities.

Table 7.11: Business Capabilities in Deal Execution

Activity: Announcement	
Method	**Capability Relevance**
n/a	n/a
Deliverable	**Capability Relevance**
Official Announcement	n/a
Tentative Agreements	n/a
Activity: Signing	
Method	**Capability Relevance**
n/a	n/a
Deliverable	**Capability Relevance**
Sales Agreement	n/a
Activity: Closing	
Method	**Capability Relevance**
Antitrust Audit	n/a
Deliverable	**Capability Relevance**
Antitrust Clearance	n/a
New Legal Entity	n/a

7.4.6 Summary for Transaction Phase

Figure 7.15 illustrates the sequence in which the introduced business capability models, namely Due Diligence Map (DD-Map), a group of Information

Collection Maps (IC-Map), and Company Business Capability Map (C-BCM) can be used along the process steps in the Transaction Phase. While the Due Diligence Map (DD-Map) is based on the structure of the Company Business Capability Map (C-BCM), the complementary group of Information Collection Maps (IC-Map) provides more detailed views on the relevant sections of capability level below. The Company Business Capability Map (C-BCM) itself can be applied again during the pre-merger integration planning.

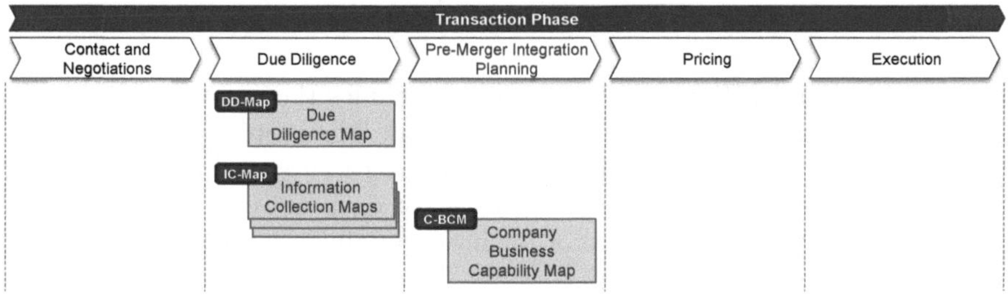

Figure 7.15: Sequence of Capability Models in Transaction Phase

Obviously, only two out of five process steps in the Transaction Phase can be supported by capability models. Both can use business capabilities as a reference structure in the methods and deliverables. The main reason for this is the emphasis of the financial, and legal management dimensions during the Transaction Phase.

However, due diligence as well as pre-closing integration planning require condensed information from different management dimensions. Therefore, likewise to the Pre-Merger Phase, the establishment of the business capability structure enables the integration of the required information across these management dimensions during the Transaction Phase. Furthermore, existing information from previous process steps is made available and the results can be integrated into integration planning.

7.5 Post-Merger Phase

7.5.1 Process Step: Post Closing Integration Planning

Building on the results of the "pre-merger integration planning", "post closing integration planning" includes the development of a concrete PMI plan and establishment of an adequate PMI organization and processes, as well as integration controlling and communication.

After a review and confirmation, the pre-closing integration plan can be finalized with a final agreement how business capabilities are integrated, which existing capabilities are replaced and which of the acquired capabilities are subject to decommissioning. Accordingly, the integration plan includes a roadmap depicting the timeline of integration steps. Each of these steps should reference to a business capability, describing the capability increment as well as its initial and target state. Business capabilities that are worked on simultaneously may be grouped, for example due to dependencies between single business capabilities. A method for the identification of dependencies is provided in section 7.6.2.

Establishing a PMI project organization includes the definition of responsibilities for each project on the PMI roadmap. The scoping of the projects can be supported with the business capability structure. Table 7.12 gives an overview on the methods and deliverables for each activity of this process step and indicates the relevance of business capabilities for each of them.

Table 7.12: Business Capabilities in Post-Closing Integration Planning

Activity: Develop PMI Plan	
Method	**Capability Relevance**
PMI Reference Process	Reference
Roadmap Planning	Reference
Deliverable	**Capability Relevance**
Integration Plan	Reference
Integration Goals	Reference
Key-Performance Indicators	Reference
Activity: Establish PMI Organization	
Method	**Capability Relevance**
PMI Project Organization Reference Model	Reference
RACI Matrix	Reference
Deliverable	**Capability Relevance**
PMI Project Organization	n/a
PMI Roles and Responsibilities	Reference
Integration Controlling Model	Reference
Activity: Establish Internal and External Communication	
Method	**Capability Relevance**
Stakeholder Management	Reference
Deliverable	**Capability Relevance**
Communication Concept	Reference

Figure 7.16 shows an example Project Portfolio Map (PP-Map). In the proposed viewpoint, the scope of each project is depicted with a dotted

line. In the given example, a portfolio of non-overlapping projects has been defined.

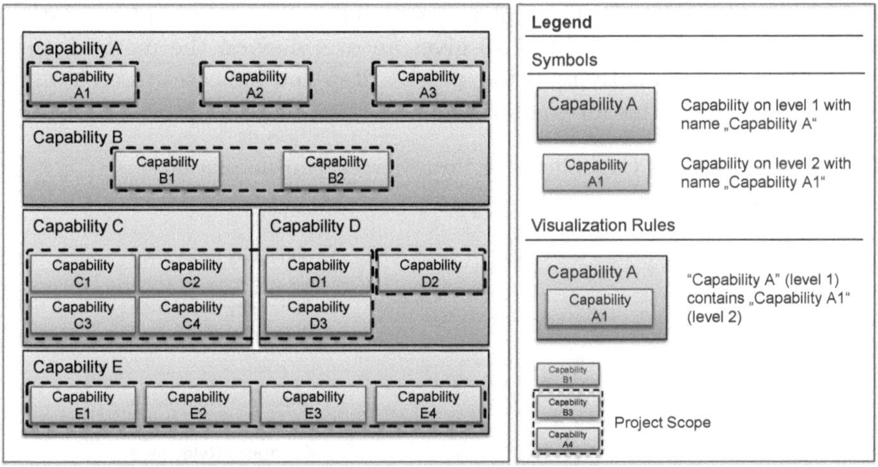

Figure 7.16: Project Portfolio Map (PP-Map)

From the perspective of a single project, the Project Portfolio Map (PP-Map) visualizes the project boundaries. It helps to identify resulting dependencies and enables communication within the project as well as with other teams. Again the proposed method for the identification of dependencies can be applied (see section 7.6.2). Within the scope of the respective project, a more detailed capability map will be used for transformation planning and implementation. Progress and results can be summarized and reported on the level of the PP-Map.

From the overarching perspective, the Project Portfolio Map (PP-Map) should be established as a means for communication and stakeholder management. On the one hand, the elaborated stakeholder map can reference to the capability structure. On the other hand, the knowledge about the influences on a certain business capability may help to identify all relevant stakeholders. During communication activities, the repetitive presentation of stakeholder-specific information on the basis of the Company Business Capability Map (C-BCM) fosters the establishment of the common language across the enterprise, especially in the newly acquired parts of the organization. Once established, it enables the exchange of information between stakeholders from different management dimensions or from the old and new organization units.

7.5.2 Process Step: Post Merger Transformation

The developed integration plan is now detailed for the strategy, business, IT and infrastructure layers. These plans are used to manage the implementation of the transformation. Table 7.13 gives an overview on the methods and deliverables for each activity of this process step and indicates the relevance of business capabilities for each of them.

Table 7.13: Business Capabilities in Post Merger Transformation

Activity: Integration of Strategies	
Method	**Capability Relevance**
n/a	n/a
Deliverable	**Capability Relevance**
Set of Common Strategies	Reference
Activity: Integration of Market Presence	
Method	**Capability Relevance**
n/a	n/a
Deliverable	**Capability Relevance**
Common Brand(s)	n/a
Common Product Portfolio	n/a
Activity: Integration of Organization and Culture	
Method	**Capability Relevance**
Target Architecture Planning (Business)	Reference
Deliverable	**Capability Relevance**
Common Organizational Structure	n/a
Employee Placement	n/a
Common Business Processes	n/a
Activity: Integration of Business Information and IT	
Method	**Capability Relevance**
Target Architecture Planning (IT)	Reference
Deliverable	**Capability Relevance**
Common Business Information	n/a
Integrated IT Architecture	n/a
Activity: Integration of Infrastructure	
Method	**Capability Relevance**
Target Architecture Planning (Infrastructure)	Reference
Deliverable	**Capability Relevance**
Integrated Infrastructure	n/a

The formulated set of strategies should reference the Company Business Capability Map (C-BCM). While the business strategy covers the complete map, functional strategies like a marketing or product strategy focus on distinct areas. Others like an IT or technology strategy may have effects on all business capabilities, for example by definition of technology standards. In all, strategies describe the relevance of certain business capabilities and define goals for their future development.

The target architecture planning activities for business, IT and infrastructure are part of an integrated EA planning approach. In this approach, business capabilities can be the leading reference structure. Section 7.6.3 describes experiences made during the application of business capabilities for consolidation of applications in a PMI project. The presented approach is based on the EA framework TOGAF [Th09], which was tailored in order to fit to the specific merger context. The idea of following the TOGAF Architecture Development Method (ADM) (see section 3.3.3) can be equally transferred to target architecture planning on the business or infrastructure level. This would require an extension of ADM phase B or D respectively.

Figure 7.17 shows an example Target Architecture Map (TA-Map) for the application level of "capability B".

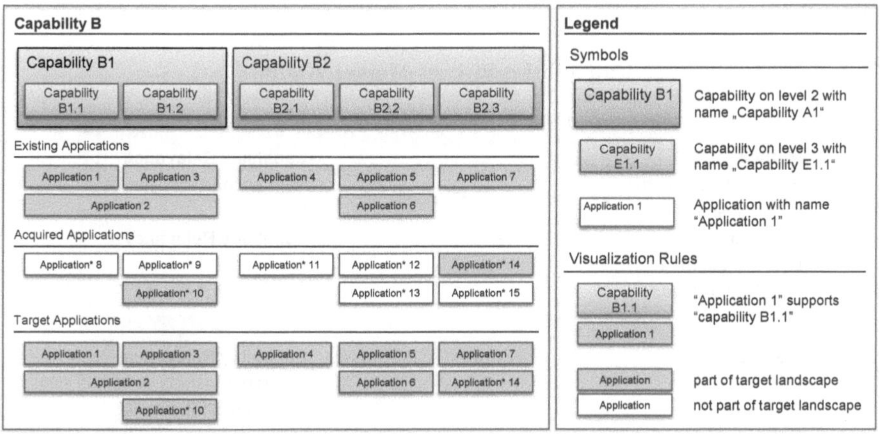

Figure 7.17: Target Architecture Map (TA-Map)

Looking on "capability B1" if the example, the existing application landscape is documented as follows: "application 1" supports "capability B1.1", "application 3" supports "capability B1.2", "application 2" supports "capability B1.1" and "capability B1.2". The acquired applications comprise "application* 8" supporting "capability B1.1", as well as "application* 9" and "application* 10" supporting "capability B1.2". The "*" symbol is used to label acquired applications. As a result of the target architecture planning, "application 1", "application 2", "application 3", and "application* 10" are selected as target applications, while "application* 8" and "application* 9" are subject to decommissioning.

As shown above, the level 2 and 3 business capability structure can be used in each of the PMI projects to document existing and newly acquired applications, as well as the selected target applications for the defined project scope. Additional information, for example on as-is costs, underlying technologies, or sourcing models can also be included as attributes. The consolidation of the single Target Architecture Maps (TA-Map) provides a complete target picture, making results comparable on capability level 1.

7.5.3 Process Step: Post-Merger Audit

As the final step of the CBMA Process, the "post-merger audit" assesses the outcomes of the Post-Merger Phase against the defined goals. Table 7.14 gives an overview on the methods and deliverables for each activity of this process step and indicates the relevance of business capabilities for each of them.

Table 7.14: Business Capabilities in Post Merger Audit

Activity: Control Achievement of Targets	
Method	**Capability Relevance**
Balanced Scorecard	Reference
KPI Assessment	Reference
Deliverable	**Capability Relevance**
Lessons Learned	n/a
Refinishing Needs	Reference
Activity: Definition of Follow-up Measures	
Method	**Capability Relevance**
Gap Analysis	Reference
Deliverable	**Capability Relevance**
Optimized Integrated Enterprise	n/a

During the Pre-Merger Phase, a Capability Condition Map (CC-Map) (see figure 7.6) has been introduced to show the initial condition of each business capability as result of the analysis of strategic potentials and gaps. Now, the achieved outcome of the integration can be assessed by matching the expected target condition with the real condition. Subsequently, during the assessment of the target candidate, an Target Enterprise Map (TE-Map) (see figure 7.11) has been elaborated to visualize the planned outcome after post merger transformation. Alternatively, a recapitulation of the gap analysis will reveal whether all gaps have been successfully closed as planned. In either case, an Integration Result Map (IR-Map) helps to visualize the achievement of targets. An example is given in figure 7.18.

An appropriate visualization method for the Integration Result Map (IR-Map) is color coding (BCM-CC). In this case, the proposed colors are used as follows:

- red: integration work not completed as planned, major refinishing needs
- yellow: integration work widely completed, minor refinishing needs
- green: integration work fully completed, no refinishing needs

The resulting refinishing needs can be allocated to the respective business capabilities and thus handed over to those responsible for completion. The capability structure also supports the clustering of follow-up activities from different PMI projects into a greater restructuring and optimization program. In this case, refinishing needs from different M&A initiatives can be consolidated for one business capability.

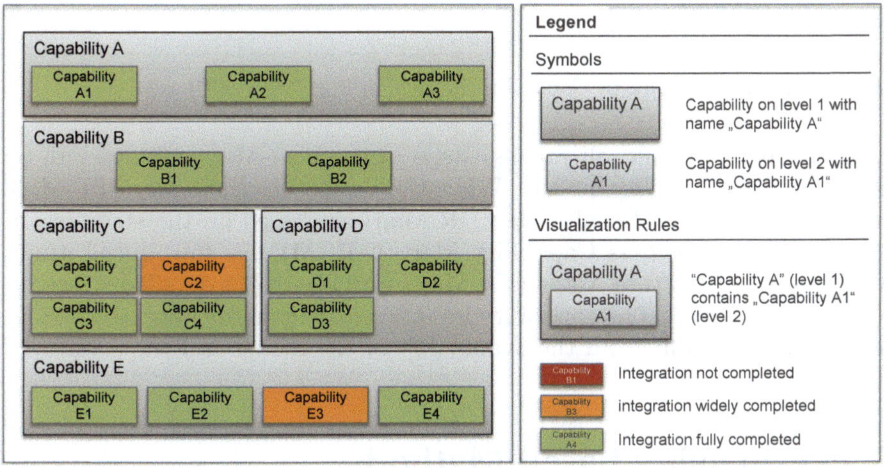

Figure 7.18: Integration Results Map (IR-Map)

The given example assumes that integration work has been fully completed for the majority of business capabilities. Even though integration work is widely completed for "capability C2" and "capability E3", minor refinishing needs have been identified.

7.5.4 Summary for Post-Merger Phase

Figure 7.19 illustrates the sequence in which the introduced business capability models, namely Project Portfolio Map (PP-Map), Company Business Capability Map (C-BCM), a group of Target Architecture Maps (TA-Map), and Integration Result Map (IR-Map) can be used along the process steps in the Transaction Phase.

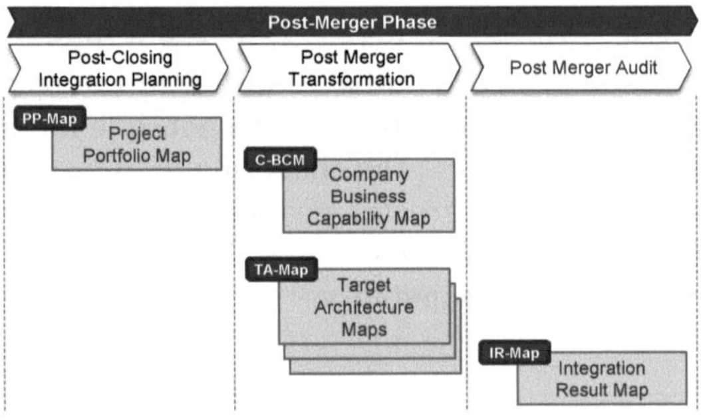

Figure 7.19: Sequence of Capability Models in Post-Merger Phase

It can be seen, that all process steps in the Post-Merger Phase can be supported by capability models. While the Project Portfolio Map (PP-Map) and the Integration Results Map (IR-Map) are based on the structure of the Company Business Capability Map (C-BCM), the introduced group of Target Architecture Maps (TA-Map) provides more detailed views on the relevant sections at capability level 2 or 3. Again, as expected not all activities can profit from the availability of the model and the connected information.

7.6 Capability-based Methods

7.6.1 Development of an Initial Capability Map

Throughout this chapter, the availability of an initial Company Business Capability Map (C-BCM) is assumed. It has been stated, that the development of a C-BCM is a one time effort and an EA Management responsibility and that it should not be part of a regular M&A process. However, as M&A can also be a reason for introducing EA Management, the C-BCM is not available at the initiation of the M&A process. In this case, an initial version of the C-BCM has to be developed. Figure 7.20 gives an overview on the method consisting in four steps that may be performed iteratively. Noteworthy, the development of a comprehensive business capability map for an individual company is an activity that includes some degree of creativity and personal experience. Therefore, the presented method can only work as a guideline.

Step	Name
1	Top-Level Business Capabilities
2	Strategy Alignment
3	Derivation of Business Capabilities Level 2
4	Refinement

Figure 7.20: Capability Map Construction

Step 1: Top-Level Business Capabilities

First of all, the meta-model has to be agreed, defining the basic elements and their relationships. Consistent with the developed theoretical foundation for business capabilities (see section 4.6), we assume three levels of business capabilities. Business entities are allocated to business capability level 2. The idea of this first step is to identify the key things a company must be able to do to make its business model work. As described in section 4.6, the capability map aims to provide a complete and non-overlapping perspective, while the key activities depicted in the business model are limited to the most important.

The initial starting point for the definition of the top level business capabilities is the analysis of available material that describes business architecture elements important to the enterprise. These can be company internal or external sources:

- Industry reference models
- Business processes, business function libraries
- Business information models, business entity libraries
- Existing capability models

The result of this step is a first draft version of the Company Business Capability Map (C-BCM).

Step 2: Strategy Alignment

Since the inputs for the first draft version of the Company Business Capability Map (C-BCM) are models or documentations that aim to describe the current state of the company, it does not reflect any capability needed in future. Therefore, it has to be aligned with the company's strategy, as well as industry and technology trends. Required refinements can be identified with an adapted quality function deployment (QFD)[34] method. The result of this step is the first agreed version of the Company Business Capability Map (C-BCM) on level 1.

Step 3: Derivation of Business Capabilities Level 2

In the next step, the defined level 1 structure can be broken down into level 2 capabilities. Again, each level 1 capability should be described by a complete set of non-overlapping level 2 capabilities. Again, the sources listed in the first step can be a valuable source for the population of the model.

There are a few criteria helping to decide on the right granularity of business capabilities:

- Redundancy in functionality or data ownership
- Interdependencies between functionality of single business capabilities
- Characteristics of capability lifecycle
- Differences in sourcing options
- Individual strategic relevance and strategy support

However, the model should be balanced. In general, all level 1 capabilities have a similar amount of level 2 capabilities. If the quantity differs to much, this is a hint for a review of the level 1 structure or the granularity of defined level 2 capabilities. Consequently, design decisions remain within the responsibility of the architect as mentioned above.

Step 4: Refinement

The further refinement of the model is achieved by practical usage and intensive stakeholder interactions in the course of normal project work. During project work, new insights gained may lead to adaptions or extensions on the lower capability level. But there may also be reasons to change the top-level structure, for example as a result of a new business strategy or

[34] The Quality Function Deployment (QFD) is an approach supporting the translation of customer requirements into technical details of a product [Ak04, Sc10]. It has been adapted by Helbig to analyze the relationships in the EA model [He07b].

the acquisition of an entity with a different business model. For both cases, a proper change management process with clear responsibilities has to be established to ensure a concerted advancement of the model.

7.6.2 Capability-based Dependency Analysis

The goal of the presented method is the identification and analysis of dependencies between business capabilities. Parts of the method as well as the underlying architecture viewpoints have been published in [Fr11]. Figure 7.21 gives an overview on the method consisting of three phases, which are described in this section. The gray boxes indicate the architecture viewpoints used in phase one and two and the use of the EA model in phase three.

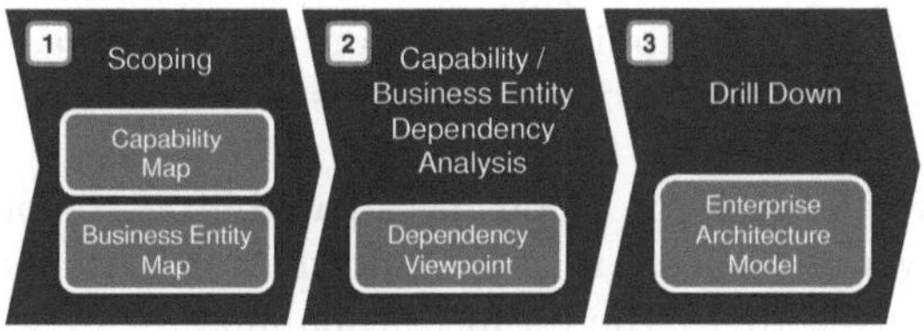

Figure 7.21: Capability Dependency Analysis

Step 1: Scoping on Business Architecture Level

The goal of the first phase is the scoping of a given problem statement using the business capability map and business entity map. The necessary input to this step is a definition of the problem which is supposed to be analyzed using the capabilities dependency analysis method. Furthermore, the documented respective maps as a common understanding of the business model and the necessary information are compulsory in order to conduct this investigation.

As a first step, the scope of the considered problem is projected on the business capability map. In the next step, a similar activity is conducted with respect to the business entity map. Dependent on the considered problem statement, the order of these two steps may differ. In cases which are strongly data centric, it may be more comfortable to start with the business entity map analysis since the stakeholders can then usually define the relevant information more easily as supposed to work with the functional view directly. On the other hand, in the process management environment, starting with the functional scoping will be more beneficial. Dependent on the required level of detail of the considered problem, scoping by drilling down different levels of capabilities or business entities may be required. The steps referred here are thus to be performed iteratively leading to development of a complete view on the referred problem.

Finally, the results of the problem scoping based on the both maps need to be documented, for example by using color coding (BCM-CC) to point out relevant business capabilities and business entities. The results of this phase are both or one of the maps on the relevant level of detail depicting the problem scope.

Step 2: Dependencies on Business Architecture Level

The subsequent phase aims to refine the scope definition by identification of dependent business capabilities based on the known assignment of the business entities. The analysis of dependencies in this phase can be considered twofold:

1. in terms of relationships of business capabilities to business entities, e.g. to answer the question which information is necessary to be provided/exchanged to/by the business capability
2. in terms of relationships between business capabilities.

For each of the above cases, an information ownership map is an indispensable input. The information ownership map informs if a given is owned by a business capability, i.e. it is owned by it or of the business entity is only used by the capability but owned by a different business capability.

In order to develop a complete picture of the dependencies of the considered business capabilities, one can proceed as follows. First, the business entities which are used by the business capability are considered in search of those which own them. The dependencies discovered in this way inform about sources of information used in the given business capability. In the second step, the business entities which are owned by the given business capability are the subject of analysis. Learning about the relations of these business entities to other business capabilities (which have them assigned as used) is significant information on the destination to which the information needs to be delivered. Conducting these steps iteratively will lead to a gradual enrichment of the preliminarily performed scoping. In the last step, it needs to be documented on the available maps. An output of this phase is therefore a refined problem scoping based on the business capability map and the business entity map.

Step 3: Dependencies across Enterprise Architecture Layers

In the last phase the scope of the problem is finally refined by identification of relevant architecture elements from other layers of the EA model. Figure 7.22 depicts the idea of using the EA model information to drill down from capability level to application or technology level.

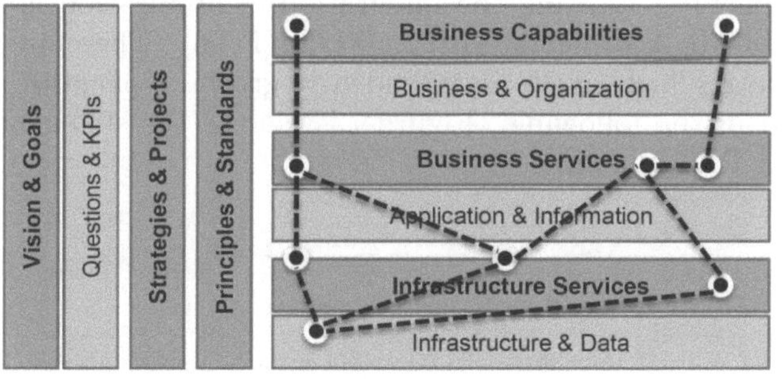

Figure 7.22: Dependencies across the EA Model

Consequently, the EA model with relations between the contained architecture elements (for instance in the sense of an architecture repository) is a required input here. The availability of the information about elements of the EA model, including their interrelations is assumed. The first step in this phase relies in analysis of business capabilities along of the EA model, i.e. across various architecture layers relevant for the considered problem.

In the course of this extensive analysis, some gaps in the availability of quality of the available information about architecture elements may be discovered. In this case, a further optional step, may take place which aims at identification of the necessary additional data to be collected. This top-down dependency analysis may be followed by a bottom-up identification of further dependencies which complete the scope definition. Finally, the documentation produced until now, the business capability map and business entity map with dependencies to each other and to other architecture elements, is updated and represents the result of the third phase.

7.6.3 Capability-based PMI Planning

The integration of IT includes the consolidation of application landscapes which previously supported different businesses and have been developed separately. In the case of the developed corporate buyer scenario (see chapter 5), a complete integration is assumed. Therefore, the application landscapes are consolidated entirely, hence coupling solutions and green field approaches are not considered. Consequently, in the target picture for the common application landscape, each single functionality is realized non-redundantly by one dedicated application.

Little literature exists (both in academia as well as in practice) providing specific artifacts facilitating the integration of application landscapes in the course of M&A projects [MB07, WL04, JY96]. Therefore, a method for consolidating historically independently grown application landscapes is presented in the following. Figure 7.23 shows the stringent top-down approach for PMI planning.

Step	Name
1	Design and Establish Governance Model
2	Understand and Document Business Target Model
3	Develop Capability Map
4	Develop Architecture Vision
5	Capture Baseline Architecture
6	Evaluate Target Scenarios
7	Evaluate Financial Impact
8	Plan Implementation Roadmap
9	Implement Governance and Change Management

Figure 7.23: Post Merger Integration Planning

The method provides an approach for consolidating application landscapes driven by a merger and acquisition activities. It is based on the EA framework TOGAF (see section 3.3.3). The TOGAF ADM has been tailored in order to fit to the specific merger context. The ADM describes the holistic development of architectures (i.e. business, information systems, and technology architecture) following 11 distinct phases. Therefore, the presented method allows to interlink IT consolidation activities with general integration work conducted in other domains, e.g. alignment of business processes, organizational changes, or change of technical resources. The artifact originates from a case study in the telecommunication industry in which two lines of business have been integrated [De07]. Parts of the method as well as examples from the case study have been published in [FMS10a].

The final deliverables of the presented method artifact consist in a "business target picture", an "architecture blueprint", and an "implementation roadmap" and are defined as follows:

- Business target picture: An explicitly documented common corporate vision for the respective functional scope
- Architecture blueprint: A description of the target application landscape on a logical level
- Implementation roadmap: A list of individual transformation steps, scheduled on a time line to show progression from the baseline to the target architecture.

Step 1: Design and Establish Governance Model

Before working on the project's core task, an overall governance model is established. The main rationale behind is to provide a binding working environment and to form a foundation for all subsequent method steps performed by the responsible project team. As major constituents, the governance model gives information about the project organization, clear responsibilities, conductive rules for collaboration, reporting, as well as effective escalation paths. Besides the formal governance model, the overall project success strongly relies on the management of multidisciplinary stakeholders and the establishment of adequate communication and information activities.

Step 2: Understand and Document Business Target Picture

During the second step, the mandate of the post merger planning project including the functional scope, rights, and responsibilities, is specified in more detail and formally agreed upon. The functional scope is defined with the help of business capabilities, using the C-BCM (see section 7.1.1) or the PP-Map (see figure 7.16). Furthermore, the business target picture is thoroughly analyzed and documented in order to derive the strategic requirements, which will drive the development of the target application landscape.

Step 3: Develop Capability Map

In this step, a common language and structure for the relevant segments of the consolidation project is established among the multidisciplinary stakeholders.

This is especially important to ensure a high degree of acceptance and sustainability for the solution to be developed in the course of the project. Again a capability map is used to break down the relevant segment of the architecture. This is achieved by refining or reconfirming the C-BCM (see section 7.1.1) on Level 2 and 3 for the respective scope.

Step 4: Develop Architecture Vision

The architecture vision depicts a high-level view on the as-is and target enterprise architecture, according to the prior elaborated business target picture. As one key element of the architecture vision, the architecture blueprint describes the target application landscape on a logical level. It is needed to analyze and compare existing application landscapes in order to support the selection of the target applications. To facilitate the comparison of the different applications, logical architecture building blocks (ABB)s which cluster functional and non-functional requirements, are assigned to the capabilities identified in previous step.

Step 5: Capture Baseline

In order to select the applications that optimally support the elaborated architecture blueprint, the baseline of existing applications is captured. Different applications are compared on the basis of information about their lifecycle, functional, non-functional, and financial criteria. Thereby, the developed architecture blueprint including capabilities and architecture building blocks is applied as a common reference structure to make results comparable.

Step 6: Evaluate Target Scenarios

To select the optimal target application landscape, different alternative scenarios are evaluated against functional and non-functional requirements attached to the respective ABBs. In each case, the required migration steps towards the target application landscape are elaborated and documented (e.g. functional extensions, data migration, or retirement).

Step 7: Evaluate Financial Impact

To support the decision for one target scenario, a corresponding business case is worked out. The calculation has to encompass estimated transformation costs, current operation and maintenance costs, as well as estimated saving potentials. Costs are structured according to established cost center structures, but for an in-depth comparison a common reference is needed. The different alternative target application landscapes can be evaluated using the formerly elaborated capability map which is extended through the application of a compatible controlling approach allowing to analyze costs and benefits of the transformation on capability level [Fr08]. Finally, the step is concluded with the decision for one target landscape.

Step 8: Plan Implementation Roadmap

Finally, an implementation roadmap for the selected target application landscape is elaborated. The business vision is broken down into major milestones, which realize concrete business value (e.g. establishment of a common information base). The required activities concerning the different application landscapes can be grouped in work packages according to these milestones. In addition, those applications that have to be modified (e.g. functional extensions, data migration, or retirement) can be assigned to each of these work packages.

Step 9: Implementation Governance and Change Management

Lastly, an adequate implementation governance has to be established in order to guide the following implementation projects. According to TOGAF [Th09], implementation governance provides an architectural supervision of the implementation. Therefore, a common set of recommendations and guidelines is formulated. Regular checkpoints are established along the implementation process to guarantee conformance with the defined target architecture and ensure the realization of the estimated business value. Furthermore, a proper change management establishes procedures to identify needs and manage changes in order to adjust the implementation roadmap if necessary. Implementation governance and change management have to be closely integrated into general integration activities.

8 Evaluation

8.1 Evaluation Goals

The goal of design science research is to produce artifacts that provide utility in a practical business environment [He04]. Offermann et al. [Of09] propose to review and either reconfirm or adapt the research questions before starting with evaluation activities. In section 1.2 seven research questions are presented which have been formulated to direct the substantiation of the problem area and artifact design. These are reconfirmed.

The goal for the evaluation part of this thesis is to discuss the practical applicability of the developed methodology. Therefore, the evaluation approach is not limited to a discussion of the single artifacts only. We also want to identify options for introducing the approach in an organization and formulate prerequisites for its successful application.

The selection of adequate evaluation methods is important and has to match the characteristics of the research topic and the environment in which it is conducted. Several authors (e.g. [He04, MS95, Of09]) provide hints to successful evaluation of artifacts in information systems research. Especially for the evaluation of reference models, such as conceptual frameworks, universal models, generic models, or model patterns, Fettke and Loos [FL03] recommend to select more than one method from multiple perspectives. The authors describe a framework comprising a set of evaluation methods that represent different evaluation perspectives. From a practical point of view, the textbook of Bortz and Döring [BD09] provides methods and suggestions for evaluation setup, guidance for conduction of evaluation activities and documentation.

Special circumstances can limit the availability of practitioner information and the applicability of certain evaluation methods [BD09]. This also applies for the evaluation of the artifacts proposed in this thesis. Section 8.1.1 describes the research environment and the circumstances which have been identified as relevant to the setup and conduction of the evaluation approach. Section 8.1.2 than identifies evaluation methods applicable for the research conducted in this thesis.

8.1.1 Research Environment

Cross-Disciplinary Research

The work conducted in this thesis spans across two research disciplines. It deals with the applicability of the business capability concept from the EA Management discipline in the context of M&A, which can be regarded as one use case for EA Management. The phenomenon of M&A is also a broad research domain, covering a multitude of management disciplines like strategic management, finance, as well as law. Consequently, the appropriate evaluation approach should include both perspectives, EA Management and M&A.

When conducting research at an information systems chair, access to M&A practitioners is limited. Noteworthy, M&A expert feedback has been integrated wherever possible during the design phase. Additionally, EA management experts brought in their secondary knowledge gained from their engagement in M&A projects. Furthermore, the developed approach has been discussed with teachers and participants during an M&A summer school training program.

Multidisciplinary Stakeholders

A main characteristic of the M&A working environment is the presence of a multitude of multidisciplinary experts and stakeholders. This fact is one of the main motivations for this work, and enhanced communication between these participants is potentially a valuable effect of applying business capabilities. However, this is a drawback for setting up a formal and technically consistent evaluation approach. It is nearly impossible to get access to experts from each of the management disciplines from one organization. This can only be achieved as an employee at a company, applying the presented artifacts while being engaged in an M&A case.

Duration of M&A Process

The typical duration of an M&A process is several years from initial planning of a transaction until full completion of the PMI phase. The completeness of the presented M&A process, from planning to integration as described in this thesis is a prerequisite to improve the communication along the process and between the different management dimensions participating in the respective phases and steps. Again, this holistic scope in which the application of business capabilities potentially helps to improve the outcome of the process is a drawback for the setup of a formal evaluation approach.

Confidentiality of Data

Many personal contacts have been very interested in the results of this research project and their applicability in practice. Along our research, they provided valuable insights by sharing their personal experiences. Unfortunately, despite great commitment of single individuals, the initiation of ex-post analysis of real-world case studies was not possible due to confidentiality obligations.

Complexity of M&A Process

Even though the developed M&A process provides a stable structure on the level of process phases, steps, and activities, the working environment is characterized as highly complex and dynamic. Therefore, the comparability of different real-world M&A projects is limited. The same applies to the repeatability of a scenario. Consequently, it would be pointless to evaluate the applicability of capabilities in the M&A process on a level below using multiple iterations. According to practitioner feedback, it is more important to focus on the general applicability by evaluating the basic idea of applying business capability models for the activities and methods in the M&A process.

Practitioner Focus of EA Management Research

EA management is one of the practice based research domains, where researchers often find themselves trailing behind practitioners in proposing changes or in evaluating methods or models. Like in many other parts of the information systems area (see [BGM87]), researchers usually learn by studying innovations generated by practitioners, rather than by providing the initial contribution for these novel ideas. As worked out in the literature study as part of the theoretical foundation for this thesis (see chapter 4), business capability models and capability-based methods are examples for these innovations put into place mainly by practitioners. Distinct research on application of EA Management methods and models in the context of M&A is still at a very early stage. This thesis represents an initial contribution to the respective body of knowledge, while being the first explicit work on the application of business capability models in M&A.

8.1.2 Evaluation Method Selection

Case Study

Case research is especially appropriate for two types of problems: first for research and theory at an early, formative stage, and second for practice based problems where the experiences of actors are important and the context of action is critical [BGM87]. As there is no standard definition of a case study, Benbasat et al. [BGM87] analyzed a set of related work (e.g. [Bo85, Ka86, St78]) to draw a definition. They state that a case study *"examines a phenomenon in its natural setting, employing multiple methods of data collection to gather information from one or a few entities (people, groups, or organizations). The boundaries of the phenomenon are not clearly evident at the outset of the research and no experimental control or manipulation is used"*. The value of case studies in the domain of M&A is discussed controversially. It has to be noted that some researchers rate the results of this research published in practitioners' rather than academic journals as case-specific and anecdotal in nature (e.g. [MH04, MM95, SJR96]).

Actually, the characteristics formulated by Benbasat et al. [BGM87] match to the research conducted in this thesis. But, unfortunately, conducting a case study approach is not feasible for the initial evaluation of the artifacts proposed in this thesis. First, the duration of an M&A process can be several years from initial planning until completion of the PMI phase. Second, the high confidentiality of information about past or ongoing M&A projects makes detailed data unavailable. Both reasons hinder a researcher to evaluate the developed artifacts along a complete execution of the M&A process. Nevertheless, in subsequent research projects, the artifacts can be applied by practitioners in their regular working environment and evaluated in an academic set-up afterwards.

As a second option, we analyzed available publications of real world M&A case studies, assuming that these help to understand the applicability of the developed approach in a real-world corporate buyer scenario. We hoped that the case studies document the status-quo which then can be used to discuss the applicability of the developed artifacts in practice. Our goal was to identify the prerequisites and potential starting points for applying the results in practice. However, the result of our literature research was disappointing.

In 2012, Bengtsson and Larsson [BL12] published a working paper on the use of case study research in the domain of M&A. The paper provides a comprehensive overview on available publications. First, the authors review methodological literature to identify strengths and weaknesses of case studies. Second, they identified M&A literature reviews and examined the importance of M&A case studies. Based on an analysis of strategic and behavioral literature, Cartwright and Schoenberg [CS06] identified three primary research streams which focus on the issues of strategic fit, organizational fit and the acquisition process itself. Haleblian et al. [Ha09b] performed a study of 167 US journal articles on M&A, comprising five case studies. The authors then performed a complementary literature study, focusing on the influence of publications indicated by the Social Science Citation Index (SSCI). The study revealed a list of eleven influential articles. Third, Bengtsson and Larsson revisited a case survey which has been analyzed by Larsson [La93] earlier. In summary, the authors confirm the earlier statement by Larsson and Finkelstein [LF99] and conclude that authors focus on single disciplines (e.g. strategic management, finance, human resources management) and provide little information that helps to integrate these perspectives. Consequently, their list of M&A case studies did not contain material which was comprehensive and detailed enough for an evaluation of the approach developed in this thesis.

Despite these findings from existing literature reviews, we performed an additional online search of case study documentation. The goal was to identify recent publications that have not been covered so far, public information, or less influential material (e.g. not high-rated in SSCI). We identified additional 20 publications. But again, the authors focus on single disciplines and give little information on the case. We conclude that available literature does not help to evaluate the applicability of the developed approach in a real-world corporate buyer scenario. Nevertheless, the resulting list of sources is included in appendix C.

Laboratory Experiment

In laboratory experiments the researcher measures dependent variables while manipulating independent variables in a controlled environment [BD09, BGM87]. Experiments can be conducted with practitioners who may use the proposed artifacts in their working environment or with neutral participants who participate in a basic training (e.g. students). It is very challenging to reconstruct the high complexity of an M&A process in a simulated setting. The high number of variables would result in a separation into a large number of single aspects, while the value of the overall evaluation becomes doubtful. Additionally, the tasks performed during the process require expert knowledge. Therefore, the set-up of a laboratory environment to perform simulations is also inappropriate for this thesis.

Survey

A survey is especially helpful to evaluate a well-known topic with a large number of participants [BD09]. In the case of this research project this would imply that participants possess knowledge and practical experiences regarding both domains, EA management as well as M&A. As stated above, there are few practitioners and researchers that have experiences in both domains. Consequently, conducting a survey, for example online, is not applicable to evaluate the developed artifacts. The expected knowledge gained would be relatively small as validity of results can not be ensured.

Expert Interviews and Questionnaires

Qualitative interviews are based on open questions that allow the adaption of the conversation to the individual counterpart [BD09]. The idea of aligning the discussion to the participants personal expertise and experiences matches to the challenge of the cross-disciplinary topic and the early state of research. Each participant will contribute to the evaluation from his individual perspective, leading to a multifaceted view on the developed approach. Questionnaires are a next step towards a repetitive, structured analysis and quantitative analysis. According to Bortz and Döring [BD09], the value of written questionnaires is especially high if participant selection and the process of data collection can be controlled. For this research project, the sample size will not be large enough for a quantitative analysis, but first trends in the results can be evaluated on a qualitative level. Consequently, expert interviews using questionnaires or interview guidelines are an adequate research method to evaluate the practical applicability of the developed approach. Kanwischer's guideline [Ka05] can be used as a guideline for setup of interviews, as well as for documentation and analysis of results.

8.2 Evaluation Approach

Given the individual circumstances in the research environment (see section 8.1.1) and the examination of evaluation methods (see section 8.1.2), the evaluation approach for this work has been set up in two phases as shown in figure 8.1.

The first part of the evaluation approach, presented in section 8.3, is focused on the developed artifacts. In order to get feedback on the developed approach to M&A, we performed a series of expert workshops including the discussion of a fictional case study, a questionnaire, and open discussions around the value of the approach for practitioners. Besides the collection of feedback on the artifacts, the workshops are designed to gain a first insight into its introduction in an organization.

The second part of the evaluation approach, presented in section 8.4, is focused on introducing the developed approach in practice. The goal of this second part of the evaluation is to identify options for introducing the approach, but also to identify limitations and prerequisites for its application in practice. As a basic structure for analysis, an exemplary application scenario shows the main actors who are directly affected when introducing the methodology. This application scenario is used to review the expert workshop results.

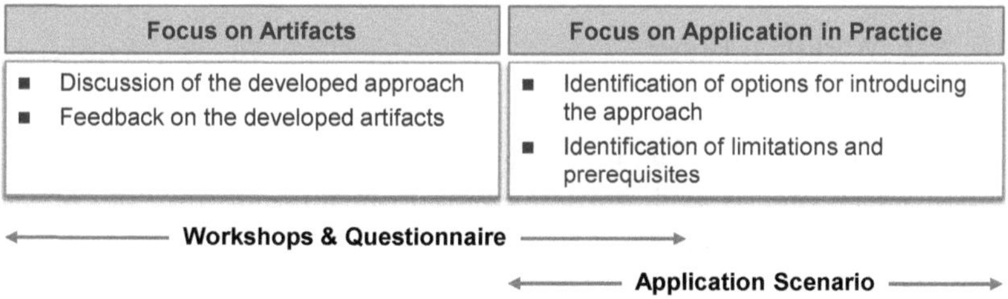

Figure 8.1: Evaluation Approach

8.3 Expert Workshops and Questionnaire

8.3.1 Combination of M&A and EA Perspective

There will be no single evaluation partner who covers the complete business capability theory and the complete M&A process in detail. Different feedbacks from workshop groups can contribute to an overall evaluation of the contributions proposed in this work. As capabilities are proposed as boundary object between the EA practice and other management disciplines, artifacts are evaluated from both perspectives. Figure 8.2 depicts the chosen approach for the expert workshops and the design of the questionnaire.

From the EA management perspective, the target group for participants are enterprise architects working in large international companies. Their starting point for the discussion of the presented artifacts is that they are aspiring to apply EA in M&A (see study results in section 3.4), while they are already familiar with capability concept. The evaluation goals for this group of participants is the validation of the developed capability foundation,

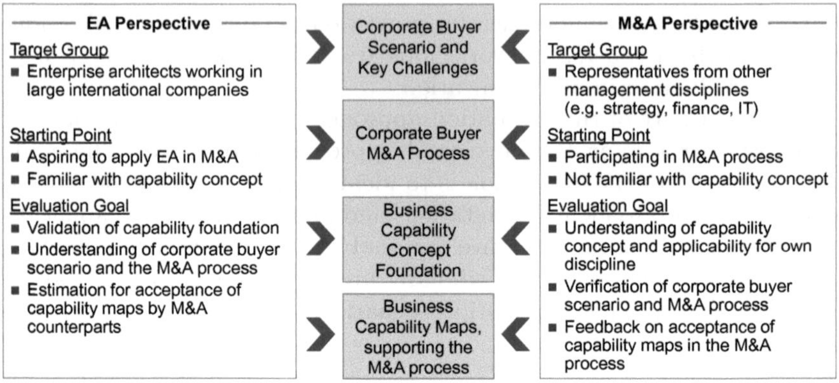

Figure 8.2: Workshop Design

the evaluation of their understanding of the corporate buyer scenario and the CBMA Process, as well as their estimation of acceptance of capability maps by M&A counterparts.

From the M&A perspective, the target group for participants are representatives from other management disciplines (e.g. strategy, finance, IT). Their starting point for the discussion of the presented artifacts is that they are participating in the M&A process, but in general not familiar with the capability concept. The evaluation goals for this group of participants is the evaluation of their understanding of the capability concept and their estimation of applicability for their own management discipline. This group of participants will also be able to verify the corporate buyer scenario and the developed CBMA Process. Additionally, they will give feedback on the acceptance of capability maps in the M&A process, also by other management disciplines.

8.3.2 National Bank Case Study

During the workshops, the developed artifacts are presented and discussed on the basis of an exemplary case study. The fictional "National Bank" is a German bank with a strong customer base of private and corporate customers operating on national scope in Germany. We assume the company has 900 branches and a customer base of 3.2 million private and 0.8 million corporate clients. The current product portfolio comprises giro accounts, private savings and pension products, small and medium size enterprise financing, and corporates&markets. As shown in figure 8.3, the company pursues a strategy of external growth to address challenges in the banking business environment.

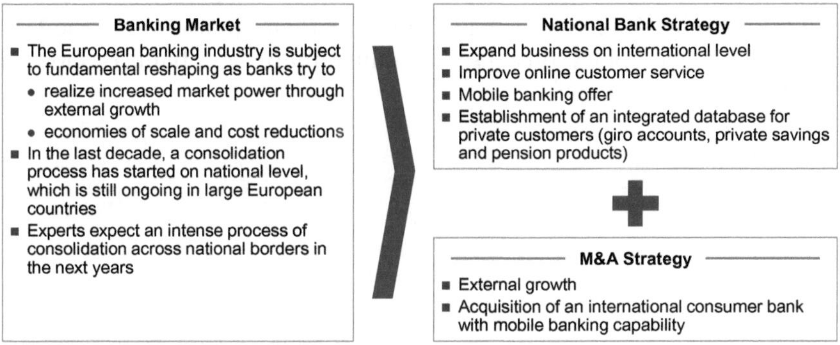

Figure 8.3: Case Study - M&A Strategy

We assume that "National Bank" plans the acquisition of an international consumer bank with a mobile banking capability. Consequently, efficient integration and holistic optimization are major goals for the M&A transaction. In the course of the case study, the market screening reveals "Target Bank" as a potential candidate matching "National Bank's" acquisition strategy. Furthermore, we assume that the transaction type is an acquisition and has aspects of horizontal and vertical integration. Furthermore, we assume a friendly deal setting with a high level of decision power on the side of "National Bank". The motivation of the deal is clearly strategic. Therefore, we assume that no exit of the investor is planned. We do not make additional assumptions on details like payment method or channel of offer submission. Figure 8.4 depicts the intended deal according to the developed M&A classification scheme (see figure 2.2).

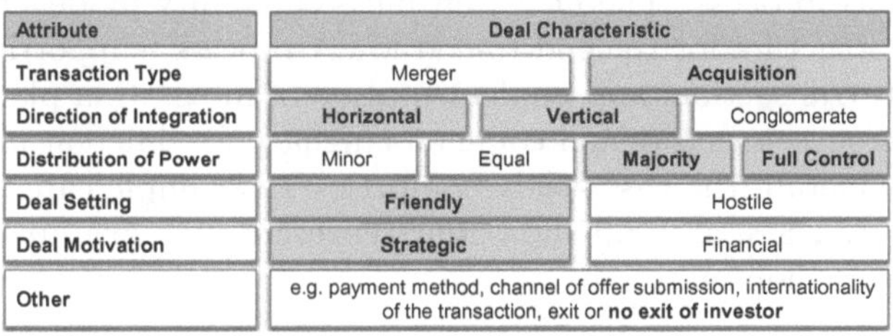

Figure 8.4: Case Study - M&A Classification Scheme

In the course of the evaluation, examples from the banking industry are applied to each conceptual description or model to make the usage of capability maps more tangible for the participants. Therefore an example capability map has been developed to illustrate their application in the M&A process. This exemplary business capability map for a bank is shown in figure 8.5.

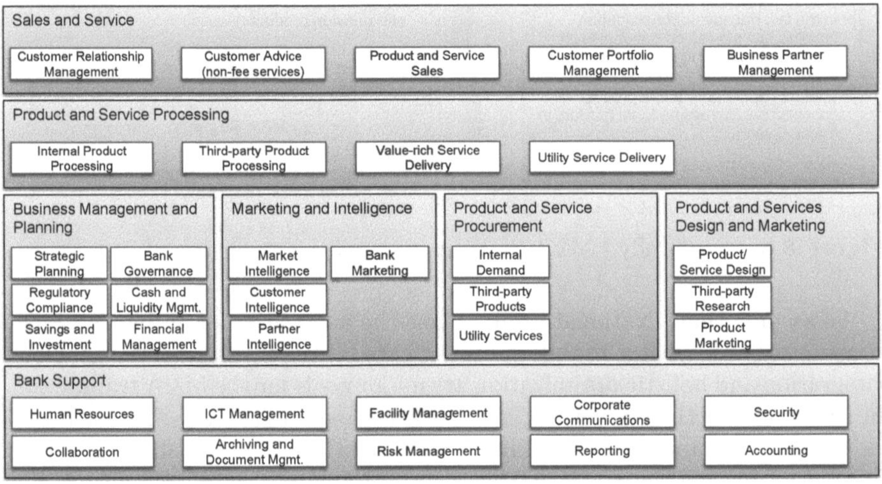

Figure 8.5: Case Study - Example Capability Map Banking

The example map has been elaborated by combining publicly available reference models and examples for the banking industry. It has to be noted, that the presented example map does not represent a comprehensive model for a bank. Table 8.1 provides a short description for each top level capability.

During the case study, "National Bank" works according to the defined M&A reference process. Therefore, business capability models are applied as reference structure for the end-to-end M&A process (supporting strategy development, transaction, and implementation of integration plan) and as a common reference structure and common language for different management disciplines. Overall, the case study comprises 11 example capability maps. Figures 8.6, 8.7, 8.8, and 8.9 show four representative examples from the evaluation workshop material.

Table 8.1: Case Study - Example Capability Map Description

Capability	Description
Sales and Service	Sales and service represents all capabilities for building and maintaining customer and business partner relationships. It includes servicing and selling to customers, potential customers, and third parties with relationships to customers as well as aspects such as customer risk, customer profitability, campaign management, and cross- and up-selling. Business partner management targets two types of business partner: corporate clients in retail banking and other financial services firms (e.g. insurance or mortgage product provider).
Product and Service Processing	Product and service processing represents the banking factory capabilities of internal or external factories as well as combinations thereof. This capability covers processing an internal bank product, a bundle of internal and/or external products, or white- or black-label products. It includes retail service delivery representing the degree of value that services deliver to customers.
Business Management and Planning	Business Management and Planning includes all capabilities of strategic management and key bank management functions.
Marketing and Intelligence	Marketing and Intelligence includes marketing and a variety of intelligence capabilities to analyze and influence customers, partners, and the market.
Product and Service Procurement	Product and Service Procurement represents the procurement capabilities, directly influencing product pricing and business flexibility, e.g. via third-party products and their support, enabling sourcing flexibility.
Product and Services Design and Marketing	Product and Services Design and Marketing represents the product management capabilities, including product-specific marketing.
Bank Support	Bank Support capabilities have a more horizontal nature and are less banking-specific than the others. They build the foundation for efficient bank operation.

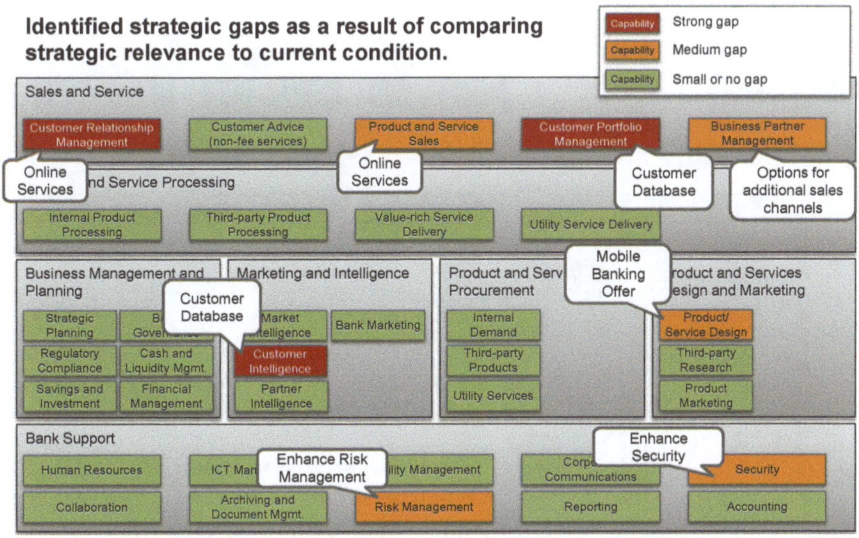

Figure 8.6: Case Study - Example Strategic Gap Map (SG-Map)

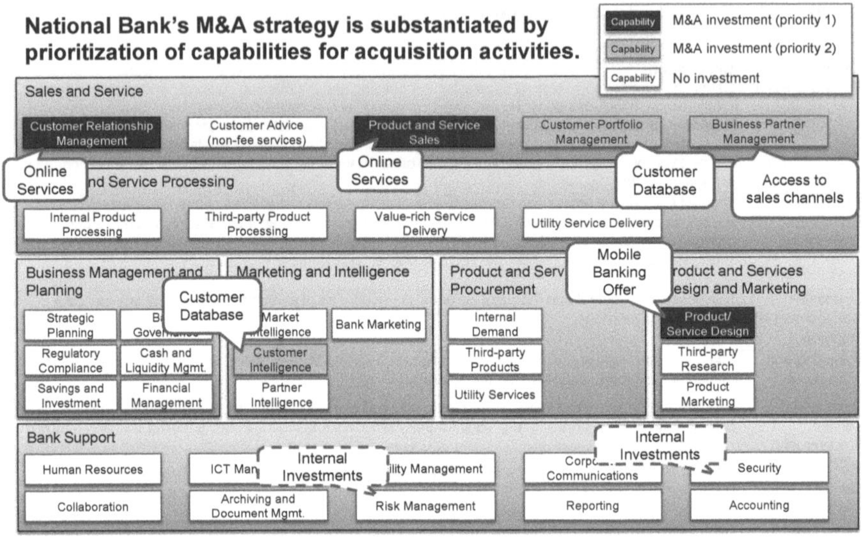

Figure 8.7: Case Study - Example Acquisition Goals Map (AG-Map)

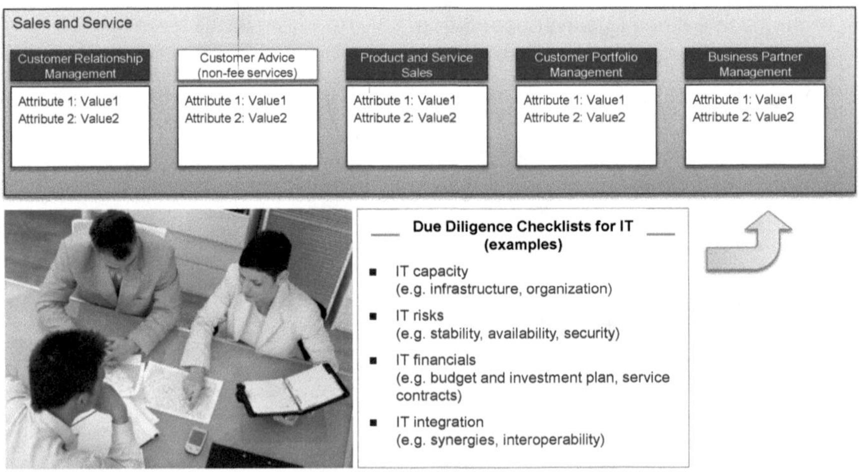

Figure 8.8: Case Study - Example Information Collection Map (IC-Map)

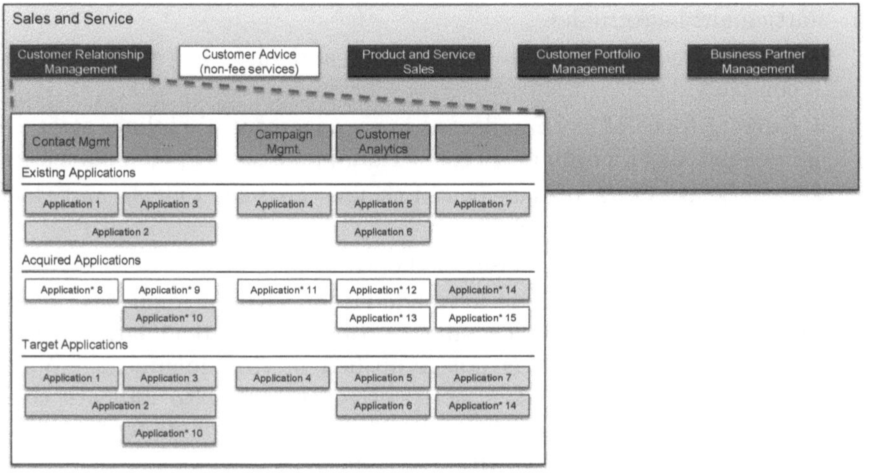

Figure 8.9: Case Study - Example Target Architecture Map (TA-Map)

8.3.3 Questionnaire

In addition to the discussion of the case study, the developed artifacts are evaluated with two questionnaires designed for enterprise architects and their M&A counterparts. The questionnaire comprises 53 questions of which 41 are common questions for both participant groups. 12 questions focus on special aspects for either the EA perspective or the M&A perspective. Thereby, the approach aims at a broad coverage of the artifacts while allowing for analysis of single aspects in greater depth for the respective participants.

The questionnaire contains three types of questions. First, the introductory questions document the participants background with free text fields, selection options (e.g. management disciplines), as well as number of years for indication of the individuals experiences. Second, closed questions with "yes/no" answers are applied in each section to capture facts about the participant's organization. Third, the questionnaire consists of questions formulated as statements with a five-level Likert scale [Li32] to document the participant's level of agreement or disagreement ("fully agree", "agree", "neutral", "disagree", "strongly disagree").

In the following the six sections of the questionnaire are described shortly, including the differences for enterprise architects and their M&A counterparts. The full questionnaire is included in appendix D.

1. Participant background
   - Background data on the participant and his role/function in his company.
   - Current focus of work, reflected in management disciplines strategy, financial, legal, products, organization, processes, IT, communication
   - Experiences in EA management, business capability models, and M&A in general
   - Experiences in single phases of the M&A process

   Answers in this section can be made either with personal data or by entering the role, function, or industry. However, personal data provided is kept confidential and is not published in this document. While participants from the M&A perspective are asked to indicate their background in the management disciplines, participants from the EA perspective are assigned to group EA per default.
2. Theoretical foundation for business capabilities
   - Knowledge about business capabilities at the participant's company
   - Comprehensiveness, scoping, detail of documentation, and formal correctness of theoretical foundation for business capabilities
   - Applicability of theoretical foundation for business capabilities in practice

   Participants from the M&A perspective are asked if they know about business capabilities or EA management at their company. For participants with an EA management background the section comprises additional questions on the application of business capabilities in EA management, the availability of a business capability definition, and the existence of a business capability model at their company.
3. Corporate Buyer Scenario
   - Comprehensiveness, completeness, and formal correctness of corporate buyer scenario
   - Usefulness of corporate buyer scenario to identify the relevant group of companies
   - Applicability for the participant's company
   - Relevance of challenges integration of pre-merger planning and post merger integration (PMI) and communication between multidisciplinary experts and stakeholders is a challenge the participant's company

No differentiation is made between enterprise architects and their M&A counterparts.

4. Corporate Buyer M&A Process (CBMA Process)
   - Knowledge about M&A process at the participant's company and other process models
   - Comprehensiveness, completeness, and formal correctness of the M&A process
   - Completeness of the developed M&A process as end-to-end approach from merger planning to integration and in terms of included management dimensions
   - Applicability of the M&A process in practice

   No differentiation is made between enterprise architects and their M&A counterparts.
5. Application of business capability models in the M&A process
   - Applicability of business capability models to support communication in the M&A process
   - Understanding and acceptance of business capability models for each management discipline
   - Applicability of business capability models for each phase of the M&A process
   - Applicability of business capability models for selected transformation challenges

   No differentiation is made between enterprise architects and their M&A counterparts.
6. Concluding questions and overall impression
   - Overall impression, if business capabilities can be established as a common reference structure along the M&A process, from merger planning to integration
   - Overall impression, if business capabilities can be established as a common reference structure between stakeholders from different management disciplines in the M&A process
   - Conclusion, if participant would apply the developed approach in practice

   No differentiation is made between enterprise architects and their M&A counterparts.

8.3.4 Open Discussion

Furthermore, each workshop comprised an open discussion of the presented artifacts. To initiate and stimulate the discussion, two leading questions are posed.

Do business capability models support integrated planning of business and IT, from early merger planning activities to completion of integration?

The first question is targeted on two aspects. On the one hand, discussing the potential of business capabilities as a stable reference structure for end-to-end process, supporting strategy development, transaction, and implementation of integration plan. On the other hand, the potential as a common reference structure and common language for different management disciplines and multiple stakeholders.

Could EA Management improve the M&A process by providing consistent information? Are business capability models a good starting point?

The question is targeted on the potential of EA Management and especially the concept of business capabilities in the context of M&A. Today, business capability models are an integral part of a modern EA Management approach, providing a reference structure applied in business and IT strategy development, implementation planning and controlling. They are established as a common language between business and IT and therefore suggested as starting point for successful collaboration with business departments in EA work. The discussion should evaluate their potential as a starting point to apply EA Management methods and models in the M&A process.

8.3.5 Expert Workshop Results

This section documents the findings of the evaluation workshops conducted. During documentation and analysis of the results the workshops are referenced as [WS#workshopnumber] (e.g. [WS1] for workshop 1) and single participants are referenced as [WS#workshopnumber#participantnumber] (e.g. [WS1a] for workshop 1, participant a).

Workshop 1: EA and M&A Representatives

The first evaluation workshop [WS1] was performed with a representative from a group EA management function and two representatives from an international integration program currently performed in one of the group's companies.

The organization is one of the world's leading passenger and logistics companies. Its group EA management function is part of the central strategic IT management department. The service offering of the EA management function comprises architecture models (e.g. a group domain model and a group catalog of technical components), basic methodologies (e.g. for IT master planning and technology standardization) and a central architecture repository. The company performing the integration project is a European freight railroad company operating one of the largest rail networks in the world. The company itself is structured as a group as well. Its headquarter is located in Germany, coordinating several regional and local structures.

Participant [WS1a] is a member of the group EA management team, responsible for business architecture. He is the owner of the group capability model. Participant [WS1b] is lead architect at the company headquarter, responsible for architecture approach in the integration project. Participant [WS1c] is consultant at the group's IT service provider. He is engaged to support Participant [WS1b] in the integration project.

Participant [WS1b] stated, that IT has a subordinated role during M&A in his organization. Other assets, for example physical assets of the logistics business, are more significant for planning and decision making during the M&A process. The other participants agreed, but remarked that this fact is industry-specific and may be less relevant for other business models. From a group perspective, participant [WS1a] added that the group operates multiple business models. The participants described that there is no organizational unit or team on group level that has end-to-end responsibility for M&A. While the Merger-Planning and Transaction Phase are managed centrally, the integration during the Post-Merger Phase is performed by the single companies. Participant [WS1a] stated that enterprise architects on group-level are not informed until the transaction has been closed. Regarding the role of IT during PMI, participant [WS1b] stated that IT is of increased significance during PMI to exploit the business opportunities endeavored with the acquisition. Later he added that a fast integration is more important than cost optimization.

Participant [WS1a] described, that business capabilities are modeled in a so-called "group domain model". This domain model is a group-wide standard comprising two levels of capabilities. The multiple business models in the group are a challenge for designing and maintaining the common model. Therefore, each company is free to refine the model on the lower levels. All participants agreed that the structure and level of detail of their group domain model on the second level is comparable to the example capability map presented during the case study. They especially stressed the value of a common company capability map but also mentioned the challenge of defining a common terminology for such a large organization. Participant [WS1a] stated that level one and two of the group domain model help to identify functional synergies, even across different business models. Participant [WS1b] stated that a third level of capabilities is required for the architecture approach applied in the integration project. Participant [WS1b] agreed. A discussion between participant [WS1a] and participant [WS1b] lead to the statement that the additional capability maps provided in the case study are viewpoints on this common company capability map. Participant [WS1c] described in other words, that they are specialized capability maps, referencing to the same structure.

Regarding the management disciplines in the M&A process, participant [WS1b] stated that the process experts in his organization are using functional views on the enterprise which are comparable to the presented capability concept. He added that the application of capability maps during the M&A process requires broad acceptance of the approach in the organization. The participants agreed that the single management disciplines can use the capability map as a common reference structure, but each discipline will need specific additional views.

The presented corporate buyer scenario, visualized with the developed M&A classification scheme, matched the setting of the integration project performed by participant [WS1b] and participant [WS1c]. The participants agreed that this scenario is the most common case for M&A transactions in the group. They mentioned that there are few cases where parts of the acquired organizations have been decommissioned. Participant [WS1a] provided additional examples of ongoing M&A activities, some national and some cross-border transactions.

Regarding the activities during the Pre-Merger Phase, participant [WS1b] stressed the importance of early analysis of dependencies. He stated that the single capabilities can not be analyzed completely individual. The group discussion lead to the finding, that the dependency analysis method (section 7.6.2) should be used as early as possible. Knowing that the level of detail for analysis is limited due to the limited amount of available information on the target enterprise, participant [WS1b] proposed to use it to identify critical areas to be taken care of during due diligence. Participant [WS1a] and participant [WS1b] assumed that the assessment of a target enterprise can be improved with a reference structure like a capability map. They added the idea of performing a mapping in the case the target enterprise does also have a capability model. As a prerequisite for the mapping, they mentioned access to business and IT representatives on executive and operational level.

Participant [WS1c] added, that the process of working out a mapping itself will give a good indication how well managed the target enterprise is.

The discussion of the activities during the Transaction Phase was kept quite short during this workshop. Regarding the application of capability maps during due diligence, the participants referenced back to the discussion of the dependency analysis method during the Pre-Merger Phase. They agreed that the same method can be applied again, in this phase with more detailed information available. Participant [WS1b] added that external consultants and service providers will be able to map their working structures to the capability map.

Regarding the activities during the Post-Merger Phase, participant [WS1b] and participant [WS1c] reported about intensive use of visualizations comparable to those presented in the case study. Viewpoints like the project portfolio map (PP-Map) are applied on management level to give an overview on the ongoing projects in the integration project. A comparable target architecture map (TA-map) is used to define target applications for the company's headquarter and regional units.

Furthermore, participant [WS1b] and participant [WS1c] reported that they use comparable visualizations for the progress of the integration project. While the presented integration result map (IR-Map) uses color coding, they recommended harvey balls due to the positive feedback received from their management. For the progress on application portfolio level, participant [WS1b] used a flip-book presentation containing yearly versions of the application architecture. This format allows to show the progress of integration, for example migration of local applications to headquarter applications or consolidation of redundant applications.

All participants contributed to the discussion of business capabilities as a stable reference structure along the end-to-end M&A process. They agreed that a capability map can be a solution for the challenge of structuring information during large transformation projects like M&A. Participant [WS1b] added the prerequisite, that the capability map has to be an established standard in the organization.

Participant [WS1a] and participant [WS1b] stated that the owner of the end-to-end M&A process should be the group M&A department, while the capability map has to be provided by the group enterprise architecture function. The statement was justified by participant [WS1c], who added that the capability map is used for a variety of other EA management tasks. He also added the possibility of using an M&A case to develop the initial version of the capability map, if a company does not have an established model. Participant [WS1b] mentioned the challenge that overarching structures like a capability map are often developed in the IT organization, leading to a lack of acceptance by business units. In his opinion, sponsorship from executives is crucial for commitment while acceptance of middle management ensures applicability of a capability map.

Participant [WS1a] concluded that the group M&A department could apply the presented approach to improve the collaboration with the single companies along the M&A process. Participant [WS1b] stated that the capability map is not an IT topic and should therefore be introduced in the Merger-Planning and Transaction Phase first. The group also discussed the approach of developing a capability map together with business and IT representatives in one M&A transaction. Provided that the pilot project is successful, the model can be debriefed and positioned in the formal M&A process as a second step.

Furthermore, participant [WS1a] concluded that the presented approach allows to use the architecture repository as information base during the M&A process. Participant [WS1a] and participant [WS1b] agreed that frameworks like TOGAF are a good starting point to extend the group's approach to enterprise architecture according to the needs arising from supporting M&A. Participant [WS1b] noted that the business side of the existing approach has to be strengthened further. All participants agreed that business capabilities are a good starting point to link the disciplines of enterprise architecture and M&A.

Besides the statements above, the participants gave three suggestions for improvement and future extensions of the developed approach. First, participant [WS1b] proposed to put more emphasis on the requirements for a functional reference structure than on business capabilities only. Referring to his organization, the available group domain model would fulfill these requirements. Even though it does not explicitly refer to a capability definition. The other participants agreed that this would offer the possibility to introduce the linkage between enterprise architecture and M&A by integrating existing models. Second, as an option for future research steps, participant [WS1b] proposed to work on the integration of more existing methods currently used by the single management domains. Third, participant [WS1a] proposed to develop a method to tailor the presented approach to an individual enterprise. All participants agreed that the developed approach needs to be applied in practice for further refinement.

Workshop 2: M&A Working Group

The second evaluation workshop [WS2] was performed with the members of the M&A working group of a large international chemicals company.

The chemical company is based in Germany, performing business around the world, being active in more than 100 countries globally and operating production plants in more than 20 countries. The business strategy includes entering attractive future-oriented markets on a regular basis.

From public information, it is known that the company has an EA Management function and operates an architecture repository. The EA Management function has been set up as part of the corporate IT department in order to manage the complexity of the IT landscape and to support strategic business decisions[35].

The M&A working group meets regularly to advance the company's M&A process and methodology. The evaluation workshop with this group comprised ten participants from different management disciplines. Due to the large group, we refrain from documenting each participant individually. During the workshops most group discussions have been initiated by the leader of the workshop group [WS2a]. Individual statements have been contributed by a compliance specialist [WS2b], a specialist for the integration process [WS2c], a security specialist [WS2d], and a mainframe specialist [WS2e]. Unfortunately, no representative of the EA Management function participated in the workshop.

Participant [WS2a] stated, that in his organization, IT has a subordinated role during M&A. Other assets, for example physical assets, are more significant for planning and decision making during the M&A process. Participant [WS2d] gave two examples for more important issues to be managed during acquisitions in the chemical industry: contaminated sites and regulatory obligations. The other participants agreed, but remarked that this is industry-dependent and may be less relevant for other companies adopting the approach.

The proposed management dimensions have been intensively discussed by the workshop participants. We have discussed the challenges arising from the compliance and human resources perspective and how they are represented in the management dimensions of the developed M&A process. Participant [WS2b] added that, in the chemicals sector, "Environment, Health and Safety

[35] Sources are not published, due to confidentiality reasons. They contain the company name and would conflict with the agreement of anonymous documentation of the workshop results.

(EHS)"[36] plays an important role. Therefore, the workshop participants identified the need to refine the proposed management dimensions to ensure an explicit representation. The workshop group agreed that this would help to communicate the approach to business representatives. Participant [WS2c] pointed out the high importance of human resources. He proposed to represent it as a distinct management dimension on top-level. In the presented M&A process it is part of the "organization" dimension.

Participant [WS2a] stated that there is no organizational unit or team that has end-to-end responsibility for M&A. He reported that the IT organization is not participating during the Merger-Planning and Transaction Phase. Participant [WS2e] stated that IT is not informed until the transaction has been closed. Participant [WS2a] added that IT is just seen as one of the main cost drivers during the integration phase, but especially in the case of delays during IT integration, its relevance for business operations becomes obvious.

The presented corporate buyer scenario, visualized with the developed M&A classification scheme, matched the common type of M&A transaction performed at the company. Participant [WS2a] noted that the recurrence of this kind of M&A transaction lead to the establishment of the M&A working group with the responsibility to documenting best practices from past M&A projects in the form of an M&A playbook.

The presented business capability concept and the example capability maps used during the case study have been well-understood by the workshop group. Overall, the participants agreed on the purpose and the benefits of using capability maps. However, the participants did not know about a capability model or a comparable model provided by the organization's enterprise architecture team. Participant [WS2a] assumed that most departments use process-oriented models.

The presentation of the activities during the Pre-Merger Phase received little specific feedback. Instead of discussing single process steps or capability maps in detail, the workshop group discussed the possibility of participating during the Pre-Merger Phase at all. Participant [WS2a] concluded, that the presented approach can be used as a basis for discussing the role of enterprise architects and the IT organization in the early M&A phases.

The discussion of the activities during the Transaction Phase during this workshop focused on due diligence, as many participants shared their experiences from past M&A projects. Participant [WS2c] emphasized the

[36] Additional information to be found in the Environmental, Health, and Safety Guidelines published by the World Bank Group [Wo07].

need to align goals and results of a due diligence with the business objectives of the M&A transaction. The group agreed that this is usually not the case today. Participant [WS2b], participant [WS2d], and participant [WS2e] gave examples for areas with proven methods for due diligence, e.g. checklists, compliance audit methods, license model analysis. The workshop group agreed that each expert is already well-prepared, but only for the individual area of analysis. Participant [WS2a] proposed to use a common structure like a capability map to coordinate the individual analyzes and link them to business goals.

The presentation of the activities during the Post-Merger Phase received little specific feedback, again. Participant [WS2e] stated that the workshop group is well positioned for PMI activities, while the approach presented for the Pre-Merger Phase and the Transaction Phase introduced a new perspective to the team.

Therefore, we spent more time on the open discussion of the presented approach. First, we approached the applicability of business capabilities as a stable reference structure along the end-to-end M&A process. Participant [WS2a] identified the access to the M&A responsible in the Pre-Merger and Transaction Phase as a challenge. In his opinion, this applies equally to enterprise architects and the IT organization as a whole. The workshop agreed and formulated the goal that the Pre-Merger and Transaction Phase has to deliver standardized results that can be used during integration work. They identified a structured business view as a prerequisite for this approach and agreed that a capability map can be a solution. Second, we discussed the applicability of business capabilities as a common reference structure and common language for the different management disciplines. Participant [WS2a] assumed that a comprehensive business capability model could replace the existing, process-oriented structures. Participant [WS2c] formulated the prerequisite that the business capability model is designed in business language and agreed by the different management disciplines.

Participant [WS2a] concluded that the working group could use the presented M&A process as a leading structure for the collection of best practices. Regarding the role of enterprise architects, participant [WS2c] concluded that the acceptance of their participation in the Pre-Merger Phase is depending on their ability to engage themselves in the think and feel of the M&A responsibles. The workshop group agreed, that if the enterprise architects are able to provide reliable information to the M&A managers they will be more than happy to collaborate.

Besides the statements above, the participants gave two suggestions for improvement and future extensions of the developed approach. First, the workshop group proposed to develop industry-specific variants of the approach, including industry-specific management dimensions and an industry-specific capability map. According to their feedback, this would support the introduction of the approach ion practice. Second, participant [WS2a] proposed the development of a method to transfer existing process-oriented structures into capability models. This suggestion is partly addressed by the method for development of an initial capability map presented in section 7.6.1. But this method was not part of the workshop presentation.

Workshop 3: Business Transformation Specialist

The third evaluation workshop [WS3] was a one-on-one session performed with a business transformation specialist. Participant [WS3a] is working as IT transformation consultant and leader of consultancy practices for a multinational professional services firm. The company is focused on assurance, tax advisory, consulting, and financial advisory services. In his role as a consultant, participant [WS3a] shares experiences gained at multiple client organizations, most of them large international organizations. Therefore, the feedback collected in this workshop is more general and not referring to one single organization.

Participant [WS3a] confirmed that achieving merger readiness has a high practical relevance, as a lot of companies are setting up an M&A practice to build up the competencies needed to perform acquisitions successfully. Additionally, he stated that EA management is an important management discipline which can strongly support the M&A process. He clearly sees the opportunity to integrate EA management when setting up a company's approach to M&A. However, according to his insights into his client organizations, the key responsible for an organization's approach to M&A is the head of the M&A department, while EA management will stay in a supporting role.

Participant [WS3a] agreed that the presented corporate buyer scenario reflects the typical setting of large international companies with an external growth strategy. Therefore, it is applicable to the most client situations he is facing. According to his opinion, the presented M&A process is complete and fully understandable. He remarked, that the practical manifestation of the management domains financial and legal will always be industry-specific, while the rest of the management domains will be applicable for any organization. He noted, that human resources are one of the most important aspects during M&A.

Regarding the selection of the case study for the workshop, he remarked that there may be a risk of misunderstanding, because banks also participate as external parties in the M&A process. By the end of the workshop he commented on the previous statement, adding that the roles have been clearly separated.

During the presentation of the activities in the Pre-Merger Phase, participant [WS3a] remarked the importance of internal measures. He emphasized the strong influence of requirements from risk and security on other management disciplines. He remarked that the presented approach to analysis of the target enterprise with a Candidate Assessment Map (CA-Map), and the simulation of the integrated enterprise with a Target Enterprise Map (TE-Map) are only feasible if a certain level of insight into the target enterprise is available. After considering the case of the corporate buyer scenario which included a friendly deal setting he concluded that the availability of information can be ensured. During the discussion of the activities in the Transaction Phase he stated, that the dependency analysis method (section 7.6.2) should also be used during merger planning. In his opinion, the available information on the target enterprise are sufficient to start identifying first dependencies. The presentation of the activities during the PMI phase comprised the Project Portfolio Map (PP-Map), a visualization for the portfolio of integration projects, their scope and dependencies on basis of a capability map. Referring to this capability map, participant [WS3a] remarked that in practice a view on the project portfolio is equally important as the view on the single M&A project.

Participant [WS3a] agreed both, the applicability of business capabilities as a stable reference structure along the end-to-end M&A process, as well as the applicability of business capabilities as a common reference structure for the different management disciplines. He added that the acceptance of the presented approach heavily depends on the way the underlying capability map is produced. He identified stakeholder participation in the model development as a key success factor. According to his experience, the application of EA models such as a capability map requires profound education of business departments. Therefore, a collaborative approach between business and IT is needed to develop of a capability map.

Participant [WS3a] concluded that the developed approach is elaborated enough to be applied in practice. He did not make any concrete suggestions for improvements or future extensions of the developed approach. In his option, any further refinement should be made according to experiences gained from practical application. Furthermore, participant [WS3a] concluded that EA management has to be positioned as a business planning discipline for successful introduction of the presented approach in practice. According to his experience, an IT-internal EA management function or a capability map which has been designed without any business involvement will not be accepted.

At the end of the workshop participant [WS3a] gave a suggestion for improvement of the workshop design. He proposed to extend the story line of the case study depending on the audience when discussing the case with practitioners. The examples included in the present version are quite general. Accordingly, he assumed that the presented achievement of targets Integration Result Map (IR-Map) may be seen as too realistic by M&A practitioners. He proposed to include some provocative examples in the case study in order to stimulate the discussion.

Additionally, he proposed an industry reference model as a starting point for introducing the approach. According to his experience this makes the general approach more comprehensible and fosters acceptance in practice. However, he added that the M&A process, the management dimensions, and the capability model has to be tailored to the individual organization.

8.3.6 Questionnaire Results

Due to the number of workshop participants (n=14), the amount of data is not sufficient for a quantitative analysis. Therefore, the questionnaire can only provide first qualitative trends. The analysis of the returned questionnaires shows interesting tendencies for some questions. However, some of them do not show a clear picture. In the following, the most obvious results are presented and commented. We focus on the general agreement or disagreement but want to provide a complete picture. Thus, we also document percentages of the distribution of answers. Noteworthy, few questionnaire sheets have not been filled out completely. In this case, single questions have not been answered.

Participant Background

The participants roles and their organizations have already been documented in section 8.3.5. They are experienced in the areas of EA management, business capabilities and M&A. Overall, 10 of 14 participants are experienced in EA Management, ranging from 1 to 15 years. They are a little less experienced in business capabilities with 6 of 14 participants having worked with this concept for 1 to 15 years. 13 of 14 participants are experienced in M&A, ranging from 1 to 15 years with an average experience of 4.6 years.

They have been working across all phases of the M&A process with an emphasis on the later phases (merger planning 21%, transaction 71%, PMI 93%).

Theoretical Foundation for Business Capabilities

Most participants (85%) know about business capabilities or EA management at their company. All EA representatives confirmed that their organizations apply business capabilities in EA management, as well as the existence of a business capability definition and a business capability model. They agree that the presented business capability definition matches their experiences in practice and that the theoretical foundation for business capabilities is compatible with their company's EA framework.

38% of participants from other management disciplines "fully agree" that the business capability concept is useful for their management discipline, 23% selected "agree", 38% selected "neutral", while no participant disagrees with this statement. The same pattern can be identified regarding the comprehensibility of the concept as well as its scope, the level of detail and the formal correctness: 20-30% "fully agree", 50-65% selected "agree", 10-20% selected "neutral", while no participant disagrees with any of these statements. In summary, more than two thirds of the respondents would apply the theoretical foundation for business capabilities in practice.

Corporate Buyer Scenario

Most participants rate the presented corporate buyer scenario as comprehensible (64% "fully agree", 29% selected "agree"). They agree that it is a complete representation of the specific situation at a strategic buyer (21% "fully agree", 71% selected "agree") and that it is formally correct (21% "fully agree", 79% selected "agree").

The results are not so straightforward with the questions on the application of the corporate buyer scenario in practice. The majority of respondents agree (29% "fully agree", 71% selected "agree") that it is useful to identify the relevant group of companies, but 29% remained neutral. Only half of the participants agree (21% "fully agree", 21% selected "agree") that the presented corporate buyer scenario matches with the situation at their company, while 50% remained neutral. However, no participant disagrees with the first and only one disagrees with the second statement.

Strong agreement is shown regarding the two challenges: integration of pre-merger planning and post merger integration (PMI) and communication between multidisciplinary experts and stakeholders: 50% "fully agree", 36% selected "agree", 14% selected "neutral", while no participant disagrees.

Corporate Buyer M&A Process (CBMA Process)

Most participant companies (71%) follow an established M&A process. Only few respondents (21%) know other M&A process models for a corporate buyer. The others reported about proprietary process models owned by investment companies or consultants and individual best practice collections. All participant agree that the presented CBMA Process is comprehensible (50% "fully agree", 50% "agree").

The majority rated the scope of the process as appropriate (36% "fully agree", 57% selected "agree"), while 7% remained "neutral". In line with that, they state that it provides a complete end-to-end approach from merger planning to integration (29% "fully agree", 57% "agree"), while 14% remained "neutral". Only one participant disagrees that the CBMA Process includes all relevant management dimensions (14% "fully agree", 43% "agree", 36% "neutral").

The statements regarding the level of detail of the process (29% "fully agree", 29% "agree", 36% "neutral", 7% "disagree") and its formal correctness (29% "fully agree", 36% "agree", 36% "neutral") do not provide a clear picture. Two respondents did not provide an answer to the second statement.

The questions which focus on the application of the M&A process in practice have a tendency to agreement. Half of the respondents agree (14% "fully agree", 43% "agree") that the M&A process matches their experiences in practice, while 36% remained "neutral" and a minority of 7% "disagree". The majority of participants would apply the M&A process in practice (21% "fully agree", 43% selected "agree"), while 29% remained "neutral" and one disagreed.

Application of Business Capability Models in the M&A Process

All participants agreed (21% "fully agree", 43% "agree") that business capability models support the communication between stakeholders from different disciplines. The responses to the statements on the understandability and the expected acceptance by the single management disciplines show an interesting pattern. The results of these questions are depicted in figures 8.10 and 8.11.

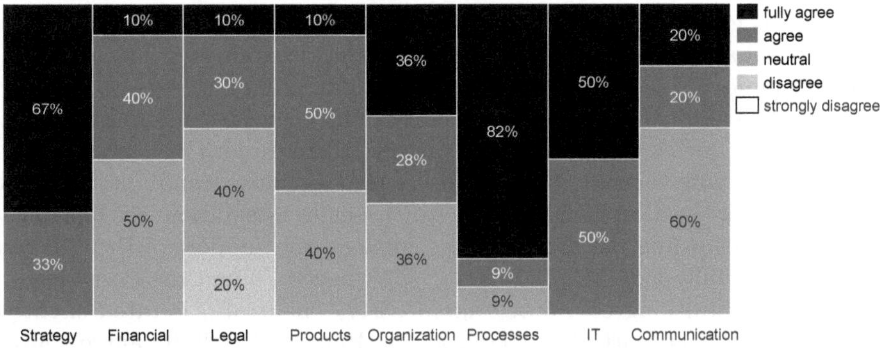

Figure 8.10: Questionnaire Result - Understandability of Capability Approach

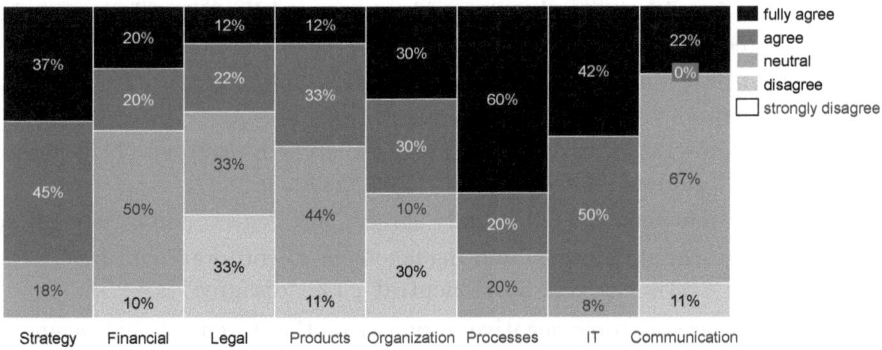

Figure 8.11: Questionnaire Result - Acceptance of Capability Approach

Looking on these results, there seem to be two groups of management disciplines. The respondents agree that the application of business capabilities in the M&A process is understandable and will be accepted by the first group, comprising strategy, processes and IT. Only few answer "neutral" and no participant disagrees. The answers for the second group, comprising financial, legal, products and communication, contain also answers of disagreement (e.g. for legal and organization) and less positive responses. Still, the overall feedback on the application of business capabilities is positive. There is few disagreement on the applicability, but a tendency that there are management disciplines with a higher affinity towards the business capability concept in the M&A process. The resulting pattern does not differ between the respondent groups. In other words, representatives with EA Management background and those from other management disciplines in M&A have a similar opinion.

The applicability of business capability models end-to-end and in single phases of the M&A process is rated positive. The majority of respondents agree (36% "fully agree", 57% "agree") that business capability models support multiple activities from merger planning to integration, 7% remained "neutral". Regarding the single process phases, the support of Pre-Merger Phase (36% "fully agree", 57% "agree", 7% "neutral") and the Post-Merger Phase (43% "fully agree", 36% "agree", 21% "neutral") is rated slightly better than the support of the Transaction Phase (21% "fully agree", 43% "agree", 29% "neutral", 7% "disagree").

The participants mainly agreed that business capability models support organizations in selected transformation challenges during M&A. These are:

- coordinated and holistic planning of business and IT (29% "fully agree", 50% "agree", 21% "neutral"),
- consistent decisions for business and IT (29% "fully agree", 42% "agree", 29% "neutral"),
- adequate knowledge management, e.g. a merger repository (21% "fully agree", 29% "agree", 43% "neutral", 7% "disagree"),
- stakeholder management (29% "fully agree", 36% "agree", 36% "neutral"),
- and effective communication and management of corporate cultures (14% "fully agree", 43% "agree", 36% "neutral", 7% "disagree").

Noteworthy, there are some negative responses on the statement that business capability models support knowledge management and communication.

Concluding Questions

As a conclusion, the participants rated the overall applicability of business capabilities in the M&A process positively. The majority of respondents agree (36% "fully agree", 43% "agree") that business capabilities can be established as a common reference structure along the M&A process, from merger planning to integration, 21% remained "neutral". The same applies to the statement that business capabilities can be established as a common reference structure between stakeholders from different management disciplines in the M&A process (36% "fully agree", 50% "agree", 14% "neutral"). From their overall impression of the presented approach, the majority of respondents (36% "fully agree", 29% "agree", 36% "neutral") would apply business capabilities in the M&A process in practice.

The final question for individual comments or further thoughts on the presented approach resulted in the following statements. One participant stated that *"business capabilities have to be understood by all involved parties"* and added that they *"should not be perceived as IT topic"* and *"have to be accepted by business"*. A second participant stated that it is *"a prerequisite that the company's business capability model is established as standard in everyday work"*. A third response contained the comment *"additional experience in carve out ("post merger separation")"*, which could either refer to his additional experiences or the proposal to extend the developed approach to this case. One participant noted that it is *"very important that "business" (a relative notion) understands capability models, so make it simple and be save that "business" recognizes itself in the models"* and that *"transparency is becoming more and more important"*.

8.4 Introduction of the Developed Approach

Overall, the workshop and questionnaire results show positive feedback regarding the developed artifacts and their applicability in practice. During the open discussions at the end of each workshop session, the participants discussed how the developed approach can be successfully applied in their organization.

First, the participants discussed the roles that are affected by the introduction of the CBMA Process. The discussion was primarily focused on the process environment, for example, the relationship to corporate management, a company's M&A responsible and the project manager for a single transaction. Therefore, we reviewed the workshop results and documented a simplified application scenario (see section 8.4.1).

Second, the participants identified prerequisites. For example, they identified the need that the artifacts of the developed approach have to be tailored and adjusted to the individual company's situation and business. Accordingly, individual business objectives, the present governance model and resources have to be considered. From a more general perspective, this implies that there are some limitations for introducing the approach and that some pre-requisites have to be fulfilled for its successful application. Therefore, we documented the identified options (see section 8.4.2) and prerequisites for introducing the approach (see section 8.4.3).

8.4.1 Application Scenario

Figure 8.12 depicts the application scenario for the developed approach, resulting from the feedback collected in the evaluation workshops. It shows the main actors who are directly affected when introducing the methodology.

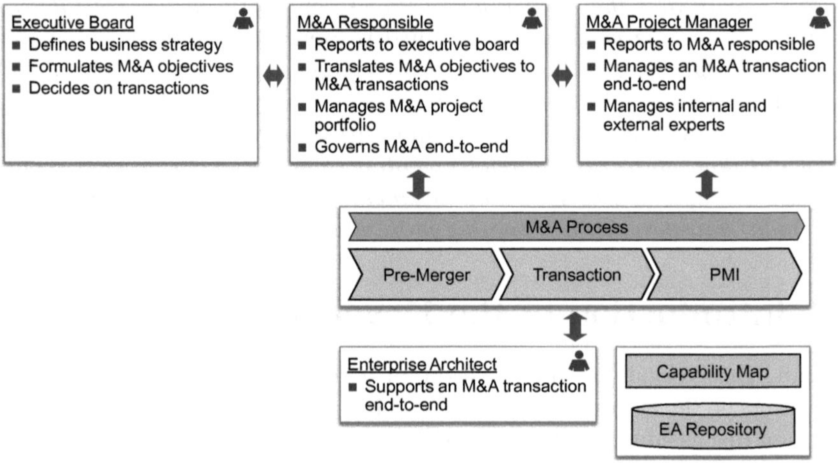

Figure 8.12: Application Scenario for Developed Approach

In the following, the responsibilities of each actor are described shortly with regard to the M&A process. Hence, they do not reflect the full set of responsibilities of these actors in the organization:

- A company's executive board defines the business strategy and formulates M&A objectives. The board represents the corporate management and decides on transactions.
- The M&A responsible reports to the executive board. This actor is responsible for the translation of the organization's M&A objectives into M&A transactions. The M&A responsible manages the portfolio of M&A projects and governs M&A transactions end-to-end.
- The M&A project manager reports to the M&A responsible and manages an M&A transaction end-to-end. This includes the responsibility to manage internal and external experts along the process.
- The enterprise architect supports an M&A transaction end-to-end. To achieve this, the architect provides information from the architecture repository in the form of capability maps.

8.4.2 Introduction Options

In the following, we document the identified options for introducing the approach in practice, as well as associated challenges. It has to be noted, that the following options have been identified during the expert workshops and that there may be more starting points.

Upcoming M&A Transaction

According to the participants, any upcoming M&A transaction offers a possibility to apply the approach in a real M&A case. The first application can then be a pilot project. After its completion, a debriefing of the project delivers two valuable outcomes. First, the approach has been proven in practice and can be refined with the experiences made during the first application. Second, a success story is the best reference for communication of the value of a new approach during sustainable anchoring in the organization. This introduction option requires strong commitment of the executive management and enthusiasm of the M&A responsible. The main challenge is to convince the participants along the M&A process to work with the new approach. This requires intensive communication activities and additional support and coaching for the regular project team. Especially the different external experts may be restrained regarding "being a pilot" and will use this fact as a justification in the event of any delay in the project. On the one hand, the stronger formal governance of a contract between the parties could make it easier to dictate a certain approach. On the other hand, especially these temporary engaged external parties have been the reason for information loss in the past.

M&A Management Initiative

Improving merger readiness is one motivation for our research. The participants confirmed that the introduction or advancement of the company's M&A process is one initiative to improve an organization's M&A practice. As possible triggers for starting such an initiative, they mentioned that the enterprise is new to external growth through acquisitions, that the M&A responsible changed, or that there is a new ownership for the M&A process.

Best Practice Collections

Ongoing knowledge management initiatives to document best practices for managing M&A can be a starting point. Some of these collections are focused on methods and tools (e.g. checklists) and labeled as "M&A framework" or "M&A handbook". Others also include additional material like reference models, standard solutions, or performance indicators and are referred to as a merger repository. The participants proposed to use the CBMA Process as a leading structure for an organization's best practice collection.

8.4.3 Prerequisites for Introduction

During the workshop discussions, we also identified some limitations and discussed prerequisites for the introduction of the developed approach.

Existence of M&A Responsible

We found out, that today the responsibility for Pre-Merger Phase and Transaction Phase is often separated from responsibility for the Post-Merger Phase. Therefore, a prerequisite for the introduction of the approach is the existence of an overarching M&A responsible as described in section 8.4.1. This role is in charge of the end-to-end process and has decision rights and resources to change and optimize the M&A process.

Awareness for M&A Process

The participants remarked that M&A are sometimes perceived as unique events which have few similarities. They argued, that this is true for many experts involved in single steps of the process. Hence, there is low awareness for the need to implement and continually improve an M&A process from this perspective. But, the participants emphasized the importance of establishing a managed M&A process from an end-to-end view. From their ongoing discussions on improving M&A, they formulated management awareness as a prerequisite for the introduction of the approach.

Maturity of EA Management

Obviously, the existence of an EA Management practice is a prerequisite to apply EA methods and models in the M&A process. In addition, the participants remarked that the EA Management team requires an adequate mandate. First, this means that the scope of EA has to include business architecture, not only applications and technology. Second, the EA approach has to be strategy-oriented and not on an operational level.

Consequently, the architecture model has to provide a complete cause-effect-chain from business to technology, for example business capabilities, business information, application portfolio, and technology portfolio. Furthermore, the participants remarked that the application of capability maps during the M&A process requires broad acceptance of the capability approach and the EA Management team in the organization.

8.5 Review of Transformation Challenges

In section 5.3.1, we listed nine transformation challenges relevant to the corporate buyer scenario (see table 5.1). As part of the evaluation, we review our research results. In the following, we document which of these transformation challenges can be addressed with the developed approach and how.

TC1 - Provide a clear business vision - committed, explicitly described, and measurable: The transformation challenge is twofold. On the one hand, it describes the need to have a business vision as a guidance throughout the M&A process. On the other hand, it formulates quality requirements. As one important view on the business model, the Company Business Capability Map (C-BCM) provides a complete and non-overlapping view on the enterprise's business capabilities. Thereby, it helps to structure and document the business vision. However, a complete business vision needs more elements to be explicitly described (see section 4.2).

Additional maps can be used to substantiate the business model. For example, the Strategic Relevance Map (SR-Map) (see figure 7.5) to highlight the most important capabilities to accomplish the business vision, or a Strategic Gap Map (SG-Map) (see figure 7.7) to indicate the most important fields of action. Indeed, additional efforts are needed to ensure commitment to the formulated business and to make it measurable.

TC2 - Support high aspiration level with definite directions and common KPIs: This transformation challenge consists in three aspects. First, target setting through a high aspiration level is the result of a management process. We did not elaborate on its relation to a capability model in this work. But the second aspect, definite directions through decision making and clear communication can be supported by the provided set of capability maps. For example through documentation of target architecture plans with a Target Architecture Map (TA-Map) (see figure 7.17) or by communication of a clear scope for the portfolio of integration projects with a Project Portfolio Map (PP-Map) (see figure 7.16).

The third aspect, a common set of KPIs has to be in place independent from the use of capability maps. But, depending on the type of KPIs, they can be attached as attributes on capabilities in the Company Business Capability Map (C-BCM). Thereby, they can be communicated into expert teams working with the capability model, for example as reference KPIs during due diligence in an Information Collection Map (IC-Map) (see figure 7.14).

TC3 - Stakeholder management, effective communication, and corporate, cultures: The management dimensions represent the different expert groups as well as internal and external stakeholders relevant for the corporate buyer organization. The feedback from our workshops showed that they have to be adjusted to an individual organization, for example due to special requirements of an industry or the individual business model. However, they were rated as a good starting point to identify the concrete disciplines that are engaged in the company's M&A process.

The use of capability maps along the M&A process helps to provide information and thereby improve communication from two perspectives. First, business capability models help to close the gap between strategic planning and PMI by supporting the end-to-end availability of information across the single phases of the M&A process. Second, business capability models improve the information exchange between experts and stakeholders from different disciplines by supporting the transfer of information across multiple disciplines and from an overarching perspective. Both options have been discussed in the workshops and have been widely approved when explicitly asked in our questionnaire.

In summary, capability maps can support a comprehensive stakeholder management approach. A complete solution has to include more elements, for example a stakeholder map and a communication plan. We did not assume an influence of capability maps on corporate culture, therefore we did not investigate this relation.

TC4 - Establish an adequate project organization (structures and processes): A well working project organization requires both, a governance model and a clear scoping of work. We presented several options to support the scoping of work with a capability map. As one example, the Due Diligence Map (DD-Map) (see figure 7.13) can be used to scope and prioritize information analysis during the Transaction Phase.

Later, during the Post-Merger Phase, a Project Portfolio Map (PP-Map) (see figure 7.16) helps to define the scope of parallel integration projects. Thereby, it helps to define a portfolio of non-overlapping projects or alternatively to clearly describe areas to be coordinated.

TC5 - Coordinated and holistic planning of business and IT: We proposed capabilities as a connecting element between the business and the IT perspective on the enterprise. For example the Target Architecture Map (TA-Map) (see figure 7.17) connects information about the application portfolio with business capabilities. The idea was taken for granted by the workshop groups. It was widely confirmed that capability models support coordinated and holistic planning of business and IT when explicitly asked in our questionnaire. Thereupon, the participants initiated a discussion about the current status of implementation of the concept in their organization. Depending on the workshop group, the application of capability maps ranges from initial awareness for the concept to an established group-wide model.

TC6 - Consistent decisions for business and IT: Taken that capabilities work as a connecting element between business and IT (see TC5), business capability models do also support consistent decisions for both domains. This is also reflected in the workshop discussions and the questionnaire results. Decisions made on the business level, like strategic planning with a Strategic Relevance Map (SR-Map) (see figure 7.5) can be transferred to priorities for IT analysis in a Due Diligence Map (DD-Map) (see figure 7.13). The capability map structure does also help to transfer this information into the planning of the target IT landscape with a Target Architecture Map (TA-Map) (see figure 7.17).

Additionally, the presented capability approach does also support a dependency analysis along a cause-effect-chain from business to technology (see section 7.6.2). Noteworthy, the workshop participants formulated a certain maturity level of the EA Management approach as a prerequisite for its application in practice (see section 8.4.3).

TC7 - Establish adequate knowledge management (merger repository): The benefits of managing the knowledge gained through past M&A transactions was a main motivation of the industry partners to participate in our evaluation workshops. The workshop participants widely agreed that business capability models support adequate knowledge management. They proposed to use the CBMA Process as a leading structure for an organization's best practice collection (see section 8.4.3). The contents of this merger repository (e.g. reference models, standard solutions, or performance indicators) can then reference the capabilities in the Company Business Capability Map (C-BCM), which is also reflected in the questionnaire results.

Furthermore, we showed how business capabilities can be used as a gateway to access the information in the organization's EA repository. Thereby, the EA repository can extend the information base in the merger repository.

TC8 - Establish adequate risk management: In the developed approach, risk management is seen as a continuous activity throughout the

CBMA Process. Therefore, it is not represented as an explicit management discipline or activity and we did not present a specific capability map for visualization of risks. Accordingly, we did not elaborate on different types of risk (e.g. market risks , risks due diligence, or risks during transformation) and responsibility for risk management (e.g. communications, financial management, or project management).

TC9 - Realize growth and demonstrate early wins: We referenced external growth as one major motivation. With the developed approach, we aim to improve the M&A process and thereby support an organization to reach the goal of growth. The demonstration of early wins has to be part of the communication strategy. We showed that business capabilities can support communication during the CBMA Process, for example with an "Integration Results Map (IR-Map)" (see figure 7.18) to show the progress of integration.

9 Summary

As a first step towards interlinking the domains of M&A and EA Management, we investigated the end-to-end applicability of business capabilities in the M&A process of a corporate buyer organization. We identified and evaluated options to apply business capabilities to close the gap between strategic merger planning and PMI and to improve communication between experts and stakeholders from different management disciplines. The leading research question, if business capabilities can be used as a boundary object between the EA practice and other management disciplines during the M&A process, was subdivided into seven research questions which guided the research presented in this thesis. Subsequently, we summarize our findings, document our critical reflection on the results, and provide some suggestions for future research.

9.1 Summary of Key Findings

Motivation and Relevance

We showed that M&A are an established management instrument for external growth, but enterprises still struggle to manage M&A efficiently and a significant number of merger projects do not reach the expected goals or fail completely. Furthermore, we pointed out that a professional M&A process can be a competitive advantage if an enterprise's corporate strategy includes external growth. We identified merger readiness as motivation and an organization's M&A process as one key concept to improve the M&A practice.

EA Management and M&A

Looking on EA Management as an approach for business and IT planning, we showed that it fosters communication by providing a consistent information base and thus, it promises to contribute to the success of business transformation challenges such as M&A. With our literature analysis and a survey among practitioners, we revealed that the application of EA Management in the context of M&A is still at the beginning. Our literature analysis documents that only little work exists on the role, benefit, and usage of EA Management in M&A. The existing body of knowledge discusses the role of EA Management in M&A only on a very general level. Our survey among EA practitioners showed that they perceive M&A as one of their application domains, but they currently do not participate in M&A activities on a regular basis.

Business Capabilities

We showed that business capabilities are an essential element of a state of the art EA Management approach. They describe the functional building blocks of an enterprise's business model and they are frequently used to work collaboratively with business and IT stakeholders. Even though there is an enormous interest in business capabilities among academics and practitioners, we demonstrated that many issues have not been subject to structured research yet. We presented a theoretical foundation for business capabilities in EA Management on the basis of a structured analysis of business capability literature and related work from strategic management. It documents the concept of a capability map and its relationship to the business model and a single capability. Additionally, it comprises a definition for business capabilities, its characteristics, attributes for description, and the dimensions that together provide the capability. Our evaluation activities showed that the application of business capabilities in practice is still at the beginning.

Corporate Buyer Scenario

The presented corporate buyer scenario was developed to clearly scope the target group for the capability-based approach developed in this thesis. It represents a buyer organization that pursues the goal of sustainable growth with an M&A transaction. It matched the M&A transactions relevant to the participants of our evaluation workshops and it was rated as a complete representation of the specific situation at a strategic buyer organization. Additionally, the participants rated the developed M&A classification scheme as a comprehensible visualization and they confirmed the list of transformation challenges.

Corporate Buyer M&A Process (CBMA Process)

We developed the Corporate Buyer M&A Process (CBMA Process), an integrated end-to-end M&A process for a corporate buyer scenario. The CBMA

Process comprises the three phases, Pre-Merger, Transaction, and Post-Merger. Each phase is described including its steps, the methods applied and resulting deliverables. We proposed eight management disciplines (strategy, financial, legal, product, organization, processes, information technology, and communication), which describe the perspectives of participants in the CBMA Process. During our evaluation, the plausibility of the proposed process phases, steps and management dimensions has been confirmed. Noteworthy, the workshop participants identified the need to refine the proposed management dimensions for introduction of the approach in practice.

Business Capabilities in the CBMA Process

We showed the applicability of different business capability maps along the developed CBMA Process. This leads to the conclusion that business capability models can support a corporate buyer's M&A process. First, they can provide a stable reference structure for the end-to-end process, supporting strategy development, transaction, and implementation of the integration plan. Second, they can be established as cross-disciplinary reference structure and common language for different management disciplines and multiple stakeholders.

Research Environment

The research environment certainly influenced our research, especially the evaluation of the developed approach. We described the main characteristics and we tried our best to align the evaluation approach to these circumstances. Our research spans across two research disciplines, M&A and EA Management. Even when looking at M&A only, we had to deal with a multitude of experts and stakeholders from different management disciplines. Furthermore, getting insights into real-life M&A transactions is extremely difficult. A typical duration of an M&A process is several years from initial planning of a transaction until full completion of the integration. At the same time, confidentiality of data is high and the working environment is characterized as highly complex and dynamic. Looking on EA Management, it is one of the practice based research domains. On the one hand, this yields to a small body of knowledge when applying the standards of formal research. On the other hand, available material is certainly of practical relevance.

Introduction in Practice

In our workshops, participants confirmed the relevance and applicability of the developed artifacts but also revealed limitations and prerequisites for introducing the approach in practice. We identified an upcoming M&A transaction, initiatives to improve an organization's M&A practice, and ongoing knowledge management initiatives to document best practices for managing M&A as possible starting points to apply the developed approach. As prerequisites for the introduction in practice, we identified the existence of an M&A responsible, a certain level of awareness for the M&A process, and a minimum maturity of EA Management.

9.2 Critical Reflection and Future Research

The presented approach is a first step towards interlinking the domains of M&A and EA Management. Given the innovative character of our research, we focused on one subarea. We investigated the applicability of business capabilities in the M&A process of a corporate buyer organization. Our research builds on available literature and feedback of practitioners. Therefore, we only covered the fundamentals. More detailed questions remain unanswered and have to be addressed during future research. In the following, we reflect our research and provide suggestions for future research.

Other M&A Scenarios

We focused our research on the corporate buyer scenario and we did not consider buyer organizations with different motivations, the perspective of the target enterprise, or other types of M&A transactions like carve out or disinvestment. Other scenarios may have different requirements. Consequently, the M&A process will look different and there may be a different relationship to EA Management and the application of business capabilities. Future research should address the influence of other settings on the design of the M&A process and the application of EA Management and business capabilities.

Industry Specifics

The research has been set up independently from a specific industry sector and the workshop participants confirmed applicability of the research results with their different industry background. However, the discussions revealed several potentials for industry-specific advancements of the methodology. During the workshops, an exemplary case study from the banking industry was presented. Based on this example, the participants reflected on the special characteristics for their individual industry sector. The participants in the evaluation workshop suspected that the business capability map may be replaced by any other model depending on the target group for the developed methodology. Future research should examine available industry reference models and should make them available to organizations wishing to introduce the presented approach.

Refinement of CBMA Process

We limited the documentation of the CBMA Process to a description of steps, methods applied and resulting deliverables. This degree of detail was sufficient for investigating the applicability of business capabilities. The presented CBMA Process could also be used for other research in the domain of M&A, for example for a refinement of roles in the process.

Evaluation in Real-World Scenario

External circumstances in the research environment certainly lead to a limited evaluation of the developed approach. Hopefully, the artifacts will be applied by practitioners in their regular working environment. Then, subsequent research projects can evaluate the experiences in an academic set-up. Alternatively, researchers could focus on evaluating single artifacts of the approach, e.g. the capability definition, the CBMA Process or single capability maps.

EA Management in M&A

The applicability of business capabilities in the M&A process of a corporate buyer organization presented a first step towards interlinking the domains of M&A and EA Management. Therefore, future research should extend the scope towards a complete picture of EA Management in the context on M&A. For example, a structured analysis of a standard EA framework like TOGAF would help to specify the special requirements for the EA Management practice.

EA Meta Model

The provision of profound information from an EA repository requires a consistent EA meta model. In our work, we described that it has to include a complete cause-effect-chain from business to technology, for example business capabilities, business information, application portfolio, and technology portfolio. Therefore, the development of a minimum information model needed for M&A could be a field for future research.

Tool Support

Most organizations use tools to support EA Management. To our knowledge, most of these tool are able to document business capabilities and to generate views like the capability map. We recommend a further evaluation, if these tools can also support the presented set of 13 business capability maps along the CBMA Process. Furthermore, the research should address options to integrate data collection with reference information outside the architecture repository.

Portfolio Level

In this thesis, we described M&A activities on the level of one transaction. Additionally, we documented first insights into the environment of the CBMA Process in the application scenario (see figure 8.12). We mentioned that serial acquirers perform complex acquisition programs with multiple interrelated acquisitions, often even in parallel. This requires a synchronization of multiple instances of the CBMA Process on the level of the M&A responsible or the executive board. Therefore, we propose to initiate research on the application of EA Management and business capabilities to support M&A activities on the portfolio level.

A Appendix: Survey on EA Management in M&A

We conducted an expert survey with conference participants at three European EA Management conferences. An excerpt of the results relevant to this thesis have been presented in section 3.4. The survey contained the following 15 questions and was subdivided into three main parts: participant's background, questions about the company's EA Management, and questions referring to M&A.

Participant Background Information

1. Which industry sector does your company belong to?
2. What is your role/function?

Enterprise Architecture Management

1. How long are you working in EAM?
2. Do architects actively collaborate with business departments?
3. If applicable, do they apply architecture models and viewpoints?
4. Do architects use business capability models in business architecture management?
5. Are architects engaged in the management of information and data?

Mergers and Acquisitions

1. Was your company involved in M&A in the past?
2. Are you expecting M&A involving your company in the future?
3. Is support of M&A projects seen as an EAM responsibility in your company?
4. Were enterprise architects engaged in M&A projects in the past?
5. If applicable, in which phases did they participate?
6. In retrospective, do you think that EAM would have made an M&A project more successful?
7. Which tasks in M&A projects are assigned to enterprise architects today?
8. How could enterprise architects support M&A projects in the future?

B Appendix: Expert Interviews on IT Integration in M&A

During the first phase of our research project (see figure 1.2), we performed an extensive literature study on the research domain of M&A. The analysis comprised more than 170 sources. To get additional insights from a practitioner perspective, we conducted explorative expert interviews with industry partners from the German banking industry, who were involved in a merger.

The literature study and the interviews have been a joint effort of the team working for the research project on "EA Management in the context of M&A" at our chair "Software Engineering for Business Information Systems (sebis)". Therefore, they did also cover other focus areas like tooling, data migration, or application integration strategies. An excerpt of the results relevant to this thesis have been presented in section 5.2.1. A complete documentation of the results is available in [FMS10b, FMS11]

In all, we performed 15 semi-structured interviews between September and December 2009. In order to structure our results of related work, we worked with the mindmap shown in figure B.1. During the interviews, we worked with the following set of open questions:

Questions relating to the interviewee

1. Could you describe your professional background, as well as some of your previous activities?
2. Could you point out some main activities you are dealing with on a regular basis?
3. Could you shortly outline your specific role in the context of M&A?
4. How would you assess your own experience with respect to M&A?

Questions relating to the enterprise

1. What have been the core businesses of the enterprises before the merger?
2. Could you shortly define the two types of the enterprises?
3. What were the different goals and strategies of the enterprises?
4. Could you briefly talk about the M&A history of the merging enterprises?

Questions relating to the merger

1. According to your opinion, what have been the main reasons for the merger?
2. Who was the main driver for the merger in your enterprise?
3. Could you shortly outline the merger strategy?
4. Which significant synergy potentials of the merger have been identified?
5. What is the target picture of the common enterprise and who is in charge of defining this picture?
6. Which measures have been carried out in advance to the merger (IT due diligence, merger readiness)?
7. Which preconditions business and IT should fulfill prior to a merger?
8. Which approach has been taken during the merger considering business and IT?
9. Could you precise the content of your merger roadmap?
10. How has this merger roadmap been communicated and implemented?
11. Could you enumerate some success factors for a merger?

Questions relating to the M&A team

1. Is there a specific M&A competence team in your organization and how is this team staffed?
2. What are the tasks of the M&A competence team?
3. How is this team positioned in the overall organization and which rights and duties has it?
4. Could you explain the specific information flows between the M&A team and the remaining enterprise?

Questions relating to IT transformation concerns

1. What goals did you define before starting to transform your IT?
2. Do you define a specific merger strategy before transforming IT?
3. How did the IT staffing policy look like before, during and after the merger?
4. In which way is IT transformation work distributed among the different stakeholders?
5. How do you deal with different business and IT terminology during the merger?
6. How have target applications been selected for the new enterprise?
7. Could you shortly explain how the different applications have been integrated in the target application landscape?

8. What role did data migration play during the merger?
9. In which manner is data migrated from one application to another?
10. Are you developing and using workarounds for mitigating risks or speeding up the transformation process?
11. How do you test your transformed IT?
12. Are you applying different metrics and KPIs for measuring the transformation results (target landscape) as well as the transformation process?
13. Is there a dedicated knowledge base where you keep your M&A knowledge?
14. Could you think of outsourcing and off-shoring IT transformation activities?
15. What are the relative costs of IT in the old and new enterprises?
16. How did you deal with the customers if IT has an impact on their products and utilized services?
17. In which way did IT complexity impact the IT transformation?

Questions relating to IT transformation methodologies, viewpoints, and tools

1. How does your IT transformation methodology look like?
2. What kinds of artifacts are generated and used during IT transformation (software maps, migration plans, etc.)?
3. What experiences did you made with these artifacts?
4. Which specific tools are you using when carrying out the IT transformation?
5. Which experience did you made with this tools?

Questions relating to the future development of M&A

1. How will M&A in the banking industry look like in the future?
2. Considering M&A, what specific problems will be relevant in the future?
3. Considering M&A, what specific problems won't be relevant in the future?

Questions relating to category other

1. What role do carve-outs play for the banking industry?
2. Regarding insurance companies, could you describe some similarities and differences in comparison to the banking business?

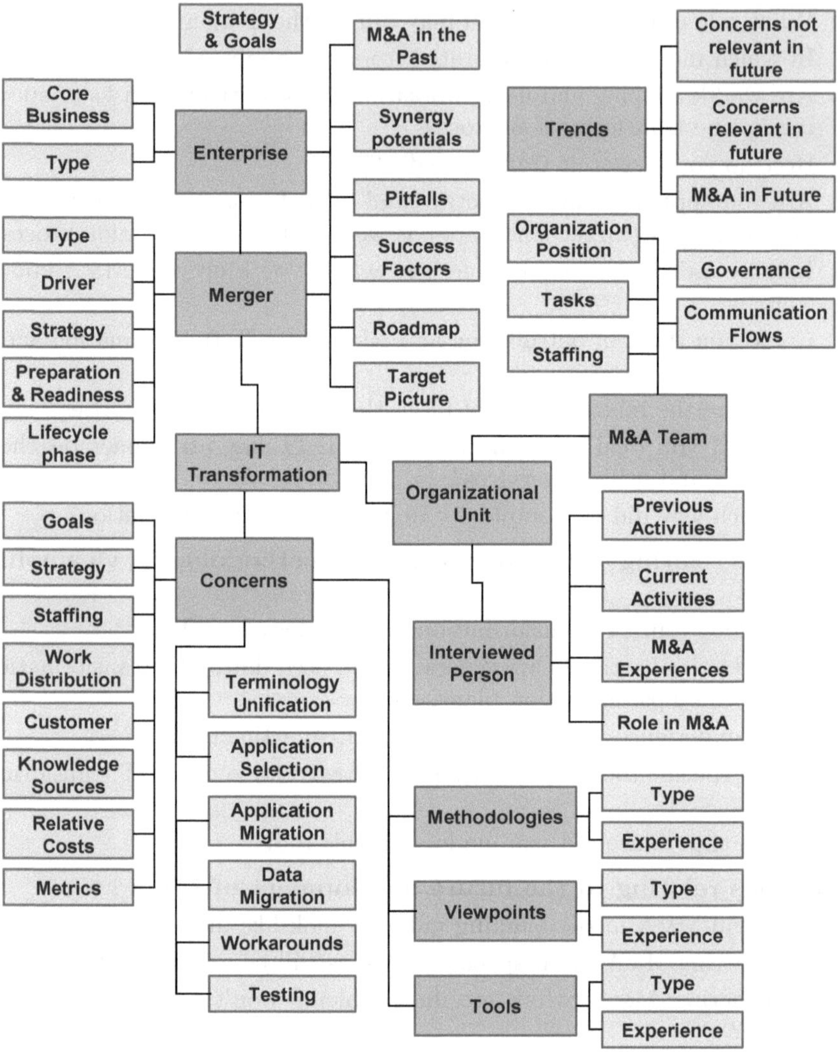

Figure B.1: Interview Mind Map

C Appendix: M&A Case Studies

During the setup phase of the evaluation approach, we performed a literature analysis on M&A case studies. After reviewing the results of available literature studies (e.g. [BL12, Ha09b]), we identified additional sources [Al05, An06, Ba02, CKB04, FGM10, Gi97, GJ12, Ha09a, HI11, HI12, HY13, JY96, KST09, Le03, Ma03, Mo13, Ni12, SHV03, SH09, ST02, Wa12].

They are listed in tables C.1 and C.2 together with the gathered information on company/industry, type of transaction, relevance of IT, covered M&A process phases and identified integration challenges.

Table C.1: M&A Case Studies

Publication			Basic Info		Industry/Company	Transaction Type(s)	IT in Scope	M&A Phases			Focus	Comments
Author	Title	Cit.	Type	Year				Pl.	Tr.	PMI		
Alaranta, Maria	Evaluating Success in Post-Merger IS Integration: A Case Study	Al05	Journal article	2005	Anonymized case from the manufacturing industry	Joint venture: one factory was transferred between the enterprises	Yes			X	IT integration	User satisfaction with the integrated IT; information quality; IT integration management; IT staff integration; IT ability to support the underlying (business) motives of the merger
Antila, Elina M	The role of HR managers in international mergers and acquisitions: a multiple case study	An06	Journal article	2006	Three Finish industrial organizations	Multiple	No	X		X	Human resources	Organizational culture; HR due diligence; Integration of HR management; Employee selection
Barnes, Nora Ganim	Mergers and Acquisitions as the New Growth Strategy: A Case Study of the Wholesale Alcohol Industry	Ba02	Journal article	2002	American wholesale liquor industry	Multiple	No		X		Market study	Not focused on one company or case
Chevalier, A Kunsch, P L Brans, J P	A contribution to the development of strategic control and planning instruments: An acquisition case study	CKB04	Journal article	2004	BSN/Danone ("Nabisco case"), food industry	Acqusition	No	X	X	X	M&A as case for planning and control of complex socio-economic processes	Influence factors (variables); Decision models; The case is part of to evaluate and improve the adaptive control methodology (ACM).
Foley, C Fritz; Goldberg, Lena G; Meyer, Linnea N	Chrysler's Sale to Fiat	FGM10	Journal article	2010	Fiat acquired Chrysler	Acquisition	No	X	X		Financial markets, regulations and law	Chapter 11 regulations and impacts; Share market effects
Giacomazzi et al.	Information systems integration in mergers and acquisitions: a normative model	Gi97	Journal article	1997	38 cases of mergers and acquisitions in italy; Not focused on one company or case	Multiple	Yes			X	Strategies for IT Integration	Influence factors (variables); Decision support model
Goyal, K. A.; Joshi, Vijay	Merger and Acquisition in Banking Industry : A Case Study of ICICI Bank Ltd.	GJ12	Journal article	2012	ICICI Bank Ltd. (private sector bank in India) acquired nine financial firms	Series of acquisitions	No	X	X	X	Human resources	Management, communication, corporate culture; Impact on human resources; The main part of paper is a literature review on challenges and success factors in M&A.
Habibbeigi, Pooria	A Project Management Approach to M & A Deals and their Post-Integration Project Projects - A Case Study	Ha09b	Master thesis	2009	Swedish manufacturing company	Series of acquisitions (national and international)	No	X		X	Project management approach	Strategic fit vs Organizational fit; Project organization; Human resources; Governance
Henningsson, Stefan; Yetton, Philip	IT-based Value Creation in Serial Acquisitions	HY13	Conference proceedings	2013	Trelleborg Engineered Systems (TES)	Series of acquisitions	Yes	X	X	X	IT integration	IT integration strategies; IT capabilities; Business and IT alignment; Infrastructure scalability
Horie, Nobuhiro; Ikawa, Yasuo	Knowledge Integration in a Product Development Organization Accompanied by M&A: A Case Study of a Precision Device Manufacturer; Adverse Factors of Knowledge Integration in a Product Development Organization after M & A : A Case Study of a Precision Device Manufacturer	HI11, HI12	Conference proceedings	2011, 2012	Japenese precision device manufacturer	Acquisition of a new product development organization and entry into a new market	No	X		X	Knowledge integration	Different types of knowledge transfer; Limitations and success factors for Knowledge transfer; Corporate culture

Table C.2: M&A Case Studies (cont.)

Publication			Basic Info		Industry/Company	Transaction Type(s)	IT in Scope	M&A Phases			Focus	Comments
Author	Title	Cit.	Type	Year				Pl.	Tr.	PMI		
Johnston, Kim; Yetton, Philip	Integrating information technology divisions in a bank merger Fit, compatibility and models of change	JY96	Journal article	1996	Commonwealth Bank of Australia (CBA) acquired State Bank of Victoria (SBV)	Acquisition of a regional competitor	Yes	X	X	X	IT integration (but with reflection of strategy and business background)	
Konstantopoulos, Nikolaos; Sakas, Damianos; Triantafyllopoulos, Yiannis	Lessons from a case study for Greek banking M&A negotiations	KST09	Journal article	2009	Anonymized case from banking industry	Merger between two leaders of the Greek banking branch	No	X	X		Human beliefs and professional attitudes; Negotiation process;	Staff's beliefs, attitudes and social representations during the negotiation process (e.g. fear of change, the stress, the insecurity and the loss of morale)
Lecrone, Kerry	IT case study: Maintaining the billing process in a M&A environment	Le03	Article	2003	Vectren Corporation, American utility group	Multiple	Yes			X	IT system selection	Continuity of business operations (especially billing); Consolidation of IT systems; Outsourcing of solutions;
Mallon, William T	The alchemists: a case study of a failed merger in academic medicine	Ma03	Journal article	2003	Merger between Pennsylvania State University's Hershey Medical Center and Geisinger Health System (both academic health centers)	Merger of equals (and de-merger)	No	X	(X)	X	Reasons for failure	Leadership; Governance; Organizational structure; Decision Making; Organizational Culture;
Mo`meni, Mansoor; Mohaghar, Ali; Godarzi, Golamreza; Haddadi, Seyyed Mostafa	A Model for successful Integration in Inter-organizational Collaboration (Case Study: M&A in Iran)	Mo13	Journal article	2013	8 companies (qualitative analysis); Survey with 26 companies, Not focused on one company or case.	Acquisitions in the same value chain (vertical & horizontal)	No	X		X	Integration	Factors for successful Integration
Nijland, Arjan	Factors influencing a post M&A development strategy	Ni12	Masters thesis	2012	Dutch automated welding company	Acqusition of a cross-border subsidiary	Yes	X		X	Development strategies (of SMEs)	Integration aspects; Strategic factors for success of integration; Integration problems
Salama, Alzira; Holland, Wayne; Vinten, Gerald	Challenges and opportunities in mergers and acquisitions: three international case studies – Deutsche Bank-Bankers Trust; British Petroleum-Amoco; Ford-Volvo	SHV03	Journal article	2003	Three international case studies (Deutsche Bank-Bankers Trust, British Petroleum-Amoco, Ford-Volvo)	Acquisition	No	X	X	X	Success of cross-border acquisitions within related industries	Organizational culture; Learning process; Knowledge acquisition,
Salama, Alzira; Holland, Wayne	The Merger of a German Bank (G Bank) an American Bank (A Bank): An Assessment of Cultural Fit	SH09	Teaching material	2009	Large German bank acquired American investment bank	Acquisition	No	X	X	X	Integration strategy from human resource perspective	Organizational culture; Employee resistance;
Sumi, Tadao; Tsuruoka, Michio	Ramp new enterprise information systems in a merger & acquisition environment: a case study	ST02	Journal article	2002	Shibaura Mechatronics Corporation, industrial equipment manufacturer	Multiple (integration, spin-off, merger)	Yes			X	Integration of enterprise information systems	Speed of integration; Success factors for integration; Preparation of computer systems for a ramp for an integration
Walker, Sebastian	IS & Business Strategy Alignment ; The Impact on IT Integration In M&A. Case study - Technology Company	Wa12	Master thesis	2012	Large technology company with international operations	Series of acquisitions	Yes	X	X	X	IT integration (but with reflection of strategy and business background)	Integration success; Communication; Impact of resource constraints; Expectations management

D Appendix: Evaluation Workshop Questionnaire

In the following, we include the questionnaire used during the evaluation workshops (see section 8.3).

Evaluation Questionnaire: Applying Business Capability Models in a Corporate Buyer M&A Process
>>> M&A Perspective

I) Participant Background

Which company (industry) are you working for?

What is your role/position?

In which of the folowing disciplines are you working?

Strategy	Financial	Legal	Products	Organization	Processes	IT	Communi-cation

How experienced are you in...

- EA management ___ years
- working with business capability models ___ years
- Mergers & Acquisitions ___ years

If you have experiences in M&A, in which process phases?

Pre Merger	Transaction	Post Merger

II) Theoretical Foundation for Business Capabilities

	yes	no
Do you know about business capabilities or EA management at your company?		

	fully agree	agree	neutral	disagree	strongly disagree
The concept of business capabilities is comprehensible.					
The business capability concept is useful for my management discipline.					
The scope of the theoretical foundation for business capabilities is appropriate.					
The level of detail of the theoretical foundation for business capabilities is appropriate.					
The representation of the theoretical foundation for business capabilities is formally correct.					
I would apply the theoretical foundation for business capabilities in practice.					

Figure D.1: Evaluation Questionnaire - M&A Perspective Page 1/4

Evaluation Questionnaire: Applying Business Capability Models in a Corporate Buyer M&A Process
>>> M&A Perspective

III) Corporate Buyer Scenario

	fully agree	agree	neutral	disagree	strongly disagree
The corporate buyer scenario is comprehensible.					
The corporate buyer scenario is a complete representation of the specific situation at a strategic buyer.					
The representation of the corporate buyer scenario is formally correct.					
The corporate buyer scenario is useful to identify the relevant group of companies.					
The corporate buyer scenario matches with the situation at my company.					
Integration of pre-merger planning and post merger integration (PMI) is a challenge at my company.					
Communication between multidisciplinary experts and stakeholders is a challenge at my company.					

IV) Corporate Buyer M&A Process (CBMA process)

	yes	no
Does your company follow an established M&A process?		
Do you know any other M&A process model for a corporate buyer?		

If yes, which ones?

	fully agree	agree	neutral	disagree	strongly disagree
The M&A process is comprehensible.					
The scope of the M&A process is appropriate.					
The M&A process provides a complete end-to-end approach from merger planning to integration.					
The M&A process includes all relevant management dimensions.					
The M&A process matches my experiences in practice.					
The level of detail of the M&A process is appropriate.					
The documentation of the M&A process is formally correct.					
I would apply the M&A process in practice.					

Figure D.2: Evaluation Questionnaire - M&A Perspective Page 2/4

Evaluation Questionnaire: Applying Business Capability Models in a Corporate Buyer M&A Process
>>> M&A Perspective

V) Application of business capability models in the M&A process

		fully agree	agree	neutral	disagree	strongly disagree
Business capability models support the communication between stakeholders from different disciplines.						
Business capability models are understandable for experts and stakeholders from…	Strategy					
	Financial					
	Legal					
	Products					
	Organization					
	Processes					
	IT					
	Communication					
Business capability models will be accepted as a communication means in M&A by experts and stakeholders from…	Strategy					
	Financial					
	Legal					
	Products					
	Organization					
	Processes					
	IT					
	Communication					

Figure D.3: Evaluation Questionnaire - M&A Perspective Page 3/4

V) Application of business capability models in the M&A process (cont.)

	fully agree	agree	neutral	disagree	strongly disagree
Business capability models support multiple activities from merger planning to integration.					
Business capability models support the merger planning phase.					
Business capabilities support the transaction phase.					
Business capability models support the post merger integration (PMI).					
Business capability models support coordinated and holistic planning of business and IT.					
Business capability models support consistent decisions for business and IT.					
Business capability models support adequate knowledge management (e.g. a merger repository).					
Business capability models support stakeholder management.					
Business capability models support effective communication and management of corporate cultures.					

VI) Concluding questions and overall impresssion

	fully agree	agree	neutral	disagree	strongly disagree
I think that business capabilities can be established as a common reference structure along the M&A process, from merger planning to integration.					
I think that business capabilities can be established as a common reference structure between stakeholders from different management disciplines in the M&A process.					
I would apply business capabilities in the M&A process in practice.					

Do you have any individual comments or further thoughts you want to share?

Thank you for your participation. Your information will be kept confidential and used only for research purposes.

Figure D.4: Evaluation Questionnaire - M&A Perspective Page 4/4

Evaluation Questionnaire: Applying Business Capability Models in a Corporate Buyer M&A Process
>>> EA Management Perspective

I) Participant Background

Which company (industry) are you working for?

What is your role/position?

How experienced are you in...

EA management ____ years

working with business capability models ____ years

Mergers & Acquisitions ____ years

	Pre Merger	Transaction	Post Merger
If you have experiences in M&A, in which process phases?			

II) Theoretical Foundation for Business Capabilities

	yes	no
Do you apply business capabilities in EA management at your company?		
Do you have a business capability definition in place at your company?		
Do you have a business capability model in place at your company?		

	fully agree	agree	neutral	disagree	strongly disagree
The business capability definition is comprehensible.					
The business capability definition matches my experiences in practice.					
The scope of the theoretical foundation for business capabilities is appropriate.					
The level of detail of the theoretical foundation for business capabilities is appropriate.					
The representation of the theoretical foundation for business capabilities is formally correct.					
The theoretical foundation for business capabilities is compatible with the EA framework of my company.					
I would apply the theoretical foundation for business capabilities in practice.					

Figure D.5: Evaluation Questionnaire - EA Perspective Page 1/4

Evaluation Questionnaire: Applying Business Capability Models in a Corporate Buyer M&A Process
>>> EA Management Perspective

III) Corporate Buyer Scenario

	fully agree	agree	neutral	disagree	strongly disagree
The corporate buyer scenario is comprehensible.					
The corporate buyer scenario is a complete representation of the specific situation at a strategic buyer.					
The representation of the corporate buyer scenario is formally correct.					
The corporate buyer scenario is useful to identify the relevant group of companies.					
The corporate buyer scenario matches with the situation at my company.					
Integration of pre-merger planning and post merger integration (PMI) is a challenge at my company.					
Communication between multidisciplinary experts and stakeholders is a challenge at my company.					

IV) Corporate Buyer M&A Process (CBMA process)

	yes	no
Does your company follow an established M&A process?		
Do you know any other M&A process model for a corporate buyer?		
If yes, which ones?		

	fully agree	agree	neutral	disagree	strongly disagree
The M&A process is comprehensible.					
The scope of the M&A process is appropriate.					
The M&A process provides a complete end-to-end approach from merger planning to integration.					
The M&A process includes all relevant management dimensions.					
The M&A process matches my experiences in practice.					
The level of detail of the M&A process is appropriate.					
The documentation of the M&A process is formally correct.					
I would apply the M&A process in practice.					

Figure D.6: Evaluation Questionnaire - EA Perspective Page 2/4

Evaluation Questionnaire: Applying Business Capability Models in a Corporate Buyer M&A Process
>>> EA Management Perspective

V) Application of business capability models in the M&A process

		fully agree	agree	neutral	disagree	strongly disagree
Business capability models support the communication between stakeholders from different disciplines.						
Business capability models are understandable for experts and stakeholders from...	Strategy					
	Financial					
	Legal					
	Products					
	Organization					
	Processes					
	IT					
	Communication					
Business capability models will be accepted as a communication means in M&A by experts and stakeholders from...	Strategy					
	Financial					
	Legal					
	Products					
	Organization					
	Processes					
	IT					
	Communication					

Figure D.7: Evaluation Questionnaire - EA Perspective Page 3/4

Evaluation Questionnaire: Applying Business Capability Models in a Corporate Buyer M&A Process
>>> EA Management Perspective

V) Application of business capability models in the M&A process (cont.)

	fully agree	agree	neutral	disagree	strongly disagree
Business capability models support multiple activities from merger planning to integration.					
Business capability models support the merger planning phase.					
Business capabilities support the transaction phase.					
Business capability models support the post merger integration (PMI).					
Business capability models support coordinated and holistic planning of business and IT.					
Business capability models support consistent decisions for business and IT.					
Business capability models support adequate knowledge management (e.g. a merger repository).					
Business capability models support stakeholder management.					
Business capability models support effective communication and management of corporate cultures.					

VI) Concluding questions and overall impresssion

	fully agree	agree	neutral	disagree	strongly disagree
I think that business capabilities can be established as a common reference structure along the M&A process, from merger planning to integration.					
I think that business capabilities can be established as a common reference structure between stakeholders from different management disciplines in the M&A process.					
I would apply business capabilities in the CBMA process in practice.					

Do you have any individual comments or further thoughts you want to share?

Thank you for your participation. Your information will be kept confidential and used only for research purposes.

Figure D.8: Evaluation Questionnaire - EA Perspective Page 4/4

Bibliography

[ADF01] Ashkenas, R. N.; Demonaco, L. J.; Francis, S. C.: *Making the Deal Real.* In *Harvard Business Review on Mergers and Acquisitions.* chapter VII, pages 149–180. Harvard Business School Press. Boston, USA. 2001.

[AF01] Ashkenas, R. N.; Francis, S. C.: *Integration Managers.* In *Harvard Business Review on Mergers and Acquisitions.* chapter VIII, pages 181–204. Harvard Business School Press. Boston, USA. 2001.

[AFW11] Aier, S.; Fischer, C.; Winter, R.: *Construction and Evaluation of a Meta-Model for Enterprise Architecture Design Principles.* In *Proceedings of 10th International Conference on Wirtschaftsinformatik.* pages 637–644. Zurich, Switzerland. 2011.

[AH08] Alaranta, M.; Henningsson, S.: *An approach to analyzing and planning post-merger IS integration: Insights from two field studies. Information Systems Frontiers.* 10(3):307–319. 2008.

[Ak04] Akao, Y.: *QFD: Quality Function Deployment - Integrating Customer Requirements into Product Design. Information Systems Frontiers.* page 387. 2004.

[Al05] Alaranta, M.: *Evaluating Success in Post-Merger IS Integration: A Case Study. Journal of Information Systems.* 8(3):143–150. 2005.

[Al11a] Alfabet AG: *Company Website.* `http://www.alfabet.com`. 2011. Accessed: 2011-07-17.

[Al11b] Alfabet AG: *Verbesserung der IT durch Fokussierung mittels Business Capabilities.* 2011.

[An75] Ansoff, I. H.: *Managing Strategic surprise by response to weak signals. California Management Review.* 18(2):21–33. 1975.

[An92] Ankli, R. E.: *Michael Porter's Competitive Advantage and Business History. Business and Economic History.* 21(2):228–236. 1992.

[An06] Antila, E. M.: *The role of HR managers in international mergers and acquisitions: A multiple case study. International Journal of Human Resource Management.* 17(6):999–1020. 2006.

[An07] Ansoff, I. H.: *Strategic Management.* Palgrave Macmillan. New York, USA. Classic edition. 2007.

[An09] Anello, M.: *Acquisition of an International Financial Institution: IT Integration Capabilities of Credit Suisse for a "no-regret" Move.* Master's thesis. phw Business School, Department of International Management. 2009.

[ARW08] Aier, S.; Riege, C.; Winter, R.: *Unternehmensarchitektur - Literaturüberblick und Stand der Praxis. Wirtschaftsinformatik.* 50(4):292–304. 2008.

[AS93] Amit, R.; Schoemaker, P. J. H.: *Strategic assets and organizational rent. Strategic Management Journal.* 14(1):33–46. 1993.

[AS07] Aier, S.; Schönherr, M.: *Integrating an Enterprise Architecture using Domain Clustering.* In *Proceedings of Trends in Enterprise Architecture Management (TEAR).* pages 23–30. 2007.

[As09] Assmann, M.: *Model-Based Evaluation of Service-Oriented Enterprise Architectures.* PhD thesis. University of Paderborn. 2009.

[Au11] Auer, G.; Basten, D.; Berneaud, M.; Däberitz, D.; Freitag, A.; Haas, H.; Kröber, G. et al.: *Enterprise Architecture Management - neue Disziplin für die ganzheitliche Unternehmensentwicklung.* Bundesverband Informationswirtschaft, Telekommunikation und neue Medien e.V. (BITKOM). 2011.

[AW09] Aier, S.; Winter, R.: *Virtual Decoupling for IT/Business Alignment – Conceptual Foundations, Architecture Design and Implementation Example. Business Information Systems Engineering.* 1(2):150–163. 2009.

[Ba91] Barney, J.: *Firm Resources and Sustained Competitive Advantage. Journal of Management.* 17(1):99–120. 1991.

[Ba92] Barney, J.: *Integrating organizational behavior and strategy formulation research: A resource based analysis.* In (Shrivastava, P.; Huff, A.; Dutton, J., Ed.): *Advances in Strategic Management, Vol 8.* pages 39–62. JAI Press. Greenwich, USA. 1992.

[Ba02] Barnes, N. G.: *Mergers and Acquisitions as the New Growth Strategy: A Case Study of the Wholesale Alcohol Industry. American Business Review.* pages 126–131. 2002.

[Ba05] Barker, I.: *What is information architecture?* KM Column. 2005.

[Ba10] Barney, J.: *Gaining and Sustaining Competitive Advantage.* Prentice Hall. Upper Saddle River, USA. 4th edition. 2010.

[BBH07] Brits, J.-P.; Botha, G.; Herselman, M.: *Conceptual Framework for Modeling Business Capabilities.* In *Proceedings of 2007 Informing Science and IT Education Joint Conference.* pages 151–170. 2007.

[BC08] Bartels, E.; Cosack, S.: *Integrationsmanagement.* In (Picot, G., Ed.): *Handbuch Mergers & Acquisitions.* chapter C/X, pages 450–470. Schäffer-Poeschel. Stuttgart, Germany. 4th edition. 2008.

[BD09] Bortz, J.; Döring, N.: *Forschungsmethoden und Evaluation.* Springer. Heidelberg, Germany. 4th edition. 2009.

[Be94] Becker, G.: *Mergers and Acquisitions als Instrument zur Umsetzung von Konzernstrategien. Das Wirtschaftsstudium (WISU).* 3:198–200. 1994.

[Be05] Bernard, S. A.: *An Introduction to Enterprise Architecture.* AuthorHouse. Bloomington, USA. 2nd edition. 2005.

[Be08] Bergmann, H.: *Zusammenschlusskontrolle.* In (Picot, G., Ed.): *Handbuch Mergers & Acquisitions.* chapter B/IX, pages 400–448. Schäffer-Poeschel. Stuttgart, Germany. 4th edition. 2008.

[Be09a] Becker, J.; Pöppelbuß, J.; Stolze, C.; Asgarian, C.: *Developing a framework for IT governance in the post-merger integration phase.* In *Proceeding of 17th European Conference on Information Systems.* 2009.

[Be09b] Berneaud, M.: *Der Unterschied liegt in der IT. GI-Geldinstitute.* 2009.

[BES09] Buckl, S.; Ernst, A.; Schweda, C.: *Complementing TOGAF with the EAM Pattern Catalog. Architecture & Governance Magazine.* 5(11). 2009.

[BG09] BOC-Group: *Business Capability Management.* 2009.

[BGM87] Benbasat, I.; Goldstein, D. K.; Mead, M.: *The Case Research Strategy in Studies of Information Systems. MIS Quarterly.* 11(3):369–386. 1987.

[Bl11] Bloomberg: *M&A Outlook.* `http://about.bloomberg.com/pdf/manda.pdf`. 2011. Accessed: 2011-07-17.

[BL12] Bengtsson, L.; Larsson, R.: *Researching Mergers & Acquisitions with the Case Study Method: Idiographic Understanding of Longitudinal Integration Processes.* CSIR Electronic Working Paper Series, Blekinge Institute of Technology, Center for Strategic Innovation Studies (CSIR), Karlskrona, Sweden. 2012.

[BLWP92] Buck-Lew, M.; Wardle, C. E.; Pliskin, N.: *Accounting for information technology in corporate acquisitions. Information & Management.* 22(6):363–369. 1992.

[BMP10] Barroero, T.; Motta, G.; Pignatelli, G.: *Business Capabilities Centric Enterprise Architecture.* In (Bernus, P.; Doumeingts, G.; Fox, M., Ed.): *Enterprise Architecture, Integration and Interoperability.* volume 326. pages 32–43. Springer. Boston, USA. 2010.

[BMS11] Buckl, S.; Matthes, F.; Schweda, C. M.: *Building Blocks for Enterprise Architecture Management Solutions (BEAMS)*. `http://wwwmatthes.in.tum.de/wikis/beams/`. 2011. Accessed: 2011-05-07.

[BN95] Brandenburger, A. M.; Nalebuff, B. J.: *The right game: Use game theory to shape strategy. Harvard Business Review*. July/August:57–71. 1995.

[BNW96] Bernus, P.; Nemes, L.; Williams, T. J.: *Architectures for Enterprise Integration*. Chapman & Hall. London, UK. 1996.

[Bo85] Bonoma, T. V.: *Case Research in Marketing: Opportunities, Problems, and a Process. Journal of Marketing Research*. 22(2):199–208. 1985.

[Br90] Brand, M.: *Kauf und Verkauf von Unternehmen - Wie man "Mergers and Acquisitions" erfolgreich realisiert*. Industrielle Organisation. Zürich, Switzerland. 3rd edition. 1990.

[Br01] Brown, D.: *Don't overlook IT in the merger*. `http://www.computerweekly.com/Articles/2001/05/31/180596/dont-overlook-it-in-the-merger.htm`. 2001. Accessed: 2011-05-07.

[Br03] Bredemeyer, D.; Malan, R.; Krishnan, R.; Lafrenz, A.: *Enterprise Architecture as Business Capabilities Architecture*. `http://www.bredemeyer.com/pdf_files/Presentations/EnterpriseArchitectureAsCapabilitiesArch.pdf`. 2003. Accessed: 2011-05-07.

[Br06] Brunetto, G.: *Integrating information systems during mergers: integration modes typology, prescribed vs. constructed implementation process*. In *Proceedings of 2006 European Conference on Information Systems (ECIS)*. 2006.

[BS08] Bachmann, H.; Stölzle, W.: *Post Merger Integration von Logistikdienstleistern: Konzeptionelle und empirische Analyse branchenspezifischer Integrationskompetenzen*. Gabler Verlag. Wiesbaden, Germany. 2008.

[BS10] van den Berg, M.; van Steenbergen, M.: *Building an Enterprise Architecture Practice: Tools, Tips, Best Practices, Ready-to-Use Insights*. Springer. Dordrecht, Netherlands. 2010.

[BS11] Buckl, S.; Schweda, C. M.: *On the State-of-the-Art in Enterprise Architecture Management Literature*. Technical report. Chair for Software Engineering of Business Information Systems. Technische Universität München. München, Germany. 2011.

[BU05] Burger, A.; Ulbrich, P.: *Beteiligungscontrolling*. Oldenbourg. Munich, Germany. 2005.

[Bu06] Bucher, T.; Fischer, R.; Kurpjuweit, S.; Winter, R.: *Analysis and Application Scenarios of Enterprise Architecture: An Exploratory Study.* In *Proceedings of 10th IEEE International Enterprise Distributed Object Computing Conference Workshops (EDOCW06).* 2006.

[Bu09] Buckl, S.; Ernst, A. M.; Kopper, H.; Marliani, R.; Matthes, F.; Petschownik, P.; Schweda, C. M.: *EA Management Patterns for Consolidations after Mergers.* In *Proceedings of Workshop on Patterns in Enterprise Architecture Management (PEAM).* pages 67–78. Kaiserslautern, Germany. 2009.

[Bu11] Buckl, S.: *Developing Organization-Specific Enterprise Architecture Management Functions Using a Method Base.* PhD thesis. Technische Universität München. 2011.

[BW07] Braun, C.; Winter, R.: *Integration of IT Service Management into Enterprise Architecture.* In *Proceedings of 2007 ACM symposium on Applied computing (SAC07).* pages 1215–1219. Seoul, Korea. 2007.

[Ca80] Caves, R. E.: *Industrial organization, corporate strategy and structure. Journal of Economic Literature.* 18(1):64–92. 1980.

[Ca03] Carr, N. G.: *IT Doesn't Matter. Harvard Business Review.* 81(5):41–49. 2003.

[Ca05] Caudle, S. L.: *Homeland Security Capabilities-Based Planning: Lessons from the Defense Community. Homeland Security Affairs.* I(2):15–38. 2005.

[CDV08] Chen, D.; Doumeingts, G.; Vernadat, F.: *Architectures for Enterprise Integration and Interoperability: Past, Present and Future. Computers in Industry.* 59(7):647–659. 2008.

[CFP07] Cypra, S.; Fletcher, C.; Piché, M.: *M&A and the CIO: Why earlier Involvement of IT Improves Integration Success. DM Review.* 2007.

[CG98] Clemente, M. N.; Greenspan, D. S.: *Winning at Mergers and Acquisitions: The Guide to Market Focused Planning and Integration.* Wiley. New York, USA. 1st edition. 1998.

[Ch05] Cherbakov, L.; Galambos, G.; Harishankar, R.; Kalyana, S.; Rackham, G.: *Impact of service orientation at the business level. IBM Systems Journal.* 44(4):653–668. 2005.

[CKB04] Chevalier, A.; Kunsch, P. L.; Brans, J. P.: *A contribution to the development of strategic control and planning instruments: An acquisition case study. Operational Research.* 11:155–168. 2004.

[CL04] Carleton, R. J.; Lineberry, C. S.: *Achieving Post-Merger Success: A Stakeholder's Guide to Cultural Due Diligence, Assessment, and Integration.* Wiley/Pfeiffer. San Francisco, USA. 1st edition. 2004.

[CL09] Chao, R.-d.; Lin, F.-r.: *A Multiple Case Study on Post-Merger IT Integration with IT Culture Conflict Perspective.* In *Proceedings of 42nd Hawaii International Conference on System Sciences HICCS 2009.* IEEE Computer Society. 2009.

[Co94] Collis, D. J.: *How Valuable are Organizational Capabilities? Strategic Management Journal.* 15:143–152. 1994.

[Co07] Cook, D.: *Business-Capability Mapping: Staying Ahead of the Joneses.* http://msdn.microsoft.com/en-us/library/bb402954.aspx. 2007. Accessed: 2011-05-07.

[CS06] Cartwright, S.; Schoenberg, R.: *30 Years of Mergers and Acquisitions Research: Recent Advances and Future Opportunities. British Journal of Management.* 17(S1):S1–S5. 2006.

[Da02] Davis, P. K.: *Analytic Architecture for Capabilities-Based Planning, Mission-System Analysis, and Transformation.* RAND, National Defense Research Institute. Santa Monica, USA. 2002.

[Da09] Dama International: *The DAMA Guide to The Data Management Body of Knowledge.* Technics Publications. Bradley Beach, USA. 1st edition. 2009.

[Da10] Data Governance Institute: *Assigning Data Ownership.* http://www.datagovernance.com/gbg_assigning_data_ownership.html. 2010. Accessed: 2011-05-07.

[De07] Detecon International GmbH: *Case Study CRM Architecture 2010.* http://www.detecon.com/media.php/references/en/CRM_Architecture_KR_08_en.pdf. 2007. Accessed: 2011-05-07.

[De09] DePamphilis, D.: *Mergers, Acquisitions, and Other Restructuring Activities, Fifth Edition: An Integrated Approach to Process, Tools, Cases, and Solutions (Academic Press Advanced Finance Series).* Academic Press. Burlington, USA. 5th edition. 2009.

[DKZ02] Deans, G.; Kröger, F.; Zeisel, S.: *Merger Endgames - Strategien für die Konsolidierungswelle.* Gabler Verlag. Wiesbaden, Germany. 2002.

[Dr02] Drejer, A.: *Strategic Management and Core Competencies: Theory and Application.* Greenwood Publishing. Westport, USA. 2002.

[DS09] Drukarczyk, J.; Schüler, A.: *Unternehmensbewertung.* Vahlen. München, Germany. 6th edition. 2009.

[DT07] Dudas, M.; Tobisson, P.: *Information Systems Integration in Mergers and Acquisitions.* Master's thesis. Lund University. 2007.

[Ec12] Eckert, M.-L.; Freitag, A.; Matthes, F.; Roth, S.; Schulz, C.: *Decision support for Selecting an Application Landscape Integration Strategy in Mergers and Acquisitions.* In *Proceedings of 20th European Conference on Information Systems (ECIS).* Barcelona/Spain. 2012.

[EE03] Evernden, R.; Evernden, E.: *Third Generation Information Architecture. Communication of the ACM.* 46(3):95–98. 2003.

[EM00] Eisenhardt, K. M.; Martin, J. a.: *Dynamic Capabilities: What are they? Strategic Management Journal.* 21(10-11):1105–1121. Oct 2000.

[EN07] Ernest, M.; Nisavic, J. M.: *Adding value to the IT organization with the Component Business Model. IBM Systems Journal.* 46(3):387–403. 2007.

[En08] Engels, G.; Hess, A.; Humm, B.; Juwig, O.; Lohmann, M.; Richter, J.-P.; Voß, M. et al.: *Quasar Enterprise: Anwendungslandschaften serviceorientiert gestalten.* Dpunkt Verlag. Heidelberg, Germany. 1st edition. 2008.

[Ep04] Epstein, M. J.: *The Drivers of Success in Post-Merger Integration. Organizational Dynamics.* 33(2):174–189. 2004.

[Er09] Ernst, A. M.: *A Pattern-based Approach to Enterprise Architecture Management.* PhD thesis. Technische Universität München. 2009.

[EST10] Ernst, D. E.; Schneider, S.; Thielen, B.: *Unternehmensbewertungen erstellen und verstehen.* Vahlen. München, Germany. 4th edition. 2010.

[Fä10a] Fähling, J.; Böhm, M.; Leimeister, J. M.; Yetton, P.; Krcmar, H.: *IT Challenges in M&A Transactions – The IT Carve-Out View on Divestments.* In *Proceedings of 31st International Conference on Information Systems 2010 (ICIS2010).* Saint Louis, USA. 2010.

[Fä10b] Fähling, J.; Böhm, M.; Leimeister, J. M.; Yetton, P. W.; Krcmar, H.: *Managing the IT carve-out in a SBU divestment.* In *Proceedings of 18th European Conference on Information Systems (ECIS).* 2010.

[Fe07] Feurer, S.: *The Future Role of the Enterprise Architect - Survey Results.* Technical report. SAP AG. 2007.

[FGM10] Foley, C. F.; Goldberg, L. G.; Meyer, L. N.: *Chrysler's Sale to Fiat. Harvard Business Review.* 2010.

[FH09] Freitag, A.; Helbig, R.: *Finanzplanung und Steuerung von Unternehmensarchitekturen.* `http://www.controllingportal.de/upload/iblock/8ef/7340bd61a3309f83d3e9a913388beef3.pdf`. 2009.

[FL00] Frazer, L.; Lawley, M.: *Questionnaire design & administration.* John Wiley & Sons. Milton, Australia. 2000.

[FL03] Fettke, P.; Loos, P.: *Multiperspective Evaluation of Reference Models - Towards a Framework.* In *Conceptual Modeling for Novel Application Domains, volume 2814 of Lecture Notes in Computer Science.* pages 80–91. Springer Verlag. 2003.

[FM06] Franck, E.; Meister, U.: *Vertikale und horizontale Unternehmenszusammenschlüsse.* In (Wirtz, B. W., Ed.): *Handbuch Mergers & Acquisitions Management.* chapter A/3, pages 79–108. Gabler Verlag. Wiesbaden, Germany. 2006.

[FMS10a] Freitag, A.; Matthes, F.; Schulz, C.: *A Method for Consolidating Application Landscapes during the Post-Merger-Integration Phase.* In *Proceedings of 2010 International Multiconference on Computer Science and Information Technology (IMCSIT).* pages 241–248. 2010.

[FMS10b] Freitag, A.; Matthes, F.; Schulz, C.: *IT Transformation in the Context of Mergers & Acquisitions - Findings from a Series of Expert Interviews in the German Banking Industry.* Technical report. Technische Universität München. München, Germany. 2010.

[FMS11] Freitag, A.; Matthes, F.; Schulz, C.: *M&A driven IT Transformation: Empirical Findings from a Series of Expert Interviews in the German Banking Industry.* In *Proceedings of 10th International Conference on Wirtschaftsinformatik (WI2011).* pages 508–517. 2011.

[Fr08] Freitag, A.: *A Controlling Model for the Enterprise Architecture and SOA: Increased Cost Transparency for Modular IT Architectures.* Vdm Verlag Dr. Müller. Saarbrücken, Germany. 2008.

[Fr11] Freitag, A.; Matthes, F.; Nowobilska, A.; Schulz, C.: *A Method for Business Capability Dependency Analysis.* In *Proceedings of International Conference on IT-enabled Innovation in Enterprise (ICITIE2011).* pages 27–37. 2011.

[Fr12] Freitag, A.: *Erfolg in Post-Merger-Projekten.* In (Amberg, M.; Lang, M.; Kammerer, S., Ed.): *Management komplexer IT-Projekte.* chapter Transformationsprojekte und Risikomanagement, page 293. Symposion Publishing. Düsseldorf, Germany. 2012.

[FS12] Freitag, A.; Schulz, C.: *Investigating on the role of EA management in Mergers & Acquisitions.* In *Proceedings of Second International Symposium on Business Modeling and Software Design (BMSD).* 2012.

[Ga01] Gauthier, E. M.: *Post-merger and acquisition integration in an enterprise solutions environment.* 2001.

[GB09] Gopalan, S.; Balasubramanian, V.: *Enterprise Level Business Architecture. SETLabs Briefings.* 7(6):35–42. 2009.

[GH08] Galpin, T.; Herndon, M.: *Merger repair: when M&As go wrong. Journal of Business Strategy.* 29(1):4–12. 2008.

[GH10] Glaum, M.; Hutzschenreuter, T.: *Mergers & Acquisitions - Management des externen Unternehmenswachstums.* Kohlhammer. Stuttgart, Germany. 2010.

[Gi97] Giacomazzi, F.; Panella, C.; Pernici, B.; Sansoni, M.: *Information systems integration in mergers and acquisitions: A normative model. Information & Management.* 32(6):289–302. 1997.

[Gi01] Giaglis, G. M.: *A taxonomy of business process modeling and information systems modeling techniques. International Journal of Flexible Manufacturing Systems.* 13(2):209–228. 2001.

[GJ12] Goyal, K. A.; Joshi, V.: *Merger and Acquisition in Banking Industry: A Case Study of ICICI Bank Ltd. International Journal of Research in Management.* 2(2):30–40. 2012.

[Gö06] Görtz, B.: *Due Dilligence als Schlüssel zum Erfolg von Mergers & Acquisitions.* In (Wirtz, B. W., Ed.): *Handbuch Mergers & Acquisitions Management.* chapter B/3.1, pages 519–532. Gabler. Wiesbaden, Germany. 2006.

[Gr91] Grant, R. M.: *Prospering in Dynamically-Competitive Environments: Organizational Capability as Knowledge Integration. Organization Science.* 7(4):375–387. 1991.

[GS09] Gerds, J.; Schewe, G.: *Post Merger Integration: Unternehmenserfolg durch Integration Excellence.* Springer. Berlin, Germany. 3rd edition. 2009.

[GSV06] Göttgens, O.; Steinwaerder, D.; Vogel, F.: *M&A Kommunikationsmanagement.* In (Wirtz, B. W., Ed.): *Handbuch Mergers & Acquisitions Management.* chapter A/4, pages 229–262. Gabler Verlag. Wiesbaden, Germany. 2006.

[Gu09a] Gur, N.: *Using Enterprise Architecture for forecast and implementation of Mergers and Acquisitions (M&A).* `http://www.theeagroup.net/ea/Default.aspx?tabid=1&newsType=ArticleView&articleId=159`. 2009. Accessed: 2011-07-17.

[Gu09b] Gur, N.: *Using Enterprise Architecture for Mergers and Acquisitions Planning.* `http://weblogs.asp.net/ngur/archive/2009/06/05/enterprise-architecture-work-case-studies.aspx`. 2009. Accessed: 2011-07-17.

[Gu10] Guggenberger, J. M.: *Aufbau und Ablauf einer IT-Integration: Phasenmodell und Vorgehenskonzept unter Berücksichtigung rechtlicher Aspekte.* Gabler Verlag. Wiesbaden, Germany. 2010.

[Ha05] Harmon, K.: *The Systems Nature of Enterprise Architecture.* In *Proceedings of 2005 IEEE International Conference on Systems Man and Cybernetics.* pages 78–85. 2005.

[Ha09a] Habibbeigi, P.: *A Project Management Approach to M & A Deals and their Post-Integration Project Projects - A Case Study.* PhD thesis. Umeå School of Business. 2009.

[Ha09b] Haleblian, J.; Devers, C. E.; McNamara, G.; Carpenter, M. A.; Davison, R. B.: *Taking Stock of What We Know About Mergers and Acquisitions: A Review and Research Agenda. Journal of Management.* 35(3):469–502. 2009.

[Ha09c] Hanschke, I.: *Strategic IT Management: A Toolkit for Enterprise Architecture Management.* Springer. Berlin, Germany. 2009.

[HC94] Henderson, R.; Cockburn, I.: *Measuring Competence? Exploring Firm Effects in Pharmaceutical Research. Strategic Management Journal.* 15:63–84. 1994.

[HC06] Henningsson, S.; Carlsson, S. A.: *Governing and Managing Enterprise Systems Integration in Corporate M&A.* In *Proceedings of 14th European Conference on Information Systems (ECIS).* Göteborg, Schweden. 2006.

[He04] Hevner, A. R.; March, S. T.; Park, J.; Ram, S.: *Design Science in Information Systems Research. MIS Quarterly.* 28(1):75–105. 2004.

[He07a] Helbig, R.: *Using Quality Function Deployment and TOGAF ADM to Manage EA-based Business Transformation.* In *Proceedings of Open Group Architecture Practitioners Conference.* Paris, France. 2007.

[He07b] Heutschi, R.: *Serviceorientierte Architektur: Architekturprinzipien und Umsetzung in die Praxis (Business Engineering).* Springer. Berlin, Germany. 2007.

[HG08] Hommel, U.; Grass, G.: *Unternehmensbewertung.* In (Picot, G., Ed.): *Handbuch Mergers & Acquisitions.* chapter B/VIII, pages 374–399. Schäffer-Poeschel. Stuttgart, Germany. 4th edition. 2008.

[HHS03] ten Have, S.; ten Have, W.; Stevens, Frans, Van Der Elst, M.: *Handbuch Management-Modelle.* Wiley-VCH. Weinheim, Germany. 1st edition. 2003.

[HI11] Horie, N.; Ikawa, Y.: *Knowledge Integration in a Product Development Organization Accompanied by M&A: A Case Study of a Precision Device Manufacturer.* In *Proceedings of PICMET '11: Technology Management In The Energy-Smart World (PICMET).* pages 1807–1814. Portland, USA. 2011.

[HI12] Horie, N.; Ikawa, Y.: *Adverse Factors of Knowledge Integration in a Product Development Organization after M&A: A Case Study of a Precision Device Manufacturer.* In *Proceedings of PICMET '12: Technology Management for Emerging Technologies.* pages 2570–2576. Vancouver, Canada. 2012.

[HJ92] Haspeslagh, P. C.; Jemison, D. B.: *Akquisitionsmanagement: Wertschöpfung durch strategische Neuausrichtung des Unternehmens.* Campus Fachbuch. Frankfurt, Germany. 1992.

[HJ06] Höpner, M.; Jackson, G.: *Revisiting the Mannesmann takeover: how markets for corporate control emerge. European Management Review.* 3(3):142–155. 2006.

[HKT02] Habeck, M. M.; Kröger, F.; Träm, M.: *Wi(e)der das Fusionsfieber. Die sieben Schlüsselfaktoren erfolgreicher Fusionen.* Gabler. Wiesbaden, Germany. 2nd edition. 2002.

[Ho96] Hooke, J. C.: *M&A: A Practical Guide To Doing the Deal.* John Wiley & Sons. New York, USA. 1st edition. 1996.

[Ho00a] Hoffman, N. P.: *An Examination of the "Sustainable Competitive Advantage" Concept: Past , Present , and Future. Academy of Marketing Science Review.* 4(2000):1–16. 2000.

[Ho00b] Homburg, C.: *Kundenbindung im Umfeld von Fusionen und Akquisitionen.* In (Picot, A.; Nordmeyer, A.; Pribilla, P., Ed.): *Management von Akquisitionen.* pages 169–180. Schäffer-Poeschel. Stuttgart, Germany. 2000.

[Ho06] Homann, U.: *A Business-Oriented Foundation for Service Orientation.* `http://msdn.microsoft.com/en-us/library/aa479368.aspx`. 2006. Accessed: 2011-07-17.

[Ho08] van Houwelingen, J. W.: *Relevance and Usability of Enterprise Architectures during Post Merger IT Integrations.* Master's thesis. University of Twente. 2008.

[HP94] Hayes, R. H.; Pisano, G. P.: *Beyond World-Class: The New Manufacturing Strategy. Harvard Business Review.* 72(1):77–86. 1994.

[HP96] Hamel, G.; Prahalad, C. K.: *Competing for the Future.* McGraw-Hill. Boston, USA. 1996.

[HP03] Helfat, C. E.; Peteraf, M. A.: *The dynamic resource-based view: capability lifecycles. Strategic Management Journal.* 24(10):997–1010. 2003.

[HT06] Homann, U.; Tobey, J.: *From Capabilities to Services: Moving from a Business Architecture to an IT Implementation.* `http://msdn.microsoft.com/en-us/library/aa479075.aspx`. 2006. Accessed: 2011-07-17.

[Hu99] Hubbard, N.: *Acquisition Strategy and Implementation.* Purdue University Press, Ichor Business Books. Lafayette, USA. 1999.

[HW10] Hunger, J. D.; Wheelen, T. L.: *Essentials of Strategic Management.* Prentice Hall. Upper Saddle River, USA. 5th edition. 2010.

[HY13] Henningsson, S.; Yetton, P.: *IT-based Value Creation in Serial Acquisitions.* In *Proceedings of 13th European Academy of Management (EURAM) Conference 2013.* volume 2013. Istanbul, Turkey. 2013.

[IF99] IFAC/IFIP Task Force on Architectures for Enterprise Integration: *Generalised Enterprise Reference Architecture and Methodology (GERAM).* http://www.ict.griffith.edu.au/~bernus/taskforce/geram/versions/geram1-6-3/GERAMv1.6.3.pdf. 1999. Accessed: 2011-07-17.

[In07] International Organization for Standardization: *ISO/IEC 42010:2007 Systems and software engineering - Recommended practice for architectural description of software-intensive systems.* 2007.

[Ja99] Jansen, S. A.: *Post Merger Integration: Die Härte der weichen Faktoren.* Handelsblatt 1999-08-06. 1999.

[Ja08] Jansen, S. A.: *Mergers & Acquisitions: Unternehmensakquisitionen und -kooperationen. Eine strategische, organisatorische und kapitalmarkttheoretische Einführung.* Gabler. Wiesbaden, Germany. 5th edition. 2008.

[JB08] Jansen, S. A.; Brugger, C.: *Trends, Tools, Thesen und empirische Test zum Integrationsmanagement bei Unternehmenszusammenschlüssen.* In (Picot, G., Ed.): *Handbuch Mergers & Acquisitions.* chapter XIX, pages 565–598. Schäffer-Poeschel. Stuttgart, Germany. 4th edition. 2008.

[JE07] Johnson, P.; Ekstedt, M.: *Enterprise Architecture: Models and Analyses for Information Systems Decision Making.* Studentlitteratur. Lund, Sweden. 2007.

[Jo10] Josey, A.; Harrison, R.; Homan, P.; Rouse, M. F.; van Sante, T.; Turner, M.; van der Merve, P.: *TOGAF (TM) Version 9 - Ein Pocket Guide.* Van Haren Publishing. Zaltbommel, Netherlands. 2010.

[JS86] Jemison, D. B.; Sitkin, S. B.: *Corporate Acquisitions: A Process Perspective. Academy of Management Review.* 11(1):145. 1986.

[Ju99] Jung, W.: *Praxis des Unternehmenskaufs.* Schäffer-Poeschel. Stuttgart, Germany. 3rd edition. 1999.

[JY96] Johnston, K.; Yetton, P.: *Integrating information technology divisions in a bank merger: Fit, compatibility and models of change. The Journal of Strategic Information Systems.* 5(3):189–211. Sep 1996.

[Ka86] Kaplan, R. S.: *The Role of Empirical Research in Management Accounting. Accounting, Organizations and Society.* 11(4-5):429–452. 1986.

[Ka93] Kay, J.: *Foundations of Corporate Success: How Business Strategies Add Value.* Oxford University Press. New York, USA. 1993.

[Ka05] Kanwischer, D.: *Experteninterviews - die Erhebung, Verwaltung und Dekonstruktion von Expertenwissen.* Jena, Germany. 2005.

[Ka08] Kappelman, L.; McGinnis, T.; Pettite, A.; Sidorova, A.: *Enterprise Architecture: Charting the Territory for Academic Research.* In *Proceedings of Americas Conference on Information Systems (AMCIS) 2008.* pages 96–110. Toronto, Canada. 2008.

[Ka11] Kalex, U.: *Business Capability Management: Your Key to the Business Board Room The Confusion of Tongues.* In *Proceedings of Open Group Architecture Practitioners Conference.* Johannesburg, South Africa. 2011.

[Ke04] Keller, W.: *Managing Application Portfolios in Merger Situations.* In (Dadam, P.; Reichert, M., Ed.): *INFORMATIK 2004 - Informatik verbindet, Band 1, Beiträge der 34. Jahrestagung der Gesellschaft für Informatik.* Ulm, Germany. 2004. Gesellschaft für Informatik e.V. (GI).

[Ke06] Keller, W.: *IT-Unternehmensarchitektur. Von der Geschäftsstrategie zur optimalen IT-Unterstützung.* Dpunkt Verlag. Heidelberg, Germany. 1st edition. 2006.

[Ke09a] Keller, W.: *Using Capabilities in Enterprise Architecture Management.* `http://www.objectarchitects.biz/ResourcesDontDelete/CapabilityBasedEAMWhitepaper.pdf`. 2009. Accessed: 2011-07-17.

[Ke09b] Kerzner, H.: *Project management: A systems approach to planning, scheduling, and controlling.* Wiley. Hoboken, USA. 10th edition. 2009.

[Ke11] Kengelbach, J.; Klemmer, D. C.; Schwetzler, B.; Sperling, M. O.; Roos, A.: *Does Practice Make Perfect? How the Top Serial Acquirers Create Value.* Leipzig Graduate School of Management, http://www.bcg.com/documents/file74843.pdf. 2011.

[KHG06] Keuper, F.; Häfner, M.; von Glahn, C.: *Der M&A Prozess.* Gabler. Wiesbaden, Germany. 2006.

[KHK09] Kluge, R.; Hering, T.; Klinkmüller, C.: *Geschäftsanalyse mit CM-Tools - Geschäftsanalyse auf der Basis von Geschäftsfähigkeiten mit Unterstützung von CMTools.* Technical report. Universität Leipzig. 2009.

[KK01] Koslowski, F.; Kohlmeier, U.: *Controlling-Wörterbuch der Praxis.* Lucius & Lucius. Stuttgart, Germany. 2001.

[Kl10] Klinkmüller, C.; Ludwig, A.; Franczyk, B.; Kluge, R.: *Visualising Business Capabilities in the Context of Business Analysis.* In (Aalst, W.; Mylopoulos, J.; Sadeh, N. M.; Shaw, M. J.; Szyperski, C.; Abramowicz, W.; Tolksdorf, R., Ed.): *Business Information Systems (Lecture Notes in Business Information Processing).* pages 242–253. Springer. Berlin, Germany. 2010.

[KM05] Kim, W. C.; Mauborgne, R.: *Blue Ocean Strategy: How to Create Uncontested Market Space and Make Competition Irrelevant.* Harvard Business Press. Boston, USA. 2005.

[KN96] Kaplan, R. S.; Norton, D. P.: *The Balanced Scorecard.* Harvard Business School Publishing. Boston, USA. 1996.

[Ko05a] Koetter, M.: *Evaluating the German bank merger wave.* Deutsche Bundesbank, Research Centre, Discussion Paper Series 2: Banking and Financial Studies. 2005.

[Kö05b] König, W.; Beimborn, D.; Martin, S. F.; Homann, U.: *Capability Map: Eine alternative Darstellungsweise für Unternehmensprozesse aus ressourcenorientierter Sicht.* In (Beyer, J.; Mönch, L., Ed.): *Aspekte der Wirtschaftsinformatik: Methoden, Werkzeuge und Anwendungen.* SCS-European Publishing House. Erlangen, Germany. 2005.

[Ko05c] Kossakowski, P.: *Capabilities-Based Planning: A Methodology for Deciphering Commander's Intent.* In *Proceedings of 10th International Command and Control Research and Technology Symposium (ICCRTS).* Virginia Beach, USA. 2005.

[KO09] Kamogawa, T.; Okada, H.: *Enterprise Architecture Create Business Value.* In *Proceedings of 2009 Ninth Annual International Symposium on Applications and the Internet (SAINT).* pages 205–208. Seattle, USA. 2009.

[Kr90] Kramer, R. J.: *Organizational aspects of Postmerger Integration. M&A Europe.* 2(4):24–32. 1990.

[Kr06] Krüger, W.: *Projektmanagement in der Post-Merger-Integration.* In (Wirtz, B. W., Ed.): *Handbuch Mergers & Acquisitions Management.* chapter C/2, pages 805–826. Gabler Verlag. Wiesbaden, Germany. 2006.

[KS02] Kromer, G.; Stucky, W.: *Die Integration von Informationsverarbeitungsressourcen im Rahmen von Mergers & Acquisitions. Wirtschaftsinformatik.* 44(6):523–533. 2002.

[KST09] Konstantopoulos, N.; Sakas, D.; Triantafyllopoulos, Y.: *Lessons from a case study for Greek banking M&A negotiations. Management Decision.* 47(8):1300–1312. 2009.

[Ku06] Kumar, D.: *A Framework for SOA Adoption in the Enterprise.* `http://download.microsoft.com/download/A/F/E/AFECCEB9-C0F5-4B92-AA6C-3BFFF9CD5BFF/Teched2006/Day%202%20-%20Dev_Architect/Architecture%20Track/Day%202_Session%202/Architecture%20Track%20-%20Motion%20-%20Dinesh%20Kumar.pdf`. 2006. Accessed: 2011-07-17.

[La93] Larsson, R.: *Case Survey Methodology: Qualitatove Analysis of Patterns across Case Studies. Academy of Management Journal.* 36(6):1515–1546. 1993.

[La05a] Lankhorst, M.: *Enterprise Architecture at Work: Modelling, Communication and Analysis.* Springer. Berlin, Germany. 2005.

[La05b] Larsen, M. H.: *ICT Integration in an M&A Process.* In *Proceedings of Pacific Asia Conference of Information Systems (PACIS).* pages 1146–1159. Bangkok, Thailand. 2005.

[La08] Land, M. O.; Proper, E.; Waage, M.; Cloo, J.; Steghuis, C.: *Enterprise Architecture: Creating Value by Informed Governance (The Enterprise Engineering Series).* Springer. Berlin, Germany. 2008.

[Le03] Lecrone, K.: *IT case study: Maintaining the billing process in a M&A environment. Electric Light & Power.* 81(9):28. 2003.

[Le06] Lewis, J.: *Project Planning, Scheduling & Control: A Hands-On Guide to Bringing Projects in on Time and on Budget.* McGraw-Hill. New York, USA. 2006.

[LF99] Larsson, R.; Finkelstein, S.: *Integrating Strategic, Organizational, and Human Resource Perspectives on Mergers and Acquisitions: A Case Survey of Synergy Realization. Organization Science.* 10(1):1–26. 1999.

[Li32] Likert, R.: *A technique for the measurement of attitudes. Archives of Psychology.* 22(140):1–55. 1932.

[Li06] Lindstädt, H.: *Ziele, Motive und Kriterien für Unternehmenszusammenschlüsse - Wertorientierung aus strategischer Perspektive.* In (Wirtz, B. W., Ed.): *Handbuch Mergers & Acquisitions Management.* chapter A/3, pages 57–78. Gabler Verlag. Wiesbaden, Germany. 2006.

[LK08] Laamanen, T.; Keil, T.: *Performance of serial acquirers: toward an acquisition program perspective. Strategic Management Journal.* 29(6):663–672. 2008.

[LM02] Lucks, K.; Meckl, R.: *Internationale Merger und Acquisitions: Der prozessorientierte Ansatz.* Springer. Berlin, Germany. 2002.

[LMW05] Lankes, J.; Matthes, F.; Wittenburg, A.: *Softwarekartographie als Beitrag zum Architekturmanagement.* In (Aier, S.; Schönherr, M., Ed.): *Unternehmensarchitekturen und Systemintegration.* pages 305–330. GITO-Verlag. Berlin, Germany. 2005.

[Lu02] Lucks, K.: *Nur systematisches Vorgehen bringt Erfolg. Harvard Business Manager.* 3:44–53. 2002.

[Lu03] Lucks, K.: *Project Management for Mergers & Acquistions.* Technical report. Fachhochschule Ingolstadt. Ingolstadt, Germany. 2003.

[Ma87] Mann, R.: *Praxis strategisches Controlling mit Checkliste und Arbeitsformularen: Von der strategischen Planung zur ganzheitlichen Unternehmensführung.* Moderne Industrie. Landsberg/Lech, Germany. 4th edition. 1987.

[Ma03] Mallon, W. T.: *The Alchemists: a Case Study of a failed Merger in Academic Medicine. Academic Medicine: Journal of the Association of American Medical Colleges.* 78(11):26–37. November 2003.

[Ma08a] Matthes, F.; Buckl, S.; Leitel, J.; Schweda, C. M.: *Enterprise Architecture Management Tool Survey 2008.* Chair for Informatics 19 (sebis), Technische Universität München. München, Germany. 2008.

[Ma08b] Mayer, H. O.: *Interview und schriftliche Befragung: Entwicklung, Durchführung und Auswertung.* Oldenbourg Wissenschaftsverlag. München, Germany. 5th edition. 2008.

[Ma09] Malik, N.: *Why Business Capabilities are not in the Zachman Framework.* `http://blogs.msdn.com/b/nickmalik/archive/2009/08/13/why-business/capabilities-are-not-in-the-zachman-framework.aspx`. 2009. Accessed: 2011-07-17.

[Ma11] Matthes, D.: *Enterprise Architecture Frameworks Kompendium: Über 50 Rahmenwerke für das IT-Management.* Springer. Berlin, Germany. 2011.

[MB07] Miklitz, T.; Buxmann, P.: *IT standardization and integration in mergers and acquisitions: a decision model for the selection of application systems.* In *Proceedings of 15th European Conference on Information Systems (ECIS).* pages 1041–1051. St. Gallen, Switzerland. 2007.

[Mc99] McDavid, D. W.: *A standard for business architecture description. IBM Systems Journal.* 38(1):12–31. 1999.

[Me06] Meckl, R.: *Organisation und Steuerung des Akquisitionsprozesses.* In (Wirtz, B. W., Ed.): *Handbuch Mergers & Acquisitions Management.* chapter B/2.2, pages 405 – 428. Gabler. Wiesbaden, Germany. 1st edition. 2006.

[MH04] Mehta, M.; Hirschheim, R.: *A framework for assessing IT integration decision-making in mergers and acquisitions.* In *Proceedings of 37th Annual Hawaii International Conference on System Sciences.* volume 8. pages 264–274. Washington, USA. 2004. IEEE.

[Mi08] Minoli, D.: *Enterprise Architecture A to Z: Frameworks, Business Process Modeling, SOA, and Infrastructure Technology.* Auerbach Publications. New York, USA. 2008.

[MM95] McKiernan, P.; Merali, Y.: *Integrating Information Systems After a Merger. Long Range Planning.* 28(4):54–62. 1995.

[MM10] Marks, M. L.; Mirvis, P. H.: *Joining Forces: Making One Plus One Equal Three in Mergers, Acquisitions, and Alliances.* John Wiley & Sons. Hoboken, USA. 2nd edition. 2010.

[MN09] Mo, J.; Nemes, L.: *Issues in using Enterprise Architecture for Mergers and Acquisitions.* In (Doucet, G.; Gø tze, J.; Saha, P.; Bernard, S., Ed.): *Coherency Management.* chapter 9, pages 239–266. Authorhouse. Bloomington, USA. 2009.

[Mo09] Moyer, K.: *The Looming Failure of Post-Merger Integration.* http://blogs.gartner.com/kristin_moyer/2009/01/23/the-looming-failure-of-post-merger-integration/. 2009. Accessed: 2011-07-17.

[Mo13] Mo'meni, M.; Mohaghar, A.; Godarzi, G.; Haddadi, S. M.: *A Model for successful Integration in Inter-organizational Collaboration (Case Study: M&A in Iran). World of Sciences Journal.* 4:18–30. 2013.

[MS95] March, S. T.; Smith, G. F.: *Design and natural science research on information technology. Decision Support Systems.* 15:251–266. 1995.

[MS00] Meier, A.; Spang, S.: *Merger Readiness als Erfolgsfaktor in der New Economy. Information Management & Consulting.* 15(3):7–12. 2000.

[MS06] Müller-Stewens, G.: *Konzeptionelle Entscheidungen beim Post-Merger-Management.* In (Wirtz, B. W., Ed.): *Handbuch Mergers & Acquisitions Management.* chapter C/2, pages 785–803. Gabler Verlag. Wiesbaden, Germany. 2006.

[MT06] Merrifield, R.; Tobey, J.: *Motion Lite: A Rapid Application of the Business Architecture Techniques Used by Microsoft Motion.* http://www.microsoft.com/indonesia/msdn/motionlite.aspx. 2006. Accessed: 2011-07-17.

[My11] Mykhashchuk, M.; Buckl, S.; Dierl, T.; Schweda, C. M.: *Charting the Landscape of Enterprise Architecture Management - An extensive Literature Analysis.* In *Proceedings of 10th International Conference on Wirtschaftsinformatik (WI2011).* pages 570–577. Zürich, Switzerland. 2011.

[Na05] Namba, Y.: *City Planning Approach for Rebuilding Enterprise Information Systems.* PhD thesis. Tokyo Institute of Technology. 2005.

[Ne10] NetAcad GmbH: *Proceedings of EAMKON - Informationsplattform Enterprise Architecture Management, Stuttgart, Germany.* March 2010.

[Ni08] Niemann, K. D.: *From Enterprise Architecture to IT Governance: Elements of Effective IT Management.* Vieweg Verlag. Wiesbaden, Germany. 1st edition. 2008.

[Ni12] Nijland, A.: *Factors influencing a post M&A development strategy.* Master's thesis. University of Twente. 2012.

[NMP91] Nunamaker, J. F.; Minder CHen, J.; Purdin, T. D.: *Systems development in Information Systems Research. Journal of Management Information Systems.* 7(3):89–106. 1991.

[No07] North Atlantic Treaty Organization: *NATO Architecture Framework (NAF), Version 3.* **http://www.nhqc3s.nato.int/architecture/_docs/naf_v3/annex1.pdf**. 2007. Accessed: 2011-07-17.

[Of09] Offermann, P.; Levina, O.; Schönherr, M.; Bub, U.: *Outline of a design science research process.* In *Proceedings of 4th International Conference on Design Science Research in Information Systems and Technology (DESRIST).* New York, USA. 2009. ACM.

[OP10] Osterwalder, A.; Pigneur, Y.: *Business Model Generation.* John Wiley & Sons. Hoboken, USA. 2010.

[Os04] Osterwalder, A.: *The Business Model Ontology - A Proposition in a Design Science Approach.* PhD thesis. Université de Lausanne, France. 2004.

[OWB09] Österle, H.; Winter, R.; Brenner, W., Ed.*Management von Integrationsprojekten: Konzeptionelle Grundlagen und Fallstudien aus fachlicher und IT-Sicht (Business Engineering) (German Edition).* Springer. St. Gallen, Switzerland. 1st edition. 2009.

[Pa03] Pandza, K.; Horsburgh, S.; Gorton, K.; Polajnar, A.: *A real options approach to managing resources and capabilities. International Journal of Operations & Production Management.* 23(9):1010–1032. 2003.

[Pe59] Penrose, E. T.: *The Theory of the Growth of the Firm.* Oxford University Press. New York, USA. 1959.

[Pe93] Peteraf, M. A.: *The cornerstones of competitive advantage: A resource-based view. Strategic Management Journal.* 14(3):179–191. 1993.

[Pe99] Penzel, H.-G.: *Post Merger Management in Banken - und die Konsequenzen für das IT-Management. Wirtschaftsinformatik.* 41(2):105–115. 1999.

[Pe07] Peffers, K.; Tuunanen, T.; Rothenberger, M. a.; Chatterjee, S.: *A Design Science Research Methodology for Information Systems Research. Journal of Management Information Systems.* 24(3):45–77. Dec 2007.

[PF08] Picot, G.; Fuhrmanns, A.: *Rechtliche Parameter der Integrations- bzw. Implementierungsmaßnahmen, insbesondere der Restrukturierungsmaßnahmen.* In (Picot, G., Ed.): *Handbuch Mergers & Acquisitions.* chapter C/X, pages 471–495. Schäffer-Poeschel. Stuttgart, Germany. 4th edition. 2008.

[PH90] Prahalad, C. K.; Hamel, G.: *The Core Competence of the Corporation. Harvard Business Review.* pages 79–91. 1990.

[Pi98] Picot, G.: *Unternehmenskauf und Restrukturierung. Handbuch zum Wirtschaftsrecht.* C.H. Beck Verlag. München, Germany. 3rd edition. 1998.

[Pi08a] Picot, G.: *Das vorvertragliche Verhandlungsstadium bei der Durchführung von Mergers & Acquisitions.* In (Picot, G., Ed.): *Handbuch Mergers & Acquisitions.* chapter B/V, pages 156–205. Schäffer-Poeschel. Stuttgart, Germany. 4th edition. 2008.

[Pi08b] Picot, G.: *Handbuch Mergers & Acquisitions.* Schäffer-Poeschel. Stuttgart, Germany. 4th edition. 2008.

[Pi08c] Picot, G.: *Vertragliche Gestaltung des Unternehmenskaufs.* In (Picot, G., Ed.): *Handbuch Mergers & Acquisitions.* chapter B/VI, pages 206–269. Schäffer-Poeschel. Stuttgart, Germany. 4th edition. 2008.

[Po79] Porter, M. E.: *How competitive forces shape strategy. Harvard Business Review.* 57(2):137–145. 1979.

[Po85] Porter, M. E.: *Competitive Advantage. Management Information Systems.* 19(4):487–505. 1985.

[Po87] Porter, M. E.: *From Competitive Advantage to Corporate Strategy. Harvard Business Review.* 65(3):43–59. 1987.

[Po96] Porter, M. E.: *What Is Strategy? Harvard Business Review.* 74(4134):61–78. 1996.

[Po01] Popovich, S. G.: *Meeting the pressures to accelerate IT integration. The Dealermakers Journal.* 36(12). 2001.

[Po04a] Porter, M. E.: *Competitive Advantage.* Simon & Schuster. New York, USA. 2004.

[Po04b] Porter, M. E.: *Competitive Strategy: Techniques for Analyzing Industries and Competitors.* Simon & Schuster. New York, USA. 2004.

[Po05] Pohle, G.; Korsten, P.; Ramamurthy, S.; Foecking, S.: *The specialized enterprise. A fundamental redesign of firms and industries.* `http://www-935.ibm.com/services/multimedia/specialization_en.pdf`. 2005.

[Po08] Porter, M. E.: *The five competitive forces that shape strategy. Harvard Business Review.* 86(1):78–93. 2008.

[PP00] Penzel, H.-G.; Pietig, C.: *MergerGuide.* Gabler Verlag. Wiesbaden, Germany. 2000.

[Pu07] Pulvermueller, E.; Ludwig, A.; Belter, R.; Zyskowski, D.; Heindl, U.; Nguyen, X. T.: *A Capability Oriented Management Approach for Business Integration.* In (Abramowicz, W.; Maciaszek, L., Ed.): *Proceedings of 1st International Working Conference on Business Process and Services Computing (BPSC).* pages 218–221. Gesellschaft für Informatik. 2007.

[PW81] Panzar, J. C.; Willig, R. D.: *Economies of Scope in Multi-Output Production. The American Economic Review.* 71(2):268–272. 1981.

[RKK03] Rumelt, R. P.; Kunin, H.; Kunin, E.: *What in the World is Competitive Advantage?* Policy Working Paper 2003-105. UCLA Anderson School of Management. Los Angeles, USA. 2003.

[RS99] Robbins, S.; Stylianou, A. C.: *Post-merger systems integration: the impact on IS capabilities. Information & Management.* 36(4):205–212. 1999.

[Ru91] Rumelt, R. P.: *How much does industry matter? Strategic Management Journal.* 12(3):167–185. 1991.

[RWR06] Ross, J. W.; Weill, P.; Robertson, D.: *Enterprise Architecture As Strategy: Creating a Foundation for Business Execution.* Harvard Business Press. Boston, USA. 2006.

[Sa04] Saha, P.: *Analyzing The Open Group Architecture Framework from the GERAM Perspective.* `http://www.opengroup.org/architecture/wp/saha/TOGAF_GERAM_Mapping.htm`. 2004. Accessed: 2011-07-17.

[SB09] Strohkark, C.; Brozy, L.: *Post Merger Integration bei Banken und Versicherungen.* `http://www.detecon.com/media.php/publications/spotlight/2009/Detecon_Spotlight_PMI_bei_Banken_und_Versicherungen.pdf`. 2009. Accessed: 2011-07-17.

[Sc00] Scholz, J.: *Wert und Bewertung internationaler Akquisitionen.* Gabler Verlag. Wiesbaden, Germany. 2000.

[Sc06] Schekkerman, J.: *How to Survive in the Jungle of Enterprise Architecture Frameworks: Creating or Choosing an Enterprise Architecture Framework.* Trafford Publishing. Victoria, Canada. 2nd edition. 2006.

[Sc08a] Schekkerman, J.: *Enterprise Architecture Good Practices Guide: How to Manage the Enterprise Architecture Practice.* Trafford Publishing. Victoria, BC, Canada. 2008.

[Sc08b] Schöenherr, M.: *Towards a Common Terminology in the Discipline of Enterprise Architecture.* In (Aier, S.; Johnson, P.; Schelp, J., Ed.): *Pre-Proceedings of the 3rd Workshop on Trends in Enterprise Architecture Research.* pages 107–123. Sydney, Australia. 2008.

[Sc09] Schwarzer, B.: *Enterprise Architecture Management: Verstehen - Planen - Umsetzen.* Books on Demand. Norderstedt, Germany. 2009.

[Sc10] Schilling, M. A.: *Strategic Management of Technological Innovation.* Mcgraw-Hill Higher Education. New York, USA. 3rd edition. 2010.

[SCA10] Scott, J.; Cullen, A.; An, M.: *The Anatomy Of A Capability Map.* 2010.

[SES92] Stalk, G.; Evans, P.; Shulman, L. E.: *Competing on Capabilities: The New Rules of Corporate Strategy. Harvard Business Review.* 70(2):57–69. 1992.

[SG10] Simon, H.; von der Gatten, A.: *Das große Handbuch der Strategieinstrumente - Werkzeuge für eine erfolgreiche Unternehmensführung.* Campus Verlag. Frankfurt am Main, Germany. 2nd edition. 2010.

[SH09] Salama, A.; Holland, W.: *The merger of a German Bank (G Bank) an American Bank (A Bank): an Assessment of Cultural Fit.* Cass Business School, London, UK. 2009.

[SHG10] Schmidt, A.; Hüner, K.; Grewe, A.: *Fallstudie Deutsche Telekom AG - Einheitliche Datenarchitektur als Grundlage für unternehmensweites Datenqualitätsmanagement.* Hochschule für Wirtschafts-, Rechts-, und Sozialwissenschaften (HSG), Institut für Wirtschaftsinformatik. St. Gallen, Switzerland. 2010.

[SHV03] Salama, A.; Holland, W.; Vinten, G.: *Challenges and opportunities in mergers and acquisitions: three international case studies - Deutsche Bank-Bankers Trust; British Petroleum-Amoco; Ford-Volvo. Journal of European Industrial Training.* 27(6):313–321. 2003.

[SJR96] Stylianou, A. C.; Jeffries, C. J.; Robbins, S.: *Corporate mergers and the problems of IS integration. Information & Management.* 31(4):203–213. 1996.

[St78] Stone, E. F.: *Research Methods in Organizational Behavior.* Scott Foresman and Company. Illinois, USA. 1978.

[St93a] Steinöcker, R.: *Akquisitionscontrolling: Strategische Planung von Firmenübernahmen. Konzeption. Transaktion. Integration.* Walhalla. Berlin, Germany. 1993.

[St93b] Storck, J.: *Mergers & Acquisitions: Marktentwicklung und bankpolitische Konsequenzen.* Gabler Verlag. Wiesbaden, Germany. 1993.

[ST02] Sumi, T.; Tsuruoka, M.: *Ramp new enterprise information systems in a merger & acquisition environment: a case study. Journal of Engineering and Technology Management.* 19(1):93–104. March 2002.

[SW09] Schelp, J.; Winter, R.: *Language Communities in Enterprise Architecture Research.* In *Proceedings of 4th International Conference on Design Science Research in Information Systems and Technology (DESRIST).* New York, USA. 2009.

[SZ92] Sowa, J. F.; Zachman, J. A.: *Extending and formalizing the framework for information systems architecture. IBM Systems Journal.* 31(3):590–616. 1992.

[TB08] Timmreck, C.; Bäzner, B.: *Mergers & Acquisitions als strategisches Instrument im Rahmen der Branchenkonsolidierung.* In (Picot, G., Ed.): *Handbuch Mergers & Acquisitions.* chapter A/II, pages 48–82. Schäffer-Poeschel. Stuttgart, Germany. 4th edition. 2008.

[TGS09] Thompson, A. A.; Gamble, J. E.; Strickland, A. J.: *Crafting and Executing Strategy: The Quest for Competitive Advantage: Concepts and Cases.* McGraw-Hill. New York, USA. 17th edition. 2009.

[Th09] The Open Group: *TOGAF Version 9.* `http://www.opengroup.org/architecture/togaf9-doc/arch/`. 2009.

[Th11] The Open Group: *Proceedings of Open Group Architecture Practitioners Conference, London, UK.* May 2011.

[To02] Toms, E. G.: *Information interaction: Providing a framework for information architecture. Journal of the American Society for Information Science and Technology.* 53(10):855–862. 2002.

[TPS97] Teece, D. J.; Pisano, G.; Shuen, A.: *Dynamic Capabilities and Strategic Management. Strategic Management Journal.* 18(7):509–533. Jan 1997.

[Tr11] Troux Technologies: *Company Website.* `http://www.troux.com`. 2011. Accessed: 2011-07-17.

[TW93] Treacy, M.; Wiersema, F.: *Customer Intimacy and Other Value Disciplines Customer Intimacy and Other Value Disciplines. Harvard Business Review.* 71(1):83–94. 1993.

[US99] US Federal CIO Council: *Federal Enterprise Architecture Framework (FEAF).* `http://www.cio.gov/documents/fedarch1.pdf`. 1999. Accessed: 2011-05-07.

[US10] US Department of Defense: *The Department of Defense Architecture Framework (DoDAF) Version 2.02.* `http://cio-nii.defense.gov/sites/dodaf20/index.html`. 2010. Accessed: 2011-05-07.

[Va11] Vaniya, N.: *Building Preparedness for Mergers and Acquisitions - The role of Enterprise Architecture Practice.* Master thesis. Griffith University. 2011.

[VP09] Varnus, J.; Panaich, N.: *EA Framework Survey Results Presentation.* In *Proceedings of 23rd Enterprise Architecture Practitioners Conference.* Toronto, Canada. 2009.

[VV08] de Vries, M.; Van Rensburg, A. C. J.: *Enterprise Architecture - New Business Value Perspectives. South African Journal of Industrial Engineering.* 19(1):1–16. 2008.

[Wa05] Wagter, R.; van den Berg, M.; Luijpers, J.; van Steenbergen, M.: *Dynamic Enterprise Architecture: How to Make It Work.* John Wiley & Sons. Hoboken, USA. 2005.

[Wa12] Walker, S.: *IS & Business Strategy Alignment; The Impact on IT Integration In M&A. Case study - Technology Company.* Master's thesis. Aalto University School of Economics. 2012.

[We84] Wernerfelt, B.: *Resource based view of the firm: measures of reputation among health service-sector businesses. Strategic Management Journal.* 5(1):171–180. 1984.

[Wh04] White, S. A.: *Introduction to BPMN. BP Trends.* 2004. Accessed: 2011-05-07.

[Wi03] Winter, S. G.: *Understanding dynamic capabilities. Strategic Management Journal.* 24(10):991–995. 2003.

[Wi06a] Wijnhoven, F.; Spil, T.; Stegwee, R.; Fa, R. T. A.: *Post-merger IT integration strategies: An IT alignment perspective. The Journal of Strategic Information Systems.* 15(1):5–28. 2006.

[Wi06b] Wirtz, B. W.: *Handbuch Mergers & Acquisitions Management.* Gabler. Wiesbaden, Germany. 1st edition. 2006.

[Wi10] Wiehle, U.; Diegelmann, M.; Deter, H.; Schömig, P. N.; Rolf, M.: *Unternehmensbewertung - Methoden, Rechenbeispiele, Vor- und Nachteile.* Cometis Publishing. Wiesbaden, Germany. 4th edition. 2010.

[WL04] Wirz, P.; Lusti, M.: *Information Technology Strategies in Mergers and Acquisitions: an Empirical Survey.* In *Proceedings of Winter International Symposium on Information and Communication Technologies (WISICT).* volume 58. Trinity College Dublin. 2004.

[Wo07] World Bank Group: *Environmental, Health, and Safety Guidelines.* `http://www1.ifc.org/wps/wcm/connect/Topics_Ext_Content/IFC_External_Corporate_Site/IFC+Sustainability/Sustainability+Framework/Environmental%2C+Health%2C+and+Safety+Guidelines/`. 2007. Accessed: 2011-05-07.

[WS06] Wirtz, B. W.; Schilke, O.: *Struktur und Ablauf des Akquisitionsmanagements.* In (Wirtz, B. W., Ed.): *Handbuch Mergers & Acquisitions Management.* chapter B/1, pages 317–337. Gabler Verlag. Wiesbaden, Germany. 2006.

[WW02] Webster, J.; Watson, R. T.: *Analyzing the Past to Prepare for the Future: Writing a Literature Review. MIS Quarterly.* 26(2):xiii—-xxiii. 2002.

[Za87] Zachman, J. A.: *A framework for information systems architecture. IBM Systems Journal.* 26(3):276–292. 1987.

[Za96] Zachman, J. A.: *Enterprise Architecture: The Issue of the Century. Database Programming and Design Magazine.* 10(3):44–53. 1996.

[Za01] Zachman, J. A.: *Enterprise Architecture: A Framework.* www.zifa.com/framework.pdf. 2001. Accessed: 2011-05-07.

[Za11] Zachman, J. P.: *The Zachman Framework Evolution.* http://www.zachman.com/ea-articles-reference/54-the-zachman-framework-evolution. 2011. Accessed: 2011-05-07.

[ZH08] Zimmermann, R.; Herres, J.: *Interne und externe Kommunikation.* In (Picot, G., Ed.): *Handbuch Mergers & Acquisitions.* chapter C/XII, pages 534–564. Schäffer-Poeschel. Stuttgart, Germany. 4th edition. 2008.

MIX
Papier aus verantwortungsvollen Quellen
Paper from responsible sources
FSC® C105338

FSC
www.fsc.org

If you have any concerns about our products,
you can contact us on
ProductSafety@springernature.com

In case Publisher is established outside the EU,
the EU authorized representative is:
Springer Nature Customer Service Center GmbH
Europaplatz 3, 69115 Heidelberg, Germany

Printed by Libri Plureos GmbH
in Hamburg, Germany